Standards Strategy and Policy

Cases and Stories

PETER GRINDLEY

OXFORD UNIVERSITY PRESS

1995

Oxford University Press, Walton Street, Oxford OX2 6DP

Oxford New York
Athens Auckland Bangkok Bombay
Calcutta Cape Town Dar es Salaam Delhi
Florence Hong Kong Istanbul Karachi
Kuala Lumpur Madras Madrid Melbourne
Mexico City Nairobi Paris Singapore
Taipei Tokyo Toronto
and associated companies in
Berlin Ibadan

Oxford is a trade mark of Oxford University Press

Published in the United States
by Oxford University Press Inc., New York

© *Peter Grindley 1995*

British Library Cataloguing in Publication Data
Data available

Library of Congress Cataloging in Publication Data
Grindley, Peter.
Standards, strategy, and policy : cases and stories / Peter Grindley.
1. Standardization—Case studies. 2. Commercial products—
Standards—Case studies. 3. Electronic industries—Standards—
Case studies. I. Title.
HD62.G696 1995 94-45527
389'.6—dc20
ISBN 0-19-828807-7

1 3 5 7 9 10 8 6 4 2

Typeset by Best-set Typesetter Ltd., Hong Kong
Printed in Great Britain
on acid-free paper by
Biddles Ltd., Guildford & King's Lynn

STANDARDS, STRATEGY, AND POLICY

PREFACE

This book in concerned with the relationship between standards, technology, business strategy, and policy. Standards provide a valuable opportunity to combine economic analysis and business strategy. The economic forces at work apply clearly and often overwhelm other issues. In a large number of industries, including major new products such as the video cassette recorder and the personal computer, standards have become central to business success. Compatibility standards also apply in industries where they may not at first glance be expected, such as airline routes, international railway timetables, bank credit cards, and automobile service networks. There is now a large and growing body of economic theory dedicated to understanding standards. Yet this has not made its full impact on business strategy, practised or taught, which has still not fully absorbed the implications of standards. Industry analysts and policy-makers often see standards as a technical problem, to be left to technical committees and research departments. Technical aspects are only part of the reasons for standards success. Standards imply very different strategies than those for conventional products. The objective of this book is to help bring standards more fully within the realm of business strategy and policy, as a component of analysis alongside the many other more conventional aspects.

The book aims to help the business strategist and policy-maker understand how standards work, and how they can be used to ensure success. It contains a collection of analyses and case-studies which interpret the economics of standards in practical settings. It explains the market processes associated with standards and uses these as the basis for strategic analysis. It approaches the issues first from the point of view of an innovating firm, and the problems it faces winning standards contests and establishing its products in the market. It also considers the parallel problems of how to maximize the profitability of a standard, and how to compete within a market once standards have been established. This is later extended to policy issues, and recommendations for combining directive action by industry standards bodies and government regulators with market processes.

The book contains an introduction to the problems of standards and two extended chapters laying out a framework for strategy and policy, followed by six case-studies illustrating different aspects of standards. Chapter 1, 'An Introduction to Strategy and Policy', outlines the need for a new look at standards, and introduces the main themes to be brought out later in the case-studies. The second chapter 'Framework for Standards Strategy', looks at standards strategy in detail. It presents a framework for identifying network effects and using them to win standards contests, maximize returns to the firm from standards and continue to compete effectively once standards are established. The third chapter, 'Standards Policy and Regulation', presents a similar framework for evaluating official and market standards from a policy viewpoint, and examines possible hybrid policies which combine the two.

The next six chapters present the case-studies. The cases are primarily in high-technology industries, where compatibility standards are strongest, but the lessons are intended to be universal. The first four cases—video cassette recorder, digital audio, personal computer, and open computer systems—look at standards which are almost purely market determined, and illustrate the effectiveness or otherwise of firms' strategies, with little government intervention. The two later cases—high-definition television and telepoint cordless telephone—have a stronger mix of market strategy and government policy, and illustrate ways in which the two may be combined to work with or against each other. Each of the chapters is self-contained and may be read independently, though it is recommended that at least the introductory chapter is read first. At the risk of some repetition each contains a brief summary of the standards theory needed to understand the particular case.

The book may be used in business strategy courses as a self-contained introduction to the use of standards in strategy, combining a framework for understanding the economics of standards with a series of analysed cases. At the same time, the approach is intended to be broad enough to appeal to the general business reader with an interest in new product markets, and to the strategy practitioner, who may be aware of the importance of standards but wishes to know more about how they work. The book should also be of interest to policy-makers and regulators, seeking a framework and case analyses, to illustrate and inform current strategy and policy issues. Particular subject areas for which the book may provide a useful reference are hi-tech manufacturing industries, computer science, telecommunications, and regulation.

The book has its origins within a research programme at the Centre for Business Strategy, London Business School, with the general objective of using economics to understand questions of strategy and policy. Research was completed at the Center for Research in Management at the University of California, Berkeley. I am particularly grateful to John Kay for his guidance as Director of the Centre for Business Strategy, to David Teece for his support while revising the manuscript during my stay as Visiting Scholar at the University of California, Berkeley, and to the Gatsby Foundation and the Sloan Foundation for financial support at different stages of preparing the book. I thank Ronnie McBryde for his assistance as co-author of earlier studies for the video cassette recorder, digital audio, and the personal computer, and Saadet Toker as co-author of the original study for telepoint, on which the relevant current chapters have built. The book has benefited from discussions with Charles Baden-Fuller, John Cubbin, Paul David, Joseph Farrell, Landis Gabel, Paul Geroski, Heather Hazard, Barry Karlin, Edwin Kelliher, Jackson Nickerson, Josephine Ohlson, Alan Robertson, David Sainsbury, William Schreiber, Edward Sherry, Charles Steinmetz, Edward Steinmuller, Paul Stoneman, Peter Swann, Rob Wilmott, and others. I also thank participants at conferences and workshops where early versions of some of the cases have been presented, including INSITS (Braunschweig, 1989), EARIE (Budapest, 1989, and Ferrara, 1991), and ITS (Nice, 1992). It goes without saying that responsibility for any errors and opinions expressed here lies solely with the author.

CONTENTS

LIST OF FIGURES

LIST OF TABLES

1

An Introduction to Strategy and Policy: *Winning with Standards*

SUMMARY   Compatibility standards have been the key to the successful introduction of some of the most significant product innovations of recent years. Products such as the video cassette recorder, compact disc, and personal computer have depended crucially on the adoption of common standards across an industry, while disappointments such as digital audio tape, video disc, and telepoint portable phone have shown the risks of failing to establish standards in an adequate time frame. Yet traditional business strategy has often been of limited help in understanding the forces at work. The strategic problems for the firm are threefold: to establish standards for a new product; to maximize returns from standards for the individual firm; and to compete effectively once standards are established. These call for different strategies from conventional competition. There are parallel problems for government policy for setting standards, including the role of official standards bodies and whether standards are best set by government authority or market forces. This chapter introduces a framework for these decisions based on an understanding of the unique economics of standards. The strategy and policy issues are illustrated by some recent cases.

1. INTRODUCTION

Standards have often been seen as a technical problem, to be left to standards committees and technical departments. But standards are central to business strategy. Being accepted as the common standard across an industry may be the single most important component of new product success. Standards have been vital in the introduction of some of the most significant innovations of recent years, such as the video cassette recorder (VCR), compact disc (CD), and personal computer (PC). They have also contributed to some major product disappointments, such as digital audio tape (DAT) and video disc (VD), and have at least delayed the introduction of others such as telepoint and high-definition television (HDTV). They are a key concern in current standards contests such as those for open computer systems, digital portable stereo, mobile communications, and satellite broadcasting, as well as for the integration of computers, television, and telecommunications now underway. Once standards are established they continue to affect competition. A standardized design, unless it can be kept proprietary, makes product differentiation more difficult, allows easy entry to the market, and reduces profit margins. The current upheavals in the computer industry bear witness to the impact standards can have on market behaviour. Also standards not only affect manufacturers—they are of equal concern to producers of complementary goods and to users, none of whom want to be left supporting an obsolete standard.

The common feature in these cases is not that they are all new electronic products, though many of the strongest standards are in electronics. They are all examples of products which depend on compatibility. Standards enable products to be used with complementary goods and services or to be linked with similar products. Computers need software, VCRs need tapes, compact disc players need discs, and televisions need programmes. In the same way, telecommunications services need transmission networks and other users to call, and computers may need to be connected with other computers and peripherals.

But standards do not apply only to high-technology products. They affect more mundane items such as lamp batteries, razor blades, electrical voltages, and typewriter keyboards. Railway networks need the same gauge lines, skis need bindings, and electrical plugs need sockets. They also apply in less obvious cases. Airline routes need connecting flights, calling for networks with compatible schedules (and landing rules). Similarly, household appliances and automobiles need service networks, competing credit card systems need retailers willing to accept them and accounting systems to process them, even prescription drugs need doctors familiar with their use. These all rely on compatibility standards of some sort, and many 'non-technological' systems depend for their success on standards just as much as do VCRs and personal computers.

The main characteristic of standards is that the larger the network of users adopting a standard, the more valuable belonging to the standard usually becomes. A standard which builds up an installed base ahead of its competitors becomes cumulatively more attractive, making the choice of standards 'path dependent', and highly influenced by a small advantage gained in the early stages. Thus, the more PCs there are using the IBM PC standard, the more software applications are written for it, and the harder it is for competing standards to get established. The larger a telecommunications network the more users there are to call. And the more extensive a railway or airline network, the more chances there are of finding a train or flight connecting with the right destination at the right time.

The problem for the strategist is that because of these network effects, standards follow very different rules from those for conventional products. For example, it is often thought that for a new product the firm should get it to market early, differentiate the product, protect it from imitation, and charge high prices. Yet with standards the successful firms have often done the exact opposite of this. The main objective is to build up the installed base quickly, which may mean holding back the product launch until all the obvious flaws are ironed out, encouraging other manufacturers to adopt the same standard design, and lowering prices to maximize early sales. In VCR, JVC made the specifications of its VHS format openly available to other manufacturers and defeated Sony's Betamax. In personal computers, IBM was a late entrant but outstripped competitors by using an open design which other manufacturers and software producers copied freely. In both cases the innovator shared the market with many competitors but still made high profits.

Decisions such as whether to use one's own design or a competitor's, whether to protect or allow open access, and whether to subsidize production of complementary goods and early sales rather than invest in product development, are examples of standards strategy. Despite their importance standards are not well understood. Traditional business strategy is often not much help. The reasons for success may be misattributed, while the success of even some of the most powerful standards has sometimes been the result of luck as much as conscious strategy. Meanwhile firms continue to invest huge amounts of time and money in unsuccessful standards. Similar problems occur in government policy, where the unpredictability of the standards-setting process and its sensitivity to small events in the early stages, may make attempts to direct standards unreliable.

We may get a better idea of these problems by looking at three short examples. The first two, VCR and PC, to be discussed in detail later, demonstrate typical strategic problems. The third, direct broadcasting by satellite (DBS) in the UK, shows some of the policy problems of combining official standards and market forces.

2. NEW PRODUCTS USING STANDARDS

2.1 Video cassette recorder (VCR)

The contest between VHS and Betamax VCR formats in the late 1970s is one of the most famous standards wars, and together with the PC is probably the one most responsible for bringing standards to general attention. Sony's Betamax was introduced in 1975 and JVC's VHS in 1976. Though similar in design, tapes from one format could not be played on the other's machine. VHS outstripped Betamax and eventually drove it from the market. VHS's success was clear as early as 1978, as its sales drew away. Yet it was another nine years before Sony admitted defeat and began producing to VHS format, in 1987. Philips, the only European contender, had already dropped its format in favour of VHS in 1984. The success of VHS was total: by 1987 all but 5 per cent of the 200 m. VCRs in use world-wide were VHS. That only a single standard prevailed, rather than dividing the market between standards, shows the power of standardization over other product differences. The key was the availability of pre-recorded tapes in each format, and the ability to swap tapes with other machines. Once pre-recorded tapes began to appear primarily in VHS format, sales of Betamax fell precipitately, even though Betamax was by then considered technically superior.

VHS's success resulted from a superior standards strategy. It succeeded despite Betamax's earlier entry, superior picture quality, and backing of Sony's greater size and reputation. Some of JVC's strategies were conventional—it was more careful than Sony to lengthen the playing time to two hours, as users preferred; VHS was cheaper to manufacture than Betamax; and JVC made more effort to educate the market about the new product. But the real difference was that it built up the VHS installed base more quickly. VHS was effectively an open standard, with specifications supplied willingly to other firms at moderate licence fees. As a weak player JVC needed the support of Japan's major manufacturers to give it the capacity and distribution to establish a large base of users. This also gave VHS credibility with distributors and users, and with the Japanese Ministry of International Trade and Industry (MITI). JVC insisted on low pricing to establish the base of VHS rapidly. Thus when the availability of pre-recorded movie tapes became important after about 1979, sales and rental outlets chose VHS, rather than stock both formats. In contrast, Sony took a more traditional route for a new product, with a high-price introduction to recover development costs and a proprietary approach to technology. It made little attempt to court other manufacturers. Yet its exclusive stance meant that Betamax had little support from other manufacturers, and in turn had too small a user base. Although initial product problems, such as a short (one hour) recording time, were corrected within two years of the launch, it was soon too late to challenge the bandwagon in favour of VHS. With any other type of product Sony should have been able to hold a large market share. Sony continued to pour funds into Betamax but failed to change the result. JVC had to share the market with other VHS manufacturers but still achieved huge sales and profits. It has managed to hold on to about a 20 per cent share by leading technical development of the standard (with Super-VHS and Compact-VHS) and has become one of the world's major consumer electronics companies. Had it tried to follow Sony's proprietary strategy, VHS would now be only a memory.

2.2 Personal computer (PC)

The PC illustrates the strategic trade-offs between market size and share, and the problems of competing within a market once a standard is set. Computers are particularly dependent on compatibility and the availability of software. Once a standard is apparent the market focuses rapidly on it.

The advent of the IBM PC in the early 1980s unleashed the huge growth of the microcomputer market, by defining a standard which triggered massive entry to manufacturing and independent software production. The key to the PC's success was that it was an open standard, with few clear intellectual property rights and a basic design which could be easily imitated. Competition and increased volumes brought down prices rapidly, and the expanding base of equipment provided a large market for software development.

As the market expanded, continuing competition was less favourable to IBM than it had been to JVC, in the VCR market. Inevitably, given the size of the market if nothing else, IBM had difficulty retaining its market share, which gradually declined. Although the new market eventually benefited competitors more than IBM, its strategy may have been its best chance of significant participation. It was not a pioneer of the microcomputer and when it introduced the PC in 1981 many competing systems had already appeared. Technically the PC was unexceptional, even backward. Yet, backed by IBM, the PC had the credibility needed to establish it as a serious machine in a market previously seen as for hobbyists. In contrast with its usual policy, IBM assembled the PC from existing components sourced from outside, as the only way to develop a product quickly enough before other systems, such as Apple, took a clear lead, and it was not able to protect the design. Initial software and other support was either commissioned by IBM or developed by collaborating producers. Active marketing did the rest. The PC came at a crucial time. It was rapidly accepted as the standard, and the market boomed. Clones not only brought down the price but also convinced manufacturers, software producers, and users that they would not become tied to IBM. By 1986 microcomputers already accounted for over a quarter by value of all computers sold; over 80 per cent were PC compatible machines. The global PC market is now over $60 bn. a year. Even though IBM has had to share the market it has had huge sales and profits. It had a 25 per cent market share in 1986, and still about 12 per cent in 1993. Only Apple, with a large installed base prior to the establishment of the PC, has been able to hold on to a market niche with a proprietary standard, with the Apple II and then the Macintosh. However, its position has gradually become harder to sustain.

Later developments have shown problems of competing within a standard and the difficulty of changing an established regime. IBM attempted to halt its decline in share and profit margins by switching to a proprietary standard with the PS/2 and Microchannel Architecture (MCA) in 1987. The market was unimpressed and IBM returned to the open standard. The technical leadership of the PC has been taken by Compaq, which has used this to increase its market share without changing the openness of the standard. However, proprietariness has found a place elsewhere in the supply chain. Intel has successfully introduced more advanced generations of the ×86 family of microprocessors used in the PC, with successively stronger protection from imitation. There is a limit to the proprietary control possible as other component producers have eventually matched each new generation. Similarly, Microsoft has increased its command over PC software standards by leading the incremental development of the DOS operating system, and introducing related products: Windows and applications software.

2.3 Direct broadcasting by satellite (DBS)

The introduction of satellite television in the UK shows that standards strategies apply to services as much as manufacturing. It illustrates some policy conflicts involved in trying to set official standards in a commercial market. The timetable for DBS introduction is given in Table 1.1. Two systems competed for services. Sky Television, owned by Rupert Murdoch's News International Corporation, began transmission in January 1989. It transmitted from Luxembourg on the Astra satellite, hence avoiding UK broadcasting restrictions. This was over a year ahead of the officially sanctioned service, British Satellite Broadcasting (BSB). Although licensed in December 1986, BSB only began broadcasting in April 1990, a crucial three-year delay, on a different satellite (Marco Polo). Sky made good use of its lead to build up an installed base of 1.5 m. homes (0.75 m. on satellite, the rest on cable) before BSB arrived. After initially using a

Table 1.1. *Timetable for UK satellite broadcasting*

Date	Event	Sky homes (m.)
1986 Dec.	BSB awarded UK DBS licence	
1989 Feb.	Sky Television starts broadcasts in PAL—4 channels	
Sept.	Sky announces low cost introductory offers	0.5
1990 Apr.	BSB starts broadcasts in D-MAC	1.5
Nov.	BSB merges with Sky—BSkyB	
1991 May	BSkyB £200 m. refinancing	2.0
1992 Mar.	Operational break-even	2.6
Sept.	Sky Sports encrypted	
1993 Jun.	Operating profit £60 m.	
Sept.	Subscription package introduced—12 channels + 2 free	3.2
1994 Apr.	Marco Polo satellite sold, ex-BSB—£10 m.	3.5
"	Further £500 m. financing—accumulated debt £1.6 bn.	
"	18 channels planned	
Jun.	Operating profit £186 m.	

conventional strategy of advertising and programming, Sky shifted to one focused on the installed base, with generous introductory offers, leasing receivers at minimal cost to new subscribers and charging low introductory rates. It had provided 500,000 dishes and decoders by the end of 1989. To use BSB a Sky user would have had to buy a new receiver and a new dish to aim at the two satellites. Sky's 'hot bird' strategy was that users would not want to switch once they had installed one system, so it was unlikely that two services could survive. BSB's late arrival was fatal since 750,000 satellite viewers were already locked into Sky.

BSB was late due largely to policy problems. The broadcasting policy was combined with other aims. It had taken a long time for BSB to obtain government approval and put together the consortium called for in the licence. Most critically BSB was required to use the D-MAC system design, the first stage of the planned European HDTV system, which was not developed until 1990. Satellite broadcasting had been planned for over ten years before the launch, and first the state-owned British Broadcasting Corporation (BBC) and then a consortium of all UK broadcasters had already turned it down, largely because of restrictions imposed by the government. In contrast, Sky bypassed official approval and used the existing PAL system. As in the cases above, quality differentiation was surprisingly unimportant. BSB tried to differentiate its product with superior programming, but this was ineffective. Sky offered what was considered adequate programming—the Sky One channel, when it started in 1989, billed one of its programmes as 'trash at its best'.

BSB attracted few subscribers and lost money quickly. It collapsed and merged with Sky within seven months, in November 1990. Enormous investments had been made by both services. Sky spent £550 m. in its first two years, with accumulated losses of £195 m. BSB had spent even more, at £700 m., much of which went on up-market programming and a lavish style, with operating costs almost treble Sky's. British Sky Broadcasting (BSkyB), as the merged company is called, is now an established service. By late 1993 it was being received in 3.5 m. homes (0.7 m. via cable), increasing at 70,000 new subscribers a month. It reached break-even on operating costs by late 1992, ahead of expectations, with a trading profit of about £60 m. in the year to June 1993. By June 1994 operating profits had risen to £186 m., which took it past genuine break-even, including loan financing. The company is expected to have repaid its entire £1.6 bn. shareholder debt by 1999, and should eventually be a huge money-spinner. BSkyB began charging full subscription rates for the basic twelve-channel package in September 1993, showing that it considered the service well established. It eventually will have a total of eighteen channels.

The case shows the overriding importance of standards and the installed base compared to conventional strategies concentrating on programme quality and other promotional efforts. It also shows some potential weaknesses of official standards-setting processes. Here the process was slow and contradictory, compared with the flexible decision-making possible with market-determined standards.

3. STANDARDS STRATEGY

3.1 Need for standards strategy

Many of the strategies and policies in these examples were unconventional, and sometimes counter-intuitive. Encouraging competition, sharing proprietary technology, and adopting a technically unexciting design to increase the size of the total market contradict some traditional approaches to strategy based on establishing and defending market positions (Ansoff, 1965; Porter, 1980; Day, 1990). The idea of a fixed standard design also seems to conflict with more recent concepts of dynamic competition, aiming to outstrip competitors in a continual technological race (Foster, 1986). Even accepting that standards benefit the whole market, questions remain as to why firms still may need costly standards wars to agree on standards, and why official intervention is not more successful. Though standards may benefit the market as a whole, the uneven distribution of benefits, as well as imperfect information and uncertainty, make it hard for firms and policy-makers to agree on new standards.

It is tempting to try to approach these issues by applying existing conceptual tools. However, this may be misleading. For example, a standard may appear to be a special case of a dominant design (as defined in Clark, 1985; Utterback, 1993). That it is, but the mechanism leading to a new standard is more focused than general design evolution—a strategy relying on, say, developing a technically superior design may fail. Similarly the importance of market share in establishing a standard has given a new lease of life to arguments for experience curves and penetration pricing (Arrow, 1962; Henderson, 1979; Spence, 1981, 1984; Olleros, 1992). Yet with new standards, share is important primarily as a measure of success in building up the installed base and credibility of the standard, which then attracts complementary support. The key measure is cumulative sales or installed base. This is a different mechanism from the reputation, scale, learning, and market foreclosure effects associated with share in conventional approaches. Another possible interpretation of standards is as a form of brand investment (Nelson, 1974; Jones, 1986). Although this interpretation is occasionally made, the market power given by a proprietary standard is not the same as that given by brand reputation, as a general indication of quality, especially in consumer markets, which may be applied to other unrelated goods from the same supplier—the usual understanding of a brand. Finally, standards wars should not be confused with other examples of general 'chaotic' change in an industry, such as when faced with new international competition or rapid innovation (Quinn, 1985; Peters, 1987). The unpredictability of standards setting, in which a small advantage in the early stages can lead to unexpected outcomes of standards contests and sudden changes in corporate fortunes, has contributed to rapid change in some industries and may cause chaos for a time. But while standards may call for flexibility and quick responses, they also require clear thinking, as the cases above indicate. Chaos may stem from a failure to identify a bandwagon until it is too late.

3.2 Standards behaviour

The types of standards we are interested in are compatibility standards, as opposed to quality or measurement standards. Compatibility standards define the interface requirements allowing different core products, often from different manufacturers, to use the same complementary goods and services, or be connected together in networks. These are sometimes called systems products. Typically complements are other products, such as VCR tapes or LP records, but they may also be services, such as maintenance networks, or direct networks of the same product, such as telephones or airline routes.

Compatibility standards depend on demand side-effects which make the core product more valuable the more users it has. The basic mechanism is that a large installed base attracts complementary production and makes the standard cumulatively more attractive. At its simplest, if a standard can establish a clear lead over competing standards it attracts increasing support and typically will sweep the market. But the conditions and the application of the mechanism vary enormously. In a contest many outcomes are possible. The greatest scope for strategy occurs as standards are being set, when small events can make a big difference to which standard wins. It is this sensitivity to small changes at the early stages which makes strategy and policy so influential. Later it is hard to change the standards regime until a new technology arrives.

The firm's strategic objectives are threefold: to establish the standard in the market; to maximize the individual firm's profits from the standard; and to compete within an established standard. These may conflict, and most cases call for a compromise. The firm must make two basic positioning decisions: whether to try to develop a standard itself or adopt one from outside, and whether to choose an open or proprietary standard. These depend on the combined chances of winning a standards contest and of maintaining profits under different regimes. The firm also needs supporting operational strategies to back its position and win a standards contest.

Establishing a standard essentially depends on being first to convince both users and co-producers that the standard will be supported. This needs building up the installed base and establishing credibility. Standards become more attractive the more users adopt them. At the same time profitability depends on some balance between protecting the product from imitators and encouraging wide adoption of the standard. To establish a design, instead of protecting it from imitation a firm may need to share its technology with competing firms, as the only way to get the design accepted. Markets tend to be 'hyperselective', dominated by a single successful standard, with the focus of competition between standards taking place over a very short time-period as the product is being introduced. Once a 'critical mass' is achieved the process becomes self-sustaining and the market quickly forms around the leading standard. An established standard is very difficult to change, so that 'normal' product competition may later be restricted. The problem for firms and users is to avoid being stranded with a minority standard. The firm will have some freedom, though not much, to change the positioning and operational decisions as the contest progresses.

There are parallel objectives for standards policy. The basic choice is between market and official standards (*de facto* and *de jure*). There are several different levels of official involvement, ranging from mandated standards to voluntary agreement by an industry committee. There are also hybrid policies, in which the authority sets ground rules for the standards but leaves market forces to resolve technical details and establish the standard.

3.3 Standards and policy issues in the literature

The basic mechanism of standards leads to many complex aspects of strategy and policy. In the existing literature, the basic economics of standards are described in Kindleberger (1983), Arthur (1987, 1988), David (1987), Farrell and Saloner (1986a), Besen and Saloner (1988), and Farrell (1990). Gabel (1991) adds some important implications for strategy. A number of theoretical studies have established the basic mechanisms of standards and network effects, and looked at specific implications for strategy and policy. Seminal studies include Katz and Shapiro (1985, 1986), who demonstrate the effectiveness of sponsorship (subsidy) of initial adopters and penetration pricing by a manufacturer in building an initial market lead, and the key role this has in influencing expectations of the eventual standards winner. Farrell and Saloner (1985, 1986c) show how 'bandwagons' and the effects of inertia may ensure the success of an otherwise inferior standard, and may make it hard to change a standard, even an inferior one, once established. Farrell and Saloner (1986b) and Matutes and Regibeau (1987, 1988) show how a reduction in individual product variety due to a standard may be offset, under certain conditions, by an ensuing increase in total systems innovation by focusing previously diverse R&D efforts. The importance of expectations, by means of which an inferior product may defeat a superior one, is studied in Krugman (1991), Katz and Shapiro

(1992), and elsewhere. Farrell and Saloner (1992) examine the use of connectors to achieve compatibility as an alternative to adopting the standard design. Swann (1987) demonstrates the strategic use of preannouncements to manipulate expectations of which new standard will be successful.

In the policy area, David (1986) analyses the problems of fragmentation and the stranding of users with minority, poorly supported standards. Farrell and Saloner (1988) show that in some cases committees may outperform market forces in co-ordinating standards by giving firms an opportunity to chose standard by negotiation before they make irreversible investments. They also argue that hybrid policies may be even more effective, in the sense that negotiated standards may be backed up by market investments, so strengthening commitments. Rosenberg (1976), Dybvig and Spatt (1983), and David (1987) consider different aspects of policy, and the potential for using official standards to avoid problems of market standards. A full review of recent research in the economics of standards is given in David and Greenstein (1990). Most of these strategy and policy issues are reflected in some way in the case-studies in this book.

A cautionary note on the limitations of standards is sounded by Liebowitz and Margolis (1994), who point out that not all network effects are beneficial—they may lead to congestion or a reduction in variety. Also, not all economic benefits observed with standardized products, such as declining costs and expanding markets, are due to the standard itself. Normal technological progress may be at work, with standards playing a supporting role.

There have been various case-studies of technical and non-technical standards. The most famous standards case is probably the QWERTY typewriter keyboard (David, 1985). Studies include general case summaries (Hemenway, 1975; Kindleberger, 1983), broadcasting (Besen and Johnson, 1986), quadraphonic sound systems (Postrel, 1990), AM and FM radio (Besen, 1992), AC/DC electric power supply (David, 1992), automated teller machines (ATM) (Saloner and Shepard, 1992), and microcomputer software (Cottrell, 1994). A useful collection of cases is given in Gabel (1987), which includes cases on AM stereo radio (Berg), colour television (Pelkmans and Beuter), microcomputers (Hergert), petrol grades (Grant), bank charge cards (Phillips), and others. Other cases are noted as they apply to those in the current book. Studies in the current book are video cassette recorders, digital audio (compact disc and digital audio tape), personal computers, open systems, high-definition television, and telepoint cordless telephone.

3.4 Strategies to avoid

The differences between standards and other economic behaviour lead to unusual strategy recommendations. Some strategies which are familiar in traditional markets often do not work in standards-dominated markets, either for winning standards contests or for maximizing profits. These give tips for 'strategies to avoid'. Such 'negative' strategy lessons are often as valuable as positive ones—firms have limited resources and time, and should not waste them.

(a) Competing by technological innovation

Strategies relying on superior technology or even product quality to win a standards war may be ineffective. Once the products have reached a basic level of acceptability other methods may have more impact, as standards forces soon overwhelm other differences. Although good technical performance and product features are essential for a new standard, this may lead to a belief that ever better technology is the key to establishing a standard. Provided the product design is adequate for market needs, further development is often surprisingly unimportant. Quality and even price differences are soon outweighed by network effects. Thus, Betamax VCR failed even though it was both technically superior to VHS and cheaper. As late as 1986 Sony president Morita was still saying that 'we think consumers will come back to Beta when they realise that they get better performance at lower prices'. The IBM PC had no pretensions to be the most advanced machine on the market, but it fulfilled the other requirements for acceptance as the standard and that made it a winner.

(b) Trial approach to product introduction

Standards-dominated products can not be introduced with a cautious, step-by-step approach, hoping to test the market and gradually lowering prices to expand the market. The firm will not be able to correct major design problems with the product one-by-one as they appear. The leader must make a strong commitment and investment in the standard, to build the installed base and convince adopters that the standard will succeed. Once the product is verified as 'acceptable', the sponsor's aim is to overcome the resistance of co-producers and users, and establish credibility. Even without a major competitor, a wholehearted approach is needed to overcome the co-ordination difficulties between core and complementary goods, and to ensure that the standard does not fragment. This may go against usual practices of test marketing and using high introductory 'skimming' prices to recover development costs. The risks associated with standard introductions may be reduced by being alert to the signs that the standard is failing, but cannot be avoided altogether. Trial and error was part of Betamax' downfall. UK telepoint services failed in part due to a lack of full commitment by the operators.

(c) Protecting technology

The firm should not always protect its technology from imitation or even insist on high licensing fees. The main aim is to recruit supporters, so that the innovator may 'give away' its design, even at the cost of bringing in competitors to a market. Contrary to appearances, this may not only increase the standard's chances of being adopted but may also increase profits via high volumes. A firm may also use openness to defend its share in an established market. The alternative may be a small niche market or no market at all. Thus protagonists may compete by making their format as open as possible, as in the current contest between Philips's digital compact cassette (DCC) and Sony's minidisc for the portable digital audio standard.

(d) Relying on official adoption

A traditional route to standards adoption—relying on adoption by the industry standards body—may not be the safe option in some markets and may be more risky than attempting to establish the standard independently. Standards have long been the preserve of standards bodies and industry associations. Yet, while these have important roles to play, they may be no substitute for market processes. Strategies which rely on official acceptance divert effort and alone are unlikely to be effective. Agreement is hard to achieve and is unlikely to be adhered to unless backed up by market pressures. Standards bodies are inherently conservative, and will tend to support existing producers. Most importantly, official adoption takes a great deal of precious time—the crucial element in standards contests. Standards bodies also tend to concentrate on the technical aspects of standards, whereas the most important factors may be on the market side. In general, standards may be too important to the firms' future to be negotiated in committees and have to be settled in the market-place. Thus, years of negotiations over DAT within standards organizations failed to resolve basic differences between manufacturers and recording companies over copying, and meetings became platforms for dissent. This delayed DAT until CD had pre-empted the digital audio market. Open standards were discussed in the computer industry for decades with little progress until market changes forced the issue. The policy counterpart of these problems is that the most effective way to establish an efficient standard may not be by refining the committee process but by turning over more of the standard setting process to the market.

4. CASE PREVIEWS

The strategic and policy frameworks are presented in detail in the next two chapters. They give a way of looking at cause and effect in the cases in the second half of the book. Each case here is some form of standards contest, though the focus also goes beyond the immediate contest to see how firms compete once standards are set. The challenge in each case is, first, to identify the network effects, and, second, to understand how these have been used to achieve the players' objectives. The positioning and operational decisions result from the firms' attempts to reconcile the three related objectives: winning contests, maximizing profits, and continuing to compete. The central decision with standards is usually one of total market size versus individual market share. There are then a number of supporting strategies. Market behaviour provides a basis from which to understand policy. Here, strategy and policy overlap in the telecommunications and broadcasting cases, where the public interest is greatest and regulatory agencies are involved. Some of the main issues in each case are summarized in Table 1.2.

(a) Video cassette recorder (VCR)

This is a contest between two closely matched standards, VHS and Betamax. JVC won the contest by using an open standard to enlist the support of other manufacturers and build up the installed base quickly. It earned profits via its share of the huge market rather than high margins, and it retained its profitability by holding on to its market share by building complementary assets in manufacturing and marketing early on, and by leading further technological development of the standard. Sony lost the contest due largely to its proprietary strategy, which led to little support from other manufacturers, and its installed base never reached critical mass. It tried to be profitable by using high margins but only managed to reach a very small market. The technical superiority of Betamax was ineffective compared to the network effects due to the greater availability of pre-recorded tapes for VHS. The contest is being revisited with camcorders, in which Sony's 8 mm. standard shares the market with C-VHS, both systems achieving compatibility with the installed base of VCRs by the use of different types of converters.

(b) Digital audio: CD versus DAT

Digital audio has seen a series of contests between new and entrenched standards. CD has successfully established itself against the old vinyl LP standard. Even though CD was perceived as an attractive product, it required substantial sponsorship of CD disk production by the manufacturers, Sony and Philips, to overcome the qualms of the music companies and provide an initial supply of recorded music. Before this context was resolved a further contest began between CD and an even newer technology, DAT, took place prospectively, before CD was fully established. The case shows the importance of timing, as the installed base of CD was approaching critical mass when DAT arrived. Although DAT may be the superior technology, due to its recording capability and greater portability, it arrived too late. CD pre-empted the digital audio standard and DAT was left with a specialist recording niche. Profit considerations were important as manufacturers had overlapping interests in both CD and DAT: they were unwilling to support both at the same time and risk confusing the market. The

Table 1.2. *Checklist of case issues*

Case	Strategy issues			Policy issues
	Setting standards	Profit maximization	Continuation	
VCR	Open vs. proprietary standards Strategic alliances Futile technological competition Premature standard	Market size vs. share Complementary assets	Technological leadership Leverage to new products	Market standards Single standard dominance New industry
Digital audio	Timing and pre-emption Complement co-ordination Radical standard (vs. LP) Possibly inferior standard	Cannibalization Linked profits Vertical integration Co-producer rent capture	Technological leadership Features outside standard Leverage to new products Vertical integration	Market standards Committee non-agreement New market
Personal computer	Open standards (PC) *De facto* market co-ordination Software sponsorship Niche standards (Apple)	Market size vs. share Co-producer rent capture	Technological leadership Inability to change regime Loss of proprietary niche	Market standards New industry Effect in related markets
Open systems	Open vs. proprietary standards Technology-induced change Market coalitions	Market size vs. share Degrees of openness Existing base	'Super-compatibility' Technological leadership Interoperable systems	Private market alliances Information provision Government procurement
HDTV	Regulation and market interaction Replacement standard Evolutionary vs. radical standards Bypassing official standards	Vertical integration Complement markets Complementary assets	Technological leadership Cross-technology linkage	Regulated standards methods Industrial policy interaction Delayed standards International competition
Telepoint	Policy and market conflicts Failure of co-operation Lack of commitment Window of opportunity 'Pre-emption' by future systems	Limited profits Market positioning Excessive differentiation	Quasi-regulated competition Limited development	Official and market standards Policy constraints Unresponsive mechanisms

music companies also came to prefer the known profits of CD and helped block DAT. This contrasts with the outcome of a similar contest in the video market, between VCR and video disc, where the tape medium arrived just before disk and pre-empted the market. There is still no established portable digital audio system, the current contenders being DCC and minidisc.

(c) Personal computer (PC)

The PC demonstrates the strength of an open standard in establishing a new design and expanding the market. Though technically similar to competing systems, the PC defeated several proprietary standards in the early 1980s and defined the microcomputer market. The open design used commonly available components, which allowed the IBM PC to be developed quickly, at a critical time in the emergence of the market. This also allowed it to be readily imitated, which expanded the installed base and attracted independent software producers. Supporting strategies by IBM, including strong marketing and sponsorship of initial software applications, overcame any doubts about the system's credibility. IBM obtained good returns from the standard due to its major share of the large new market and low-cost manufacturing. It failed to hold on to its share, by not leading technical development of the standard, instead relying on traditional competitive strategies and various marketing ploys. It made an ill-fated attempt to extend its market power over the standard without coupling this with significant technical improvement. Only Apple survived with a proprietary standard, in a niche market, thanks to its early start and the unique technical features of the Macintosh. Even Apple has eventually been forced towards PC compatibility, as the product differences have narrowed and the volume of applications available for the PC have grown. Strategies in related markets, by Intel in the components market and Microsoft in the software market, have shown the dual effectiveness of initial strategies stressing wide adoption of the standard, followed by continuation strategies stressing technological leadership and quasi-proprietary improvements within the standard.

(d) Open systems

The growth of Unix-based open systems in the high-performance computer market shows the power of an open standard in forming alliances strong enough to replace entrenched proprietary standards from manufacturers such as IBM and DEC. Even so, change has only been possible with a fundamental shift in industry technology with the advent of the microprocessor. This changed the economics of the computer industry, and provided a route to establish the new standards regime via new markets for minicomputers and workstations—which provided a base for new software and eroded the market for large and mid-range computer systems. The activities of the different consortia set up to promote different versions of Unix, with overlapping memberships, exemplify a fully fledged 'standards contest'. Firms have attempted to use different 'degrees of openness', to capture the value of common standards while still trying to lock customers into proprietary designs. Alliances supporting fully open systems have been more widely supported and have supplanted alliances promoting quasi-proprietary systems. Some of the most successful firms have used continuation strategies within the standard aimed at 'super-compatibility' with the standard, and used other product features beyond the interface standard to differentiate their products. The contest for open systems has lately been extended to fully interoperable systems, which further separate hardware and software design, and may use operating systems other than Unix.

(e) High-definition television (HDTV)

HDTV illustrates many potential issues for standards, but perhaps most important are the interactions between strategy and policy, and the contrast between 'evolutionary' and radical approaches to introducing replacement standards. Co-ordination problems for television standards are particularly difficult, as they involve at least three groups: equipment manufacturers, programme producers, and broadcasters. Agreement is further complicated by official regulation of broadcasting, which effectively requires that standards are set by industry standards bodies prior to launch. The Japanese Hi-Vision system was not accepted by international standards committees, keeping it out of European and US markets. A policy-inspired European effort to develop its own MAC standard ultimately failed, unable to get the support of the broadcasters. However, the US Federal Communications Commission (FCC) used a novel approach, involving markets in official standards by acting as evaluator of market-generated proposals, which has had more success. The FCC kept its overseer role but left the design to the market, which rapidly developed a superior digital standard. Despite earlier attempts to define an evolutionary standard, backwards-compatible with existing colour television, the proposed digital format cannot be received on existing sets. An interpretation of the role of international standards bodies is that by not agreeing to Hi-Vision, they gave an opportunity for manufacturers' and consumers' reservations about the system to surface, and so in part reflected market forces as much as nationalism. When European policy-makers tried to go further and impose their own system, they too failed. The US digital standard promises a more equal international distribution of returns, which may help its world-wide adoption. However, its market introduction, being non-backwards compatible, is likely to take a long time. Interestingly the Japanese manufacturers did not try to bypass official adoption outside Japan (e.g. by introducing stand-alone HDTV VCRs or signing up cable operators), sensing market as well as political resistance. Meanwhile they have been forced by the slow

take-up of Hi-Vision, even in Japan, to use a two-stage evolutionary introduction with extended definition television.

(f) Telepoint

The disappointing attempt to establish telepoint, a public cordless telephone system, in the UK provides further insights into the combination of
strategy and policy. This was an experiment in hybrid policy, combining
official adoption with market forces. The standards authority outlined the
system and set the ground rules for competition, but left the product details
to the manufacturers and operators. The services made some strategic
errors, using high pricing and a trial approach. But their apparent lack of
commitment may be traced to inherent policy contradictions. The market
was not given enough freedom to develop a marketable product, while the
rules for setting standards confused users and weakened credibility. The
competitive structure, with four licensed operators, left the firms little incentive to develop effective strategies, such as trading current profits for
future market size, or cooperating on standards and sharing base stations.
Telepoint had been limited to a narrow service niche so as not to conflict
with other policy aims for cellular telephone or personal communications
network (PCN) services. The original policy aim had been to establish a
public system quickly to give the UK system a chance to be adopted as a
European standard. Although the system was defined quickly, this advantage was spoiled by the market failure of the services. Hybrid policies do
not necessarily resolve conflicts between *de factor* and *de jure* standards.

5. AIMS OF THE BOOK

The aim of the book is to broaden our understanding of how standards
work, and in so doing to help establish standards as a normal component of
business strategy. Understanding the basic standards mechanisms helps
resolve some paradoxical market behaviour of new products, such as why
many markets converge to a single design; why the best product is not
always the winner; why it sometimes pays to give away R&D to competitors
to ensure that the market adopts the design; and why a trial approach to a
new market may fail. There are obvious lessons for current standards
contests. Standards strategies at times contradict other conventional aspects
of business strategy, and at other times complement them. Yet standards
strategies should be seen as extensions rather than replacements for traditional strategy.

   A message is also that with standards, perhaps to a greater extent than
other areas of strategy, each case is different. In particular, small influences
at a critical point in product introduction can have a huge influence on the
final shape of the market. The question becomes: how can changes in

strategy affect a firm's likelihood of success? Is there anything the firm can do to affect these 'small influences' in its favour? The basic economic mechanisms of standards are simple, but the practice can get complex, and the application of standards always seems to provide new perspectives. Truly, 'the devil is in the details'.

The book also explores ways in which standards policy may be made more effective. A policy dilemma is that although market forces often establish standards quickly and efficiently, they may also bring chaos in the process, due to the inherent 'instabilities' of standards setting. Yet regulated standards have their own problems, and experiments with hybrid policies so far have had mixed results. This is an area which needs further exploration.

2

Framework for Standards Strategy:
Establishing Standards and Maximizing Profits

SUMMARY   This chapter outlines the strategies for establishing compatibility standards, maximizing profits, and continuing to compete once standards are set. It describes different types of standards and outlines the economic forces at work. The firm must make basic positioning decisions for leadership and access. These form the basis for a series of enabling strategies to make sure that, whatever the positioning strategy, the chosen standard wins the contest and the firm maximizes its returns. The firm may deliberately give competitors access to proprietary technology and share the market. It may sacrifice early profits and subsidize co-producers, to build up the installed base of the new product. There are also continuation strategies for competing within the market once a standard is established. Producers of complementary goods and users have equally important decisions to make over which standard to support.

1. INTRODUCTION

The aim of strategy is to use standards for competitive advantage. The firm's objectives are threefold. It wants to ensure that whichever standard it chooses wins a standards contest. It wants to maximize its individual returns from the standard. And it must be able to compete effectively in the market once a standard is established. The firm has some basic positioning decisions to make: whether to support its own or an external standard, and whether to share the standard with competitors or keep it proprietary. There are a number of specific strategies to support these positions. Strategies are interconnected, in that in deciding which standard to support the firm must estimate the chances of winning a contest and the likely profits, which in turn depends on how it competes once the standard is set.

The primary aim is to establish the standard in the market—unless the standard is accepted then other strategies for the product are invalid. The firm's chances of winning a standards contest depend on basic *positioning decisions* made at the start. It must decide whether to develop its own standard or adopt an outside one, and whether to keep the design proprietary or share it. These form the basis for a series of *enabling strategies* for winning contests. These differ from conventional approaches and will be the main concern in the cases. At the same time the firm considers *profit-maximization strategies* for optimizing individual returns from the standard. The need to win the contest limits the scope for fine-tuning returns, and sharing the market may be unavoidable. The essential choice is between sharing a large market and dominating a small niche. The firm's main option is the degree of proprietary control it retains over the standard, to keep some edge over competitors. The firm is also concerned with *continuation strategies* for competing effectively on an on-going basis once standards are set. The firm may try to increase its proprietary control in a standards-ridden market, but there is a limit to how far it may change the standard's appropriability regime once it is in place. It may have to rely on innovating new features to enhance the standard. Although presented sequentially, the positioning decisions and the actualization strategies are interdependent. The positioning and enabling strategies are made with the profit and continuation strategies in mind. Also, if it becomes necessary to change the basic position, as when the firm's design fails in the market, then the other strategies will also change.

Co-producers and users make similar strategic decisions over which standard to support. They may prefer a standard where no single firm has strong control, but they also want to adopt a winning standard, with a large installed base. Though they may have little direct influence on the standard, their preferences are the key to the standard's success.

In this chapter, section 2 defines the different types of standards, and section 3 outlines standards theory. This prepares the way for the strategy framework in the rest of the chapter. Section 4 discusses basic positioning decisions, and section 5 describes enabling strategies. Section 6 discusses trade-offs for individual profit maximization, and section 7 discusses continuation strategies used once standards are established. Section 8 makes concluding remarks.

2. STANDARDS DEFINITIONS

2.1 Types of standards

Standards define any common set of product features. They range from loose sets of product characteristics to precise specifications for technical interfaces. The types are listed with examples in Table 2.1. There are several ways of classifying standards but the main distinction is between *quality standards,* concerned with the features of the product itself, and *compatibility standards,* concerned with the links with other products and services. Quality standards are often divided into two further groups, minimum attributes and product characteristics.

Table 2.1. *Types of standards*

Category	Type	Examples
Quality	Minimum attributes	
	Measurement and grades	Packaging, weights, and measures
	Public regulation	Health and safety, trade descriptions
	Product characteristics	
	Style and tastes	Fashion, breakfast cereals, brands
	Production economies	Raw materials, automobiles
Compatibility	Complementary products	VCR tapes, software, auto parts
	Complementary services	
	Support	Maintenance, servicing
	Knowledge	User training, experience
	Direct networks	Telephones, railways, LANs

(*a*) *Quality standards*

Minimum attributes standards cover basic product requirements for measurement and minimum quality such as packaging, sizes, and produce grades. They are often incorporated in legal standards or industry codes, and many are covered by government regulations such as health and safety, trade descriptions, and weights and measures acts, aimed to protect consumers and help the market to function. They make it easier to evaluate the product at purchase and so reduce transactions and search costs.

Product characteristics standards are more loosely defined 'bundles' of features which define a group of similar products. We often see clusters of similar, if not indistinguishable, products. These may reflect predominant tastes, as with groups of consumer products. Brands are a way of indicating consistent quality and an 'image' which fits the consumer's personal tastes. Characteristics may also reflect common production technology and components, which reduce development and manufacturing costs. Production requirements are the main reason why, say, televisions use standard-size picture tubes, cars share components, and potato crisps are all the same thickness.

(*b*) *Compatibility standards*

These define the interface requirements to allow different core products to use common complementary goods and services or be connected together in networks. *Complementary products* are items such as audio cassette tapes or computer software, often supplied by a separate industry. *Complementary services* include supporting services such as automobile maintenance or computer facilities management. Services also include less obvious complements in the knowledge and training of how to use the core product. These include how to prescribe a drug, use a washing-powder, operate a computer, or maintain an automobile, some of which may be learned by

Table 2.2. *Standards distinctions*

Category	Dimension	Property
Product scope	Degree Level Means	Significance of standard features Functional layer(s) standardized Built-in or 'gateway' converter
Market extent	Group Fragmentation	Multi-product, -generation, -firm Monolithic or fragmented
Positioning/control	Access Leadership	Open or proprietary Lead or follow (develop or adopt)
Process	Method	Market or official (*de facto* or *de jure*)

experience. The complements may also be *direct networks* of other users of the same core product, such as telecommunications networks or railway routes. Compatibility standards involve strong economic effects, acting through the demand side by making the core product easier and cheaper to use, with more complements available.

The same standard may serve more than one category. Compatibility standards are often linked with the internal design of the product, and may use common technology, for reasons of cost and availability. As a result compatibility benefits on the demand side may be found with production economies on the supply side.

2.2 Further distinctions

From now on our main concern will be with compatibility standards. Further categorizations of standards denote how deeply the standard is embedded in the design, the different market groupings adopting the standard, control over the standard, and the process by which it is established. These are shown in Table 2.2. These will affect strategic choices later.

(a) Product scope

The *degree* of standardization is the proportion of product characteristics covered by the standard and how important these are to product demand. The greater the degree the less scope remains for product differentiation. Some standards define all the relevant features, others standardize the main interfaces, which benefits all producers, but allow products to compete on others. Petrol octane ratings completely define the product, and radically changed the focus of competition when they were introduced. Direct network standards such as telephones or railways also need a high degree of standardization. Automobiles are partially standardized on non-strategic components such as tyres and light bulbs, but compete on engines and styling.

Technical compatibility standards may operate at different design *levels*. This is the 'depth' to which standards are built into the products. It may only be necessary to standardize the interface or it may be necessary to go deeper into the system architecture. Data communications standards may specify transmission formats and treat the rest of the system as a 'black box'. However, these may have hardware and software implications deeper in the system, such as processing speed and the system may need designing to fit these. It may be necessary to design-in the standard and use standardized components.

Design levels are related to the *means* of achieving compatibility. It may be built-in to the product or achieved by using a converter or adapter. This could be a physical adapter to give the product access into a network, called a 'gateway' technology, or a routine to transport software from one product over to another. With 'plug compatibility' no adapter is needed. In practice, unless systems are fairly similar, an adapter may be inconvenient in the long term and is often an interim solution or a way to deal with stranded users.

(b) Market extent

Standards apply to different product and firm groups. *Multi-firm* standards are adopted by different firms producing similar products. *Multi-product* standards apply across products from the same product line within the firm. *Multi-vintage* standards apply over different technical generations of a product, as in computers where users need to move software from earlier models. There may also be different amounts of *fragmentation* of the standard into distinct groups. One extreme is the *monolithic* standard, a single standard dominating the whole industry. Alternatively, there may be several different standards inhabiting the same market, such as initially for VCR (Betamax and VHS), 45 r.p.m. vs. 33 r.p.m. records (RCA and Columbia) and bank cards (MasterCard and Visa). Markets often fragment internationally, when each country champions its own telecommunications standard. The extent of standardization usually changes as the market develops, as in VCR where the standard eventually narrowed down from over forty potential entrants to a single standard.

(c) Positioning and control

A key strategic distinction is the control the firm has over the standard. This depends in the first place on the *access* to a standard, whether proprietary or open. With a *proprietary* standard one firm has property rights over the standard and uses this to restrict adoption by other firms. It may fight any attempt to copy the standard or may charge significant royalties. Proprietary standards usually need some intellectual property in the standard to be strongly protected, by patents, copyright, or firm-specific knowledge, such as with Kodacolor film, Xerox copiers, IBM software, and branded drugs. With an *open* standard no restrictions are placed on other firms adopting the standard, whether or not any firm has property rights over the standard. Imitation is usually encouraged. Rights on open standards may be weak, as for personal computers, screw threads, and typewriter keyboards, or intentionally waived and licensed for nominal fees. A second aspect is the *leadership* of the technological development of the standard, i.e. whether a firm develops or adopts. Even for an open standard there may be an effective *leader*, who defines the standard in the first place or leads technological changes. Some protection is secured by the emulation lag until other firms catch up—if this is long enough this becomes a 'quasi-proprietary' standard. *Followers* adopt an outside standard, either under licence or by inventing around the restrictions. We return to these issues later.

(d) Standardization process

The *method* by which the standard is set and maintained may be by market forces (*de facto*) or mediated by official standards bodies (*de jure*). The latter include government legislation, industry committees, and quasi-official standards associations. Most standards probably evolve by following the main firm in the market or as the outcome of a standards contest. Even consensus or legislated standards may have their origins with the largest firm, and what is now a universal standard was at some time contested, as with railway gauges, electrical supply voltages, screw threads, and razor blades. The boundary between official and market standards is not precise, and there is often a hybrid of the two approaches. Market-determined standards often involve private coalitions between firms and lobbying of various government authorities, and governments are often involved as purchasers of market-determined standards. Recently aspects of tradition-ally legislated standards in telecommunications and broadcasting have been turned over to market forces.

3. ECONOMICS OF STANDARDS

3.1 Standards forces

To understand strategy we must understand how standards work. Standards add value by making it cheaper to buy complements, easier for users to switch from product to product, and easier to use products in combinations. These *network externalities*, as they are called, differ from usual production economies by working via the demand side. They are 'externalities' because each adoption benefits all users, not just the individual. The main benefits of compatibility standards are shown in Table 2.3. The three elements are:

(a) *Complementary market*: Standards enlarge the market for complementary goods and services, which, by increasing the scale of pro-

Table 2.3. *Benefits of compatibility standards*

Category	Benefit
Complementary markets	Lower cost of complements
	Greater variety
	Competition reduces prices
Portability (switching)	Lower retraining and conversion costs
	Protects complementary investments
Connectivity	Direct networks
	Shared complements
	Mix-and-match components

duction, makes complements cheaper to produce and available in greater variety. It attracts more complementary producers and competition also lowers the price ('pecuniary' benefits). Savings include education costs, and the greater availability of people trained to use the standard and perform maintenance.

(b) Portability: Standards make it easier to move complements from one core product to another, increasing the value of the complements to the user. This reduces switching costs of conversion or retraining, and so protects the user's investment. If the standard applies across different suppliers, the users are less locked into a particular vendor and can shop around for the best price.

(c) Connectivity: Standards may allow core products to be joined together in networks, with direct benefits of having more users and shared components. Users may also 'mix and match' low-price components from different suppliers.

The net effect is to make core product cheaper and more convenient to use, increasing the value of the product and the market demand. Open standards shift the balance of power in favour of the user, who avoids being dependent on a single supplier, further lowering the prices of both core products and complements.

There may be other benefits due to supply-side economies, from shared inputs and development costs and learning effects in manufacture, which make the core product cheaper to produce. These add strength to demand but are not usually the driving force for compatibility standards. Production economies are exhausted once minimum efficient scale is reached, and cannot explain the near complete 'hyperselective' standardization we often see with compatibility standards. Network economies continue to increase with the size of the market, without limit. Standards also lead to purchase economies due to higher customer information and product reputation effects, which reduce search costs and risk.

Against these there are countervailing costs of standards, for development, co-ordination, and dissemination. For agreed standards there are often high negotiation costs, for the initial standard and for maintaining compatibility as developments occur. There may also be congestion costs or bottlenecks, if too many people try to use a limited resource, such as with a railway network. There may also be indirect costs of being tied to an obsolete standard, and of possible loss of variety. If these costs increase more quickly than the positive network effects then there may be a limit to the size of the network. However, at least for congestion costs, these costs are more likely to apply at the market level than to the individual standard, and may be alleviated by investment.

3.2 Dynamics of standardization

The dynamics of standards setting are very important. The outcome of any standardization process depends on the path taken, and slight differences in conditions in the early stages may lead to very different results. The mechanism is illustrated in Fig. 2.1. The larger the *installed base* of users the more complementary products are developed for the standard. A larger base with more complementary support also increases the *credibility* of the standard. Together these make the standard more attractive to new users. This brings in more adoptions, which further increases the size of the installed base. This builds up cumulative support, so that growth accelerates for the standard with the largest base. The leader gets a disproportionate number of adoptions and 'bandwagon' effects take over. The leader may soon have such a large advantage that all new users choose it, 'tipping' support towards the leading standard and sweeping the market. Only if other standards have managed to build sufficient installed base of their own

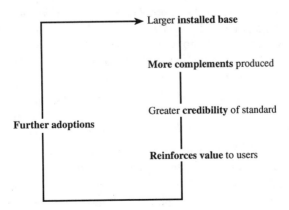

Fig. 2.1. *Standards reinforcement mechanism*

before this happens, or are very strongly differentiated, can they maintain any presence.

Standards setting is essentially a *co-ordination problem* between manufacturers, co-producers, and users, which acts as a hurdle for a new standard. The different players all make independent choices and no group wants to risk backing the wrong standard, so each holds back waiting for someone else to make the first move. This has been called the 'penguin effect', in which no one wants to be first in the water, but all jump in once it is clearly safe to do so. To get the standardization process moving its sponsor may need to make the initial investments in complements and subsidize early users.

The critical period for a standards contest is in the early stages. A small initial advantage may set the cumulative support process in motion, making chance events as well as strategy very important. Early adoption decisions depend critically on expectations of whether a standard is likely to succeed. The credibility of the standard and its package of support are crucial. Users want to select the 'right' standard to avoid being stranded with a minority, unsupported standard, while co-producers and other manufacturers want to choose the standard with the greatest market potential. If the product is new, expectations are based on whatever information is available. Expectations are to some extent self-fulfilling. Firms may influence them by preannouncements and user education, but usually these need backing up with proven features, evidence of commitment, manufacturing capability, and complementary support. Brand image may help. This underlines the importance of building an initial installed base as the best indicator of the standard's chances. Credibility is rather less important later on, once the prospects for the standards have become clearer, and the physical installed-base effect tends to take over.

A result is that there is a narrow 'window of opportunity' during which the firm may influence the standard, from the time a new product has been developed to some basic level of user acceptability until some standard has built up a dominant lead. Typically there is a period of rapid technical development of several competing products, until one or more have reached some level of market acceptability. The dynamics then take over, and once the bandwagon favours a particular standard, a 'dominant design' emerges rapidly.

3.3 Problems with standards

There are a number of potential problems which may occur because of the unpredictability of the standardization process, and the fact that once a standard is set it is difficult to change. Some of the most important are:

(a) *Fragmentation*: The market may split into several small, poorly supported standards. Each may have just enough of a niche to survive but not enough installed base to achieve full network benefits. The market as a whole is held back by not having a single fully supported standard, or at least a few well supported ones. This is 'understandardization', in which the market would be better served with fewer standards and lower costs.

(b) *Stranding*: Users of minority losing standards in standards contests, may be 'orphaned' or stranded with a poorly supported standard. There may be few complements available, but the users are locked in by their investments. In some cases the problem may be alleviated by the development of converters.

(c) *Premature standardization*: A standard may be established around a design before the basic technological development of the product has reached its full potential. This may hold back development of the product and restrict market growth.

(d) *Obsolescence*: Even a standard which was very advanced when it first appeared may persist long after it becomes technically obsolete, and hold up further development of the product.

(e) *Over-standardization*: The inverse of fragmentation is the possibly excessive reduction in product variety due to the standard. The trade-offs between fragmentation and loss of variety are rarely clear. Standards may reduce the number of types of core product offered, but may also increase the number and variety of complementary goods. The net effects on variety for the whole system are indeterminate. Also, any cost of lower variety must be set against the network benefits of a single standard.

Often problems such as these have occurred as the result of historical accidents, where markets developed before compatibility became important or before it was realized they could damage the market. This was the case for some well-known instances of persistent obsolete standards and incompatibility, such as the typewriter keyboard, incompatible railway gauges, electricity voltages, and national telephone systems. Generally, much of strategy is aimed at avoiding the problems. For example, it is the attempts by users, co-producers and manufacturers to avoid stranding which makes expectations so important. Also a realization of the effects of fragmentation often leads firms to collaborate on new standards rather than compete to the bitter end. Where problems persist there may be a role for policy to oversee the standardization process.

4. POSITIONING STRATEGIES

4.1 Positioning and control

The positioning decision determines the market control the firm is likely to have over the standard. This a dual decision covering (*a*) the *leadership* of the standard—whether the firm develops its own standard or adopts one

Access

	PROPRIETARY	OPEN
LEAD (Develop)	Sponsor/Defend	'Give Away'
FOLLOW (Adopt)	License in	Clone

Leadership

Fig. 2.2. *Strategic positioning decisions*

from outside, and (*b*) the *access* to the standard—whether the standard it supports is proprietary or open. Co-producers and users face similar choices as to which standard has the best chance of success and will offer them the best returns. The four basic options, shown in Fig. 2.2, are:

- Sponsor/defend — Develop a proprietary standard and restrict its use by competitors, charging significant licence fees
- 'Give away' — Encourage competitors to use an open standard developed by the firm, without restrictions
- License in — Adopt a proprietary standard controlled by another (competing) firm
- Clone — Adopt an open standard, without restrictions.

The leadership decision depends on whether the firm is technically and financially able to develop and introduce an acceptable standard design. It also depends on the strength of competing designs and their stage of development. The access decision concerns the market power the firm is able to exert via the standard. This depends on the strength of the intellectual property rights the firm has over the design, but more pertinently on the prospects for establishing the standard in the market as an open or proprietary standard, and the need for outside support. Together these determine how competition for and within the standard is organized. In positioning the standard the firm must balance the chances of it being adopted against the likely returns to the firm in each case. The main trade-offs between the likelihood of adoption, market size, market share, profit margins, and development costs are shown in Fig. 2.3. Thus, the positive benefits of choosing to lead the development of a proprietary standard are high market share and high unit margins. Negative considerations include the low likelihood of winning a standards contest without outside supporters, and the cost of sponsoring complementary production and initial users. For a leader of an open standard, the positive effects are greater likelihood of acceptance and larger total market, countered by the negative considera-

	PROPRIETARY	OPEN
LEAD	+ Protected market + High margins + High share + High licence earnings − Low chance of winning − Little external support − High cost − Small niche likely	+ High chance of winning + Large market + Broad external support + Shared costs − Low share − Low margins − High competition − Low licence earnings
FOLLOW	+ Proven market + Possible alliance − Secondary position − Pay high licence fees − Emulation lag − Absorption costs	+ Best chance of winning + Equalized competition + Low licence fees − High competition − Undifferentiated product − Absorption costs

Fig. 2.3. *Strategic positioning: costs and benefits*

	PROPRIETARY	OPEN
LEAD	Strong property rights Technical leader Long time lead Strong differentiation Large resources	Weak appropriability Leadership possibilities Speed essential Support needed Resources limited Proprietary threat
FOLLOW	Established standard Technical follower Late entrant Niche possible Cost competitive	Dominant proprietary standard Late entrant Product differentiation Small resources Cost competitve

Fig. 2.4. *Strategic positioning: positive selection factors*

tions of increased competition, low market share, and probably low margins.

The size of these costs and benefits in a particular case, which affect the firm's decision, depend on selection factors listed in Fig. 2.4. The more advanced the development of a competing standard and the stronger the manufacturing, marketing, and financial capabilities of the competitors, the lower the chances of a proprietary standard winning a contest. A weak

	PROPRIETARY	OPEN
LEAD	VCR Sony (Betamax) PC Apple (Macintosh) Computer IBM (S/370)	VCR JVC (VHS) PC IBM (DOS) Computer AT&T (Unix)
FOLLOW	VCR Sanyo (Betamax) PC Apricot (PS/2) Computer Fujitsu (S/370)	VCR Matsushita (VHS) PC Compaq (DOS) Computer X/Open (Unix)

Fig. 2.5. *Strategic positioning: examples*

appropriability regime makes it hard to sustain a proprietary strategy. Similarly, the threat of a strong proprietary standard increases the attractiveness of an open standard to the weaker players and raises its chances of recruiting enough support to win the contest. The selection factors include the likely effectiveness of the enabling strategies, discussed below.

Examples of positioning strategies used by different firms in some of the standards contests are given in Fig. 2.5.

The difference between standards and other forms of competition is that the individual firm's success depends on the success of the standard as a whole, which requires external support. The balance between openness and proprietariness should not be seen purely in terms of the individual firm's competitive advantage. The firm must consider the simultaneous problem of ensuring wide adoption of the standard. For example, this may mean that the firm should not defend its property rights. A proprietary strategy makes it more difficult to attract other manufacturers and to expand the installed base, even though it allows higher profit margins if the standard can get established. Users and complementary producers also prefer to avoid a potentially monopolized standard. The dilemma for the firm is that giving open access to its standard gives it more chance of winning a contest but the higher competition this brings reduces margins and market share. If neither alternative is attractive the firm may decide to adopt an external standard rather than develop its own. The firm wants the standard it supports to be established in the market, but this need not be its own design. It may be better off adopting a competitor's standard at lower cost and without risking fragmenting the market.

An important aspect is the extent to which the firm can sponsor a new standard. With a proprietary strategy, in anticipation of higher eventual profits the firm may be able to subsidize initial sales and provide initial complementary goods itself. Even so the resources of a single firm may be too limited; it may still need support from other manufacturers and co-producers. An open standard effectively recruits other manufacturers and co-producers to supply the initial capacity which the firm must otherwise provide itself. The firm then must rely for profitability on holding on to a share of a larger market. The firm may still need to combine some level of sponsorship even with an open standard, as Philips and Sony did with CD discs when the music companies were at first unwilling to support them, and IBM did with the initial software for the PC.

4.2 Positioning contests as strategic games

The firm's positioning decision depends on an analysis of its own chances of winning a standards contest against competing standards. Its strategy for leading or following, for example, depends on the relation between its own and other firms' payoffs under different standard regimes. The contest is a strategic game, in which each firm's strategic choices affect the strategic choices of its competitors. Applications of game theory to business strategy are discussed in Vickers (1985) and Kay (1993). The basic choices facing firms in a standards contest are described using a strategic game model in Besen and Farrell (1994). Although common standards benefit the industry as a whole, the differences in individual payoffs mean that there is likely to be a conflict. Contests occur when two or more firms try to lead, which is likely to happen when the winner expects a higher payoff due to first-mover advantages. Typically a firm adopts an external standard only because it has most chance of being agreed to by other manufacturers and wants to avoid a contest, even though it would prefer its own standard to be established. This is a 'battle of the sexes' game, in which the important outcome is that players agree to consistent strategies (one leads and the others follow) rather than fight. The essence of the co-ordination problem is reaching this agreement equilibrium, either by negotiation, alliance formation, or market competition. Since even identifying the payoffs is difficult for a product which is still being developed, it is not surprising that firms choose to fight standards wars, albeit 'in error'.

The 'battle of the sexes' game is shown in a simple form in Fig. 2.6, which lists the pay-offs to two competing firms according to whether they try to

Fig. 2.6. 'Battle of the sexes' game

lead or follow. For each strategy combination, payoffs are written as: (Firm A payoff, Firm B payoff). If both firms try to lead there is a leadership contest and the expected payoff to each firm is only £3 m., due to duplicated R&D costs and attempts to speed up development to preempt the standard (it is assumed that each firm has an equal chance of winning). If A leads and B follows, then A receives £6m. and B receives £4m. A Nash equilibrium occurs where neither firm has an incentive to change its strategy. If A announces first that it will lead, B's best response is to follow, and A still prefers to lead. Thus an equilibrium outcome is A leads, B follows, with payoffs (**6**, **4**) (equilibria are shown in bold). Another equilibrium is A follows, B leads, with payoffs (**4**, **6**). Thus both firms do better by agreeing to a single standard than by fighting, but the firm which gets its commitment in first does better than the follower. The total payoff for the industry if they agree is £10 m., but with a leadership contest the total payoff is only £6m. due to the resources spent in the standards war.

The most intriguing case is where the industry as a whole would be better off with a single standard but the distribution of gains in favour of the leader is so great that the follower prefers risking a standards war and fragmenting the market to an inferior position adopting an outside standard. This could be avoided if the leader is prepared to share the gains more evenly, so that the follower is not at such a disadvantage. This is a form of the 'prisoners' dilemma' game, in which all players would be better off agreeing—in this case one to lead, the other to follow—but by each trying to gain an advantage at the expense of the others they end by disagreeing, to their mutual loss (the infamous 'cut-throat defence', in which prisoners incriminate each other trying to get a lighter sentence). There are aspects of this with VCR, in which Sony would have been better off to have adopted VHS many years before it did so, but continued to try to win the standards contest. Sony perceived its payoff from following as being very low, and probably overestimated its chances of winning the contest. Other manufacturers, with less at stake, switched to VHS earlier. When payoff differences are low it may not be very important whose standard is adopted, and with no strong gains to be made by leading the industry may agree standards voluntarily. In such cases *de facto* standards may be established quickly by market forces.

This 'rather fight than switch' game is shown in Fig. 2.7, in which players jointly do better by agreeing than fighting, but the follower's payoff is now too low for it to forego the chance of winning the contest. Compared to the battle of the sexes game, the distribution of the payoffs is now more in favour of the leader, who receives £8 m. while the follower only receives £2m. The total industry payoff for an agreed standard is £10m. as before. This could occur if the leader were to charge high licensing fees for its proprietary technology. If A believes B will chose to follow, A will prefer to lead. However if A leads then B also prefers to try to lead, resulting in a

Firm B

		LEAD	FOLLOW
	LEAD	(3,3)	(8,2)
Firm A			
	FOLLOW	(2,8)	(0,0)

Fig. 2.7. *'Rather fight than switch' game*

standards war, with expected payoffs of only £3 m. to each firm and an equilibrium outcome (**3**, **3**). Total payoff to the industry is only £6 m., compared with £10 m. if they agree. Firm A (or B) could ensure agreement by changing the game, committing to making a side payment of £2 m. to B (or A) if it follows. In that case the modified payoffs would be £6 m. to the leader and £4 m. to the follower, and the outcome would be A leads, B follows, with payoffs (**6**, **4**), as in the battle of the sexes game. In practice the side payment could be a reduction in the licence fees or technical help in adopting the leading standard's technology. This is an essential part of the logic of open standards, which modify the players payoffs and hence change the combined leadership and access decisions.

These two examples merely scratch the surface of the possibilities for using games to analyse standards strategies. Most of the theoretical studies noted in Chapter 1 are based on strategic game models. Part of their value is in demonstrating basic concepts which underlie 'practical' business strategy, such as the inherent difficulties in achieving co-operation, as above, and related phenomena such as why competition may lead to premature standardization, or how committees may in some cases help to negotiate agreement. These basic forces are at work behind the scenes in the complexities of the case strategies. General descriptions of the use of game theory in business strategy are Schelling (1960), Shubik (1982), and Shapiro (1989). An outline of the new industrial economics, based in large measure on game modelling, including a section on standards, is given in Tirole (1988).

4.3 Deciding on leadership and access

To try to help the firm find a way through the positioning decisions, we will first assume that the main concern is to establish the standard, either in a niche or throughout the market. This has such a fundamental influence on

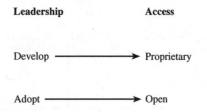

Fig. 2.8. *Sequence of positioning decisions*

the future of the product that 'fine-tuning' this decision to maximize firm profits may be considered separately. This makes the positioning decision in two steps, first to decide leadership and then access, as in Fig. 2.8, even though the decisions are in fact interdependent. The basic leadership decision is, in the first place, a question of whether the firm is technically able to develop a standard. If it believes it has a reasonable chance of developing a winning standard, the potential benefits if successful are so great that, until it becomes clear that it has no chance of winning, the firm must seriously consider trying to lead (i.e. for this case the lower two options boxes of Fig. 2.2 may be ignored). Having decided to lead, access becomes important, as the firm decides whether it should make the standard open or proprietary to establish it and maximize profits. Otherwise, if the firm does not have the resources to develop and establish the standard, especially before a competing standard is established, it must look to other sources and adopt an external standard (i.e. for the majority of firms the top two options of Fig. 2.2 are not available). The follower firm then chooses whether to adopt a proprietary or open standard depending on which gives the greatest chance of being on the winning side with the greatest competitive advantage. Thus the decision sequence is first to decide leadership, depending on whether the firm's own standard has a chance of being established, and then decide access for the chosen standard, depending on whether a proprietary or an open standard gives the best combination of winning and profitability. The firm may change its leadership decision if it later becomes clear that its standard has no chance of being accepted.

(a) Leader/Proprietary

Assuming the firm has a design available, its access decision depends on its ability to establish the standard and the returns under each option. The advantages of a proprietary standard are that, provided the protection from imitation is strong enough, the firm has monopoly control of its sub-market and can keep its share and margins high. It may choose to earn some profits by licensing the technology to other firms, rather than do all the manufacturing itself. The drawbacks are that without broad support from other manufacturers and co-producers, the standard may lose a standards contest or be limited to a niche. If intellectual property (IP) protection depends on secrecy this limits the scope for co-production. Often the firm must develop the standard alone and may have to sponsor the complementary goods as well. This leads to a small market niche with high development costs, though offset by potentially high margins and low competition. Even if a proprietary standard can be established it is not always profitable. To consider a proprietary standard the firm must have the technological capability to develop it and the manufacturing, marketing, and financial resources to establish it in the market. The standard must also be protectable. Protecting innovations from copying is notoriously difficult. In the absence of strong patents the firm must rely on hard-to-imitate manufacturing skills and lead time. For a new product the firm needs at least a head start and adequate resources.

(b) Leader/Open

With an open standard the firm chooses a smaller share of a larger market, with greater competition and lower margins. The standard is usually easier to establish because of wider support from other manufacturers and co-producers, and more users, attracted by low prices. The developing firm may be able to offset some of the effects of competition by differentiating its product in other ways and keeping ahead technically. Some development costs may be shared between manufacturers and low-cost existing components may be used. The problem is that although eventually there will be more than enough support, initially even an open standard needs a sponsor to develop and promote it. The innovator's market is shared and may be further eroded as time goes by, so it may be hard to cover development costs. The open standard is most attractive when there is little time to develop and introduce the standard against a competing standard, and when the firm's own resources are inadequate. Released from the need for IP protection there is freedom to develop the product by the cheapest and quickest means available. An important factor in obtaining outside support is the existence of a strong proprietary threat, which concentrates the minds of firms likely to be left out of the standard altogether. Otherwise they may still hope to establish their own standard and will fail to agree. The open standard does not always imply weakness, however. By uniting the industry the open standard may avoid fragmenting the market, which reduces the total market and can cause the product to fail. It also becomes more attractive if the developer can maintain some technical leadership or exploit its manufacturing and marketing assets, while getting the benefits of an open standard.

The decision between open and proprietary standards often comes down to a choice between a small protected market with high margins and a share of a much larger market with low margins, high competition, and possibly rapid (focused) technological innovation. A proprietary standard may be a high-cost, high-risk strategy, unless the product has a long lead and is well protected. It is vulnerable to being beaten by the speed and support available to an open standard. If there is a credible open threat it may be better to share the market rather than have no market at all.

(c) Follower/Proprietary

For a firm without the resources to develop a standard or entering a market where a standard already exists, there may be no choice but to adopt an outside standard. Even a firm able to develop its own standard may adopt one if it believes it has little chance of establishing its own against competing entrants. The choice of which standard to adopt depends on which appears to have the best chance of winning a contest, and will allow the follower to make reasonable profits. Adopting a proprietary standard is usually the least attractive option, unless the firm can manage to become a privileged supporter. The firm has little control over its product strategy and may remain a fringe producer competing on price. It must follow each move of the standard holder, which can only be done after an emulation lag. This puts the firm in a weak competitive position and diverts most of its development effort away from other product improvement. It may also have to pay licence fees. However, this may be the only choice other than withdrawal from the market. An added factor is that the firm must make an absorption effort to incorporate the outside standard into its design and will be less able to assume any technical leadership. There are some positive aspects. The standard may be proven and the firm may be able to survive on manufacturing and marketing ability. There may be room for a niche overlooked by the leader; this may be a foothold for further product development. Also it may be possible to form an alliance with the leader if it needs to fill gaps in its market. Adoption may still be quicker and cheaper than in-house development. Most of these comments apply to the computer mainframe industry, for many years led by the IBM S/360 and 370 standard, with various minority manufacturers of plug-compatible equipment.

(d) Follower/Open

Adopting an open standard is usually preferable to adopting a proprietary one as the firm is on an equal footing with competitors and not in a fringe position. This is preferred unless the firm is able to gain a privileged relationship with the leader. It should have broader support and greater chance of being adopted. Most of the other considerations are similar to the leader-open choice above.

5. ENABLING STRATEGIES FOR WINNING CONTESTS

The aim of strategy is to make sure that the chosen standard is adopted in the market ahead of competitors. The leadership and access decisions are preliminaries to the enabling strategies needed to establish the standard. Open access is an effective means of enlisting support and convincing users that products will be widely available. Conversely, if property rights are strong enough, the prospect of a proprietary standard may justify the full-scale commitment needed to establish it. A late-entrant firm may have no choice but to adopt an existing standard which already has timing advantages. The difficulty is that success depends as much on the availability of complements as on the product itself. The firm must ensure an adequate supply of complementary goods to make the core product worth buying. The co-ordination problem is to persuade co-producers to support the standard before there is a market, and users to buy the product before there are any complements. This may also include convincing other manufacturers to adopt the standard.

The main focus of competition is on building the *installed base* faster than competitors and establishing *credibility* with influential early adopters. Once a significant group has adopted the standard, network effects make the process self-sustaining. With sufficient installed base established the contest is in effect over, and, although the market may have only begun to grow, the loser's best strategy is to accept the new standard. Enabling strategies include direct means of building the installed base and credibility, and a number of specific supporting strategies. The main elements of enabling strategy are listed in Table 2.4, and discussed below.

(a) Build the installed base

The main priority is to establish a 'critical mass' of users more quickly than competing standards and start the network effects working for the product. It is imperative that the standard gets off to a really good start and maintains this momentum. This requires strong commitment from the sponsor. High early sales of the core product call for an aggressive strategy combining strong promotion, high-volume manufacturing, and penetration pricing. Methods to encourage early adoptions include subsidizing initial users, ensuring adequate production capacity, forming alliances with distributors and manufacturers, leveraging out existing installed bases in other segments, and other means discussed below. Distribution channels are important, as the product must be widely available once users become interested. An effective way of bringing in supporters is to make the standard open, or 'giving away' the technology. Though this means forgoing licence fees and allows in more competition, it may be the only way to establish the standard, especially if faced with strong competition.

Building the installed base makes initial sales and market share important, but the key measure of progress in establishing the standard is *cumulative* sales. Sales and even market share may be increasing, but if a competitor has an even larger share its base is growing faster and will eventually dominate the standard. The situation for a trailing standard may

Table 2.4. *Elements of standards strategy*

Strategy group	Elements
1. Basic positioning	(a) Lead or follow (develop or adopt)
	(b) Open or proprietary
2. Enabling strategies	(a) Installed base and cumulative sales
	(b) Credibility
	(c) Timing
	(d) Sponsorship
	(e) Alliances
	(f) Penetration pricing
	(g) Preannouncements
	(h) Technological design
	(i) Linkage and indirect routes
	(j) Official standards bodies
3. Profit maximization	(a) Degree of openness
	(b) Product differentiation (outside standard)
	(c) Emulation lag
4. Continuing competition	(a) Degree of openness
	(b) Supercompatibility
	(c) Technological leadership
	(d) Complementary assets
	(e) New standards products
	(f) Vertical integration

look acceptable for a while, but cumulative sales are diverging and eventually the leader's installed base will be overwhelming. A focus on the wrong measure allows the firm to continue under the illusion that its product is doing well and to expect it to hold on to a sizeable share of the market, whereas cumulative sales make it clear that the leader is building an unbeatable advantage.

(b) Establish credibility

Early purchasers must make their decisions based on expectations of the standard's prospects before the installed base and complementary market have built up. The main motive for a prospective buyer is to avoid being stranded with a product on an unsupported standard. If it is generally believed that a given standard is to be the contest winner then users will choose it. The same is true for co-producers and other manufacturers deciding which standard to support. It is vital for strategy to try to influence expectations. Part of the co-ordination problem is manipulating expectations to convince users to adopt the standard early on. This may be done directly, using advertising and promotion, and by educating the market in the use of what may be an unknown new product. Fast publication of market results helps to convince users. Credibility is not just a question of brand image, or a good track record. With new products there is no track record, and many firms with excellent reputations in an old technology have been unable to build a position in a new one. It depends on putting together a convincing package of suitable product, manufacturing capacity, financial backing, maintenance support and most important the availability of complements. Users need convincing of the firm's commitment to the standard, as they do not want to be stranded with an unsupported product. Alliances and open standards may help the standard's credibility. These convince co-producers and users that there is the capacity to meet demand and that the market will not be fragmented. Alliances with co-producers show users and manufacturers that the standard will be fully supported. Open standards reassure users that they will not later be held to ransom once they have invested in complementary goods and training.

(c) *Timing is everything*

Standards are highly dependent on the dynamics of the standardization process. There are usually many possible outcomes depending on what happens in the early stages. Timing is crucial and each aspect of strategy depends not just on the action but when it happens and how long it takes. The skill comes in recognizing the 'window of opportunity', a narrow time period between being premature, launching the standard before it is acceptable by the market, and being overdue, once some other standard is too strong to change. Operating in the window of opportunity involves flexibility as well as speed. Often the most useful ability is being able to realize when it is too late for the firm's own standard to win the contest, and time to accept the new standards regime. Timing is not all within the firm's control. Allowance must be made for the long periods of time taken for technical development, co-production, and user education, as well as for learning effects to bring down costs.

(d) *Sponsor co-producers and initial users*

To get over the co-ordination hurdle, of ensuring a supply of complements for the initial users, the manufacturer may need to sponsor early co-production. It may encourage independent complementary production by providing information, education and training, and other incentives, or form partnerships with co-producers. Open standards are usually an effective way to attract more complements, as well as hardware manufacturers and users. Otherwise the standards leader may need to produce the initial complements itself. This may be difficult, as it may take the manufacturer into an industry it is not familiar with. Alternatively, with new technology the manufacturer may be the only player at first with the skills to produce the complements. Once the initial phase is over the co-producers should respond to demand for complements without prompting. The sponsor's involvement may be limited to a basic complementary portfolio until the independent producers enter, but occasionally it leads to long-term vertical integration by the sponsor into complements. This is likely if the margins available in the complementary industry are higher than in the core product, so that CD manufacturers may continue to produce CD discs and computer makers continue to produce software.

(e) Form alliances

Establishing a support base for a standard often includes the use of alliances between manufacturers, as well as with distributors and software producers. Alliances reduce individual investment costs, and ensure adequate manufacturing capacity and distribution. They also remove potential competing standards, limit the extent of standards contests, and help avoid fragmented standards, which are expensive and hurt the market as a whole. Alliances also have a valuable role within a contest by providing a larger base, merging product features, and spreading development costs. The broadest coalitions are those for open standards, which are alliances, explicit or otherwise, often of weaker firms against a proprietary threat which they could not oppose individually. Temporary coalitions may also be used to work out problems of agreement between competitors on an *ad hoc* basis, dissolving once the object is achieved. Alliances also add to the credibility of the standard.

(f) Price for market penetration

Product pricing inevitably has an important role in introducing a standard. For conventional products a firm may use 'price skimming', charging a high initial price then gradually reducing this over time as costs fall by learning effects and bringing in users with successively lower product valuations. The aim is to maximize profits and provide cash flow for further development. However, in standards contests the first priority is to set up an installed base as quickly as possible. For standards, rather than try to recover R&D costs immediately, the firm may use 'penetration pricing', with as low prices as possible to increase volume and market share. If cash flow allows and the firm believes it can hold on to its market share, prices may be held low for years before the product comes to profitability. If the standard is successfully established the investment should eventually be paid back handsomely. Low pricing may be used even when there is no direct competitor to build up the base and get to the fast-growth phase earlier. It brings profits forward and reduces the risk of unexpected challenges from other products. The low pricing and high marketing costs unfortunately call for high up-front investment, at a time when firms often rely on high introduction prices to recover R&D costs and fund further development.

(g) Use preannouncements

Product preannouncements are a particular way of influencing expectations. They are often used to frighten off competitors or to gain time until a defending product is ready. These may reduce the impact of a competitor's innovation or at least confuse the market, especially as expectations are partly self-fulfilling. Manipulating expectations is not easy with totally new products. Users have little to go on, and firms may have to put great efforts into education and demonstrations of the product, as well as enlisting vows of support from complementary producers. Once the product is relatively well known there may be more scope. In some areas, such as microprocessors, the entire contest sometimes takes place before the product is fully developed and ends when the majority of the users have incorporated the standard in their future designs. A losing standard may never appear on the market.

Preannouncements also need to be used with care if the firm is not certain when its new product may be ready. If it preannounces a better version of its own product, then its own customers will wait for the better version, cutting off its current cash flow. This was the case for Osborne Computer, which, after a period of rapid growth in the early 1980s, was driven to bankruptcy when a new computer it had announced took a year longer to develop than expected (Osborne and Dvorak, 1984). The 'Osborne Effect' is an especially unfortunate form of cannibalization of a firm's own sales, even before it has its product on the market.

(h) 'Satisfice' the design

The winner of a standards contest is not necessarily the most technologically advanced but the one which most effectively implements the other strategies. Before the standard is brought to market technological development is clearly a central aspect of competition. However, once the product is developed to a point of user acceptability it becomes less important. The aim is an adequate standard, which 'satisfices' rather than optimizes the design, after which other aspects of strategy become more important. The standard should be brought to this point before products are launched, however. A constantly shifting design only confuses the market and a reliable, stable standard may be more important than state-of-the-art design. Technology may still be a major element in a standards contest, for cost reduction and adding performance features outside the standard. A contest may provoke rapid technical change in these areas, but should not mean that the basic interface definitions keep changing.

A firm adopting an external standard has some freedom in deciding its degree of conformity to the standard. It may clone every detail or just adopt the minimum features for basic compatibility. Also compatibility may be built into the product design or achieved by an adapter, leaving the internal design unchanged. The choice depends on a trade-off between the absorption costs to the manufacturer of redesigning the product, versus the cost and inconvenience to the user of interfacing part-compatible systems. In turn this depends on how central the standard is to the usefulness of the product. The less important the network effects the lower the degree of conformity which may be needed. Adapters are often only a temporary fix as they can be expensive and tiresome to use, but they may tide a product over until it can be redesigned. A main value of adapters is in dealing with 'orphaned' users who cannot justify switching from a stranded minority standard.

(i) Use indirect routes

There are a number of indirect means of increasing the size of the installed base. One way around the problem of building up complementary support is to make the new product compatible with an existing standard and use this as the initial installed base. This is the logic of multi-product and multi-generation/vintage standards. Adapters or translators may be used for compatibility with an existing base. The problem with evolutionary standards is that compatibility may distort the new standard too much and hold up technological advance. The product may become locked into an obsolete design. It may also be as costly to provide adapters as to build a new installed base from scratch. Eventually a radical break may be needed, with the new standard run independently, in parallel with the old system. An interesting modification of this strategy is to use a niche market to provide an 'avenue of entry' into the main market. The firm may develop a product for a specialist niche, and use the installed base to leverage out the standard into the main market. In this way the technological base of CD has made it easier to establish CD-ROM spin-offs, and the VHS standard for VCR has given VHS-C a built-in advantage for camcorders. In PC floppy discs, the 3.5-in. disc has been able to displace the 5.25-in. disk as the main standard in part by first building a base with portable machines and Apple computers.

A different aspect of linkage is joint profit maximization when a firm has interests in two competing standards, and the new standard cannibalizes sales of the old. The firm must decide whether to support both standards or only one. The total market is larger with a single standard than split between two and usually only one standard can win, so that supporting both is to be avoided. Also the firm is usually unable to sell one after the other, hoping to saturate the market with the first then repeat this with the second, as may be possible with conventional products. Once the first standard is established it blocks the second. Even with a niche this would fragment the standard, with a smaller total market.

(j) Caution—official standards bodies

Standards wars are expensive and unpredictable. Firms may try to avoid these by agreeing standards in industry committees and official standards bodies before making large investments in the market. Although standards bodies may have a useful role in policy and provide a valuable opportunity for firms to exchange information on standards and discuss common interests, a strategy which relies solely on adoption by official standards bodies is seldom effective for the individual firm compared with the other strategies above. The main reasons are that agreements are difficult to reach and once reached may not be adhered to. Committees usually rely on voluntary co-operation and unless firms are motivated by commercial interests they will not agree. Standards may be too important to the firms' futures to be agreed in committee and must be resolved by market competition. Official standards bodies, perhaps due to their traditional role in setting quality standards, tend to concentrate on technical aspects rather than commercial and strategic issues. To get agreement the standard may be ambiguously defined. Perhaps the most serious problem is that gaining official adoption is a time-consuming process and one of the key elements in setting standards is speed.

Further problems are that the standards body adds an extra player to the contest. Firms spend energy trying to influence the process rather than competing with the product. Standards authorities are poorly placed to make commercial decisions, especially in the time-frames required for new technology. Also other policy aims may interfere with the standardization process and further limit the chances of commercial success. When the standards authority is also part of government regulation, as for telecommunications and broadcasting, there may be little choice but to focus on an official approval strategy. Otherwise committees may divert effort spent more effectively elsewhere. These issues are explored further in the discussion of standards policy in Chapter 3.

6. PROFIT MAXIMIZATION AND OPENNESS

6.1 Degree of openness

Although the main determinant of firm profits is whether its chosen standard is established in the market, there is scope for maximizing profits within a given standards strategy. The key variable is the 'degree of openness' with which the firm allows access to the standard. At one extreme a fully proprietary standard has only a low chance of getting established and its market niche may be small, even though unit margins and share are high, so that expected profits (before the contest) are low. At the other extreme a fully open standard has a good chance of achieving a large total market, but with high competition and low margins and share, so that expected profits are again low. The optimal position may be somewhere in the middle, with a moderately open standard which has a good chance of being

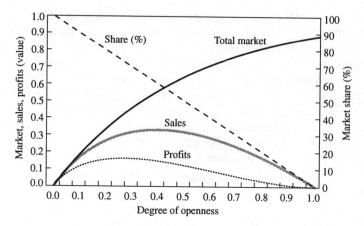

Fig. 2.9. *Openness vs. sales and profits*

established, but which still allows the leader enough control over access to retain significant market share and margin.

The essential choice for the firm is between size of total market and individual market share. The more open its strategy the larger the total market but the smaller its share and the lower the margin. A balance is needed between proprietary and open strategies. The trade-off is illustrated schematically in Fig. 2.9, which shows how sales and profits may vary with the degree of openness of the firm towards sharing the standard. Openness ranges from zero for a fully proprietary standard (no unlicensed imitation) to unity for a fully open standard (unrestricted access). Total expected market size increases as the standard is made more open, since it has a greater chance of being established and is less likely to be in a niche. In this case the market increases from zero for a fully proprietary standard (i.e. assuming it is not established at all), increasing to about 0.9 units for an open standard. The firm's expected market share decreases from 100 per cent for a proprietary standard to 0 per cent for a fully open standard (in fact the firm would expect some share of an 'open' standard since even then it would in practice have some control over its market). Multiplying total market by share gives individual firm sales, which have an inverted 'U' shape with respect to openness. This is the trade-off between size and share. As long as available market size increases faster than its share falls then the firm achieves higher revenues by allowing more openness. After a certain point further openness reduces share too much and revenues fall. Here maximum firm sales are at about 0.4 openness. Considering profitability, as the standard becomes more open it not only loses share but price competition forces down margins, so that the margin curve also falls (not shown). Combining this with the revenue curve gives the profit curve, also an inverted 'U' shape but peaking at lower openness than revenues, here at about 0.3. Sales and profit maximization occur for an intermediate point between full proprietariness and openness, and profit maximization occurs at lower openness than sales maximization.

6.2 Other methods

The openness analysis applies to the sponsors of a standard, whether 'proprietary' or 'open'. A firm adopting an external proprietary standard does not control openness. However, a firm adopting a (relatively) open standard may sometimes be able to offer a proprietary version if it has sufficient market power from other sources. If the firm is able to differentiate its product sufficiently by features outside the standard this may give it the power to influence the standard itself, even though it did not develop it. Thus a large firm may occasionally adopt an external standard and offer its own version, possibly with proprietary elements. This is part of the reason that standards are most often set by the largest firm in the industry. Following this logic, several large computer manufacturers have tried to offer proprietary versions of the open Unix operating system, though in this case without success.

Other methods available to the firm for adjusting its returns from the standard are essentially to try to increase its share of the total standards market by making its product compatible with as large a section of the market as possible, and increase its share and margin by product differentiation using features outside the standard. Different degrees of conformance to the standard are possible, so that there will be a range of products from different manufacturers more or less compatible with each other. By making its products compatible with as many of these as possible the firm gains access to a larger market. Differentiation from competitors' products is separate from the conformity choice, so that it should use product features which do not affect compatibility. It may also rely on superior complementary assets in manufacturing, marketing, and distribution to keep prices low and make acceptable margins. Examples of differentiation features are programme timers for VCRs or multi-play facilities for CD players, as well as general product quality.

7. CONTINUATION STRATEGIES: COMPETING WITHIN A STANDARD

7.1 Competitive conditions

So far our concern has been with strategies to establish a new standard. Part of the firm's profit calculation is how it expects to compete once the standard is set. We are also directly interested in continuation strategies.

Although the key period for any standard is in the early stages, the bulk of the sales and profits are made once the contest is decided. Because of the unpredictability of standards contests only a small part of what can happen with a standard can be foreseen, and there is ample scope for strategy within a given standards regime. Although the central standard itself is very difficult to change, there are other means of competition that focus on other aspects of competitive advantage as well as enhancements and extensions of the standard. Depending on the intellectual property regime and the capabilities of the firms, there may be considerable changes in market shares and who profits most from the standard. For example, PC market leadership has shifted considerably since the standard was developed and firms which have benefited most notably from the standard, such as Intel and Microsoft, were probably not the players most expected to profit from the standard at the beginning. The developers of the CD, Sony and Philips, probably did not envisage becoming as deeply involved in the music-recording industry as they eventually did, to coordinate hardware and software strategies for the standard.

Once a standard has been established the scope for competition is limited by the need for compatibility. This restricts the type of product differentiation and technical development possible. Competition is no longer to define the central standard but must work within its boundaries. Some incremental changes to the standard may be possible provided these do not affect basic compatibility. Competition is liable to rely more on basic product features of quality, service, and price. Because of the difficulty of changing an entrenched standard with a large installed base, a new standard can only be considered for a radical technical advance. However, the standard should not be seen as a problem, as it opens up large markets. Firms may make standards forces work for them not against them. There are many new opportunities for competition. Provided the standard is not limited to a niche it may lead to a large, homogeneous market with rapid technological change in both core and complementary products. It may be possible to adjust a given firm's control over the standard by introducing proprietary enhancements. Also there may be opportunities for new products built on the existing standard. Continuation strategies aim to maintain market share and to participate in new markets as they appear. There are most options within an open standards regime. Strategies within a proprietary regime may be limited, and the main aim may be to replace the old standard, as we have seen.

7.2 Continuation strategies

(a) Degree of openness

Once a standard is set the main problem for the standards leader is the gradual erosion of its market share as competitors enter the market. A

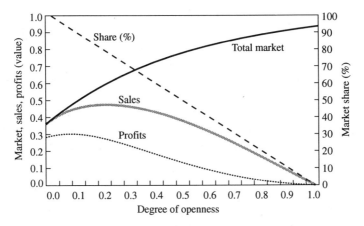

Fig. 2.10. *Openness vs. sales, profits: existing standard*

possible response is to try to increase the firm's proprietary control over the standard by restricting access, reducing the number of licensees, raising fees, and so on. We have seen that to maximize profits for a new standard the firm may allow an intermediate degree of openness—open enough to attract external support but with enough proprietary control to keep margins reasonably high. Once the standard is established there may be a similar trade-off between market size, share, and openness. Once the standard is entrenched the total market size is less responsive to changes in openness. Under some conditions the developer may be able to increase its proprietary control over the standard and so increase its market power and profits. The argument is illustrated in Fig. 2.10, which shows a possible set of relationships between market size, individual firm share, sales and profits versus openness. This is similar to the case of a new standard shown in Fig. 2.9, the difference being that the market size curve is now less responsive to changes in openness and is more horizontal. This moves the sales and profit maximization points to the left compared with the new standard, so the firm increases profits by decreasing openness after the standard is set.

Although this may look appealing, the strategy of 'closing' an open standard is difficult to implement in practice. The firm may well lose sales by trying to decrease openness. The problem is that users may be very resistant to the change, so that market size falls rapidly. Also there are now competing suppliers, and users may switch to lower-price manufacturers, unless the developer can exclude these from the market. Thus rather than increasing its market share by restricting new entrants, which was the case for the new standard, the developer may actually reduce its share by substitution from other suppliers (as happened with IBM's attempt to introduce the proprietary PS/2). The effect on share depends on the appropriability regime surrounding the standard and the developer's market strength in other areas. Often the developer has had to agree not to restrict future access as a condition for getting the standard accepted in the first place, under pressure from supporters. If a firm wants to increase proprietary control it may have to do so by adding new technological features, as below.

(b) Super-compatibility

An alternative to increasing proprietary control is to do the opposite, and make the firm's products as compatible with as broad a section of the installed base as possible. The aim is to increase the firm's share of the market by increasing the network effects working for its products. This encourages users to fill more of their systems requirements from this firm and still keeps the advantages of being able to mix products. Rather than trying to differentiate its product with non-standard features, firms may aim for more complete compatibility with the standard, to be 'super-compatible'. Non-standard features often make the product less, not more, attractive. More generally, accepting the standard as given allows the firm to concentrate on the technological development of new features rather than trying to defend its control of a static product. For example, in the computer industry many of the most successful firms have embraced open standards as fully as possible, such as ICL, Sun and Hewlett-Packard, compared with those tied to proprietary standards, such as IBM and DEC.

(c) Technical leadership

Once the standard is decided technical leadership again comes into its own as one of the main ways to compete within a standard. A firm may extend its market power by leading the technical development of features outside the standard or enhancements of the standard itself. The obvious candidate for technical leader is the original developer but other manufacturers and co-producers may also become substantial innovators, and even take over the leadership. New features should stay compatible with the standard. The installed base provides a large market, so that while standards restrict the breadth of innovation they also focus development in a certain direction and may increase total activity. Even if the new features are soon imitated, an emulation lag gives the leader some 'quasi-proprietariness' in a continual process of keeping ahead of imitators, with higher margins and market share. If broad technical leadership is not possible the firm may at least lead in some areas. If all else fails the alternative is to follow innovations as quickly as possible, and rely on the other strategies, including conventional product and manufacturing competition.

A tempting strategy is to develop new proprietary features to be incorporated in the standard, gradually increasing the firm's control. If the features are attractive enough users may be prepared to accept the proprietariness. However, there is a limit to how far a firm may change a standards regime, as noted above. Other manufacturers with the same standard technology may easily imitate most enhancements. Intellectual property rights for incremental innovations may be weak. Users will resist attempts to increase the market power of the standards leader. The greatest risk is that the proprietary 'improvements' are really incompatibilities, and separate the firm from the installed base. A more general strategy may be to lead to technological development of the standard, but encourage the adoption of these enhancements by other producers (perhaps via collaborative agreements or industry associations). The emulation lag gives the leader some market power without inducing users to reject the changes.

The standard frees resources for other development around and within the standard, reducing wasteful experimentation with new technologies in the same way that a new scientific paradigm directs research. However, it also reduces the variety of new products and eventually the standard features become 'saturated'. It is important to recognize when diminishing returns have set in for evolutionary innovation and a radical new standard is needed. Further progress may then be in a new direction with a new standards generation.

(d) Complementary assets

With a stable basic design competition tends to shift towards conventional price and quality variables. Especially with open standards the product may become 'commoditized', with many manufacturers, few means of differentiating products, and low profit margins. Even with a proprietary standard the firm is restricted in how far it may develop the product. In this situation the capabilities of the firm in quality manufacturing, marketing, and distribution, called 'complementary assets', become more important (Teece, 1986). Complementary assets and technical leadership are the two main strategy components for holding on to market share. They are interrelated in that strength in manufacturing and marketing may help the firm establish any additions to the standard, and possibly allow it to increase its proprietary control. The dynamic capabilities of the firm in innovation are in turn linked to its other capabilities in manufacturing and marketing (Teece et al., 1992).

(e) New standards products

The firm may be able to develop new products based on the standard in new areas. These have the double advantage of using tried technology and having a ready-made installed base of complementary support to start the new standard. Leadership in the new market may give high margins and other advantages. Specialization is also possible in a segment of the market served by the standard, with an existing complementary goods industry. Spin-offs include camcorders from VCR and CD-ROM and CD-I from CD.

(f) Vertical integration

The core manufacturer may vertically integrate into complementary production. This exploits its technical knowledge in developing new products and allows it to co-ordinate core and complementary strategies on a continuing basis. The firm may already have been involved in complements to co-ordinate the initial supply. Given the usual managerial differences between the two industries and the different market structures (one of the reasons interface standards are needed in the first place), successful integration may be relatively rare. The backward integration of Japanese consumer electronics manufacturers into music and movie production is well known. Having originally started producing CD discs to overcome the reluctance of the music industry, Sony later expanded its interests with a complete take-over of CBS, but kept the management of its acquisition separate.

7.3 Problem strategies

There are a number of strategies which divert effort into less effective directions and are probably best avoided. Many of these involve trying to impose proprietary control over a standard which has been established as open. These are strategies which may apply to conventional products but not to standards. Two examples, implicit in the above, are repeated here.

(a) Adding non-standard features

Adding non-standard features to differentiate the firm's version of the standard is frequently suggested, aiming to draw users into what gradually becomes a proprietary standard. The ploy is likely to fail as users may reject the 'enhancements'. Also total market demand may be reduced. The problem is that the new features may actually make the product less attractive by reducing the network benefits. The features intentionally make the firm's version less compatible with the basic standard. These subtract rather than add value to the product. 'One-way compatibility' also induces retaliation by competitors, confuses users and fragments the market, which the manufacturers do not want. Users have little difficulty seeing through the strategy and do not want to be locked into a more proprietary regime having once expressed their preference for an open standard. Examples where this route was tried and eventually rejected are the many semi-proprietary versions of Unix operating system, which have generally had low user appeal, and the introduction of the proprietary microchannel architecture (MCA) bus for the IBM PS/2, which also failed to be accepted in the market.

(b) Niche standards

A loser of a standards contest may wish to hold on to a specialist niche, where although volumes are limited it may survive on high margins. Markets tend towards a single standard. It is difficult to establish a niche standard and even more difficult to remain successful with one over time. The special attractions of a niche product have to be very high to outweigh the network advantages of the leading standard. Typically a niche is doomed to low growth and eventual elimination. If it achieves a sustainable installed base it is at a continuing and cumulative disadvantage. The leading standard has greater network advantages, more complementary support, and higher volumes to cover development costs. Niche users become stranded with an obsolete and poorly supported standard. To remain viable the niche may need eventually to become compatible with the main standard to access its base of complementary support. In VCR, Betamax failed to hold on to a niche despite quality, promotional and price advantages. In personal computers, Apple has held on to its segment of the market for many years by providing a significantly different machine from the PC, but is having difficulties now that the PC has matched many of its advantages. It has moved towards providing simpler interfaces with PC applications.

8. CONCLUSION

The main aim for the innovator is to ensure that the standard it supports is adopted in the market. Its basic decisions are whether to develop or adopt a standard and whether to make it open or proprietary. The brief discussion of strategic games indicates that the firm makes the leadership decision depending on whether it thinks it can win a contest, and adjusts access to ensure that it gets the support in needs. In determining the winner, much depends on which firm makes the first credible commitment. More generally the object is that firms agree to a common standard to benefit the whole market, and adjust individual returns to make it acceptable to all. There are a series of enabling strategies which are needed to establish the standard in the market-place. Further aspects of strategy aim to maximize profits and continue to compete effectively within a standard. The profitability decision facing a firm depends on the trade-off between total market size and individual share.

There are several themes differentiating standards strategy from that for conventional products. The focus for strategy is the complementary market as much as the product itself. The main thrust is needed in the very early stages of a new market and subsequent effort may be wasted. At this stage timing is crucial; so are expectations. Building up early volume is more important than margins. Technical development and official approval, often relied on for standards, are surprisingly unimportant. Continuation strategies within a standard are also different from the conventional products, with focused technical development and limited product differentiation and relying more on the firm's broad capabilities in production and innovation than on strategic manipulation of the market.

Many of the cases discussed in this book are open standards. Their predominance may be because of their effectiveness in attracting complementary support and winning contests. It may also be that most of the cases involve electronics and the hardware/software interface, where the widespread use of common components and dispersed intellectual property rights make proprietary strategies hard to contemplate. Competing in an open market is difficult, yet manufacturers may welcome open standards. They encourage the expansion of the market and allow freer competition. The opportunities for a successful producer are almost boundless. For example, in the computer industry, open standards have benefited users with lower prices, and manufacturers with huge new markets. Some manufacturers have been astonishingly successful in these conditions, others have had difficulty adjusting. They have created new industries in complementary goods. Rather than seeking power by manipulating proprietary standards, firms may welcome the chance to compete on equal terms. Some of the apprehension about open standards may be due to unfamiliarity with the new market structures and how to compete within them.

3

Standards Policy and Regulation: *Combining Committees and Markets*

SUMMARY   Although markets are effective in setting standards for private goods, policy intervention may be needed where the public costs of incompatibility are high. For example, driving would be chaos unless all drivers used the same side of the road. Even after drivers had settled on a common standard, the cost of dealing with occasional nonconformists or with 'stranded' users with wrong-side-drive cars would be high. In many cases, such as the use of the radio spectrum in broadcasting and interfacing with telecommunications networks, high public costs have historically led to official standards regulation. Standards committees aim to avoid standards wars and stranded users by agreeing standards before products are launched. However, official standards may bring as many problems as they solve. Vested interests make agreement difficult and time-scales may be too long for rapidly changing technology. The authority may add other policy aims which can ruin the standard. These and other problems are shown in cases where regulation has failed to set a workable standard. Mechanisms for greater involvement of markets in standards setting may help resolve some of the problems.

1. INTRODUCTION

Strategy is concerned with the decisions facing individual firms. Policy looks at the impact of standards on the industry as a whole, including manufacturers, co-producers, and users. Although markets are effective in setting standards for private goods, policy intervention may be needed when there are high public costs of incompatibility. Individual standards for, say, driving on the same side of the road would be chaotic. Even after standards had established themselves the cost of dealing with the occasional nonconformist or with stranded users with wrong-side-drive cars would be high. Here it is simpler to mandate standards. A standard may benefit an individual firm but not the rest of the economy. The market power of the standards leader may give it excellent returns but restrict new entrants to the industry and technological development. Standards wars are expensive, so that even winners may prefer to agree standards by negotiation before entering the market. Contests may lead to fragmentation, which hurts everyone, and stranded users of losing standards. Conversely the market may chose a single, technically inferior standard too early in the development cycle or provide too little variety, again holding back market growth. In such cases industry standards bodies and regulatory authorities may be used to set standards before market competition takes place. Yet they are not always successful and may bring as many problems as they solve. Some notable failures to establish official standards, such as in European high-definition television, UK telepoint, and satellite broadcasting, show that results when a regulating authority is involved may be no better than when the market is left alone.

The basic question is whether, from the point of view of individual firms and the industry as a whole, standards should be set by market forces (*de facto*), or by official standards authorities and committees (*de jure*). Regulatory committees aim to avoid standards wars and stranded users by agreeing standards before products are launched. If we see standards setting as a 'battle of the sexes' game, in which it is most important that firms agree on some reasonable standard rather than use resources contesting for leadership, then the issue is which method is most likely to reach agreement on an acceptable standard in the shortest time. The same co-ordination of decisions must take place whether by negotiations within the confines of an industry standards committee or by launching competing products in the market-place.

A difficulty with this, and a reason agreement is so hard to come by in practice, is the distribution of gains in favour of the leader. Unless some way is found to make following palatable, firms will try to pre-empt other standards to win contests. A more fundamental difficulty is lack of information. Firms may be able in principle to accept that they will be better off adopting an external standard, but not have sufficient information about technical and market potentials to make informed decisions. This is especially so for new technology still being developed as standards are set. The payoffs under the different strategies are not known with enough certainty to reach agreement. In such a case the only way to determine what standard the market will accept may be to compete with products. Standards are vital to the firms' futures, and if they cannot be sure of the outcome of the committee process they will prefer to settle their differences in the market-place. There are also a number of specific problems with official standards. The authority may be remote from the market and poorly placed to make technical and market decisions. Vested interests make agreement difficult and tend to divert the firms' efforts away from developing standards towards influencing the authority. The process may be biased towards the technical rather than business aspects of a new standard. Other policy aims may be added which can ruin the standard. Finally, time-scales may be too long for rapidly changing technology. The result is that for private goods such as computers and consumer electronics the market may be the most effective way to set standards, and the role of committees may be limited. In other industries where there is greater public interest at stake, such as in the use of the radio spectrum in broadcasting and setting up telecommunications networks, the costs of incompatibility and fragmentation are large, and may indicate the greater use of committees and official standards regulation. The choice of standards is tied in with competition to such an extent that the primary responsibility for standards may be with the authority.

In either case there are different forms of intervention and ways of organizing the committee process. These range from unofficial industry committees operating by consensus with voluntary adoption to official regulatory authorities with legal powers to mandate standards. Mechanisms for greater involvement of markets in official standards may help resolve some of the problems of official standards. Recently there have been experiments with hybrid policies, which try to combine official direction with market processes. In such cases the role of the authority becomes more one of facilitating rather than selecting standards. The authority may evaluate competing bids for new standards, as the US Federal Communications Commission (FCC) has done for high-definition television (HDTV) standards, or provide general guidelines for standards and leave market competition to determine the precise form, as the UK Department of Trade and Industry (DTI) has done with telepoint standards. It may allow the market even greater freedom to define the standard, as the FCC has done for AM stereo radio in the USA. Whatever the organization and aims, standards bodies usually also perform more general functions of collecting and disseminating information about possible standards, which help firms and users make rational choices. Any negotiating function is combined with less controversial aims such as publishing specifications and testing for conformance.

In this chapter, section 2 looks at problems with market standards as they affect the economy as a whole, and the possible need for intervention. Section 3 considers the countervailing problems of the committee process, offsetting the theoretical benefits of official standards, and gives a framework for evaluating the factors for and against official and market standards. Section 4 considers some of the possibilities for hybrid policies and their chances of combining the better features of the two extremes, while section 5 draws some conclusions and suggests some general themes for standards policy.

2. PROBLEMS WITH MARKET STANDARDS

Markets work by competition between alternative designs. They usually converge quickly to a single, proven standard. For many standards government intervention may be inappropriate and standards setting may safely be left to market competition. A large part of the success of products such as video cassette recorders and personal computers has been due to the efficiency and speed with which product design converged to a single main standard. However, this is not always the case. The market's effectiveness in generating and eliminating alternatives may become a source of problems, as noted above. Contests for new standards involve duplication of development effort, may confuse the industry, and lead to costly standards wars. They may result in fragmented standards, with stranded users locked into minority standards. Also they may settle on technically inferior standards. Finally there are questions of market power conferred by a standard, and international trade issues. From a public policy viewpoint these may justify government intervention. Problems with market standards and justification for policy intervention are discussed in Rosenberg (1976), Dybvig and Spatt (1983), David (1986, 1987), and David and Greenstein (1990), We look at the main aspects as follows, with some attempt to put the problems in context by pointing out market mechanisms which may limit the potential harm.

(a) Standards wars and duplicate development

While it is valuable to have a range of alternatives generated by the market, standards wars are costly and unpredictable. Market contests for standards are especially expensive since establishing any standard requires a high level of commitment and up-front investment, with no guarantee of winning. It is difficult for firms to hedge their bets on new technology with trial-level introductions. This means that duplicated development and promotion involve high costs and risks. At worst the risks may mean that no individual firm is prepared to make an attempt, and the product stalls. As far as this is 'wasteful' competition, resources could be saved if producers use the same standard from the beginning. However, much of the risk is inherent to standards, and cannot be avoided even with a single standard. Although the scale of investment is high it is not clear that this is fundamentally different from other aspects of competition, which are generally approved of. The outcome is at least known quickly. Also commercial risks are not necessarily reduced by trying to set standards before the technology is proven in the market-place.

(b) Fragmentation

If a leader does not emerge until late in the contest there may be several standards each with a small installed base, large enough to survive but not to attract adequate support for the long run. All users suffer by being locked into standards with smaller installed bases. Fragmented standards divide the market so that no one standard is truly successful. Each has fewer complementary goods and services, and the equipment costs are high if the standard has not reached minimum efficient scale. This holds back total market growth. The expansion of railway traffic in nineteenth-century England was retarded by the different railway gauges which had evolved for regional services, and one of these, Brunel's Great Western Railway, resisted conformity for over fifty years. Similar compatibility problems have reappeared recently on a European-wide scale with the introduction of high-speed train services. Whether fragmentation is a major danger for technologies which are widely realized to have network externalities is an open question. Many fragmented standards exist where the technology was in wide use before network effects became an issue. This is probably the case for historical standards such as railway gauges, screw threads, and fire-hose connectors (which even today are still often incompatible between neighbouring fire departments). Also, at an international level, national standards bodies have tended to use standards to promote domestic industries, leading to global fragmentation, as for most national telecommunications standards, the three different world standards for colour TV, and the potential fragmentation of HDTV standards.

(c) Stranding

Though markets may converge quickly to a single standard, they are harsh on failed standards and their supporters. The users and co-producers who have adopted a losing standard are stranded without support or complementary markets. The market provides no help for these orphans. They may not be able to justify the switching costs needed to change to the winning standard. Owners of Betamax video cassette recorders (VCR) discover that there are few pre-recorded tapes for rent, and 'diehard' owners of non-DOS-compatible personal computers have difficulty finding software, and pay high prices for it. These costs fall mainly on the users. Arguably in many cases these costs are manageable within the market system. There may be few stranded users and the winner may chose to subsidize their conversion to the main standard. A secondary market in adapters may arise to reduce the switching costs if there are enough stranded users to justify it. Technical change may soon give an opportunity to switch to the leading standard with the next upgrade. In other areas the public costs may be more severe, and call for intervention. Social costs are high if a group of drivers tries to drive on the wrong side of the road or transmissions from a non-standard television station interfere with other broadcasts. However, it is the stranding costs which make market competition effective. Avoiding being stranded is the primary reason why user expectations are so important and new standards are set quickly. Thus if it is generally known that standards are important for a new product, the number of stranded users is likely to be small. Thus only about 2 per cent of the VCR machines in existence today are on the losing Betamax standard. Also they are likely to be the first users, and possibly their support is still important to the leading standard, so the leader may subsidize conversion to bolster demand. When BSkyB was formed by merger of Sky and British Satellite Broadcasting (BSB) services in the UK it was still not clear that satellite television would be successful, though it was clear that BSB would not be. BSkyB gave special incentives for BSB subscribers to switch receivers to Sky transmissions.

(d) Technical inferiority and standards variety

The tendency for markets to converge on a single standard may mean that too few alternatives are considered before the standard is set. A standard may be chosen too early in the development of a new technology and the industry becomes locked into an inferior standard. For example, the arrangement of the QWERTY typewriter keyboard was already obsolete when it was introduced a hundred years ago but has lasted to this day. It had been designed to avoid the keys jamming, by slowing down typing speeds for the most frequently used letters, but the mechanical problem had already been corrected before typewriters were widely used (David, 1985). A problem with this argument is that it is difficult to decide what the 'best' standard is. There is more to creating a successful standard than technical superiority. It depends on the installed base as much as on the product itself. A basic level of user acceptability together with good distribution and complementary support may be more important to users. Standards established by the market have at least passed this important test. A related argument is that there may be too little variety. It is possible for the market to be better served by more than one standard but be locked into a single dominant standard. However, this must take into account the network benefits of a single standard working (strongly) against fragmentation. If the difference in the appeal of different standards to separate market segments is enough to offset the network effects then markets may support coexisting standards, as has been the case with Apple and DOS standards for personal computers. Also an 'obsolete' standard may have outlived its technical shelf life but still give great value to users through their investment in software and training.

(e) Market power

The above are essentially co-ordination problems. With a proprietary standard the design owner may restrict access and use its market power to charge high prices. This is part of a set of much broader industrial and trade policy issues with implications beyond those of setting standards. Standards certainly may bestow market power. However, standards setting is sensitive to small disturbances in the early stages so that results of policy intervention at that point are unpredictable. Policy may have more effect dealing with the results of standards contests than in directing them. Also standards are as likely to be influenced by existing market power as to create it, so that this is a longer-term problem, perhaps stretching over different technological generations, than the immediate policy issues noted above.

Whether the various problems with market standards seriously offset their advantages depends on the particular case. Whatever the balance, the fact remains that there is some level of problems with markets. Firms may become locked into standards they would like to change, often say that they would prefer a standard to be set before development to avoid wasted investment, and tend to adopt standards set by the firm with the largest resources rather than necessarily the best design. In theory such problems could be ameliorated by setting a standard by negotiation before substantial investment takes place, possibly backed by regulatory power. Alternatively an official body may try to modify the market process. The question is whether such action can be effective. Before we can make these judgements we must look at specific problems introduced by the use of committees and other forms of official standards bodies. Despite their theoretical advantages these practical problems may move the balance back in favour of market standards.

3. COMMITTEES AND REGULATED STANDARDS

3.1 Problems with regulated standards

An official standards authority aims to set standards outside the market, if possible before products are developed and launched. This is achieved by negotiation and selection using committees representing manufacturers, complementary producers, users, and government. Standards bodies are of various types, from voluntary industry associations with no direct legal powers to regulatory authorities with strong enforcement capability. A distinction is sometimes made between modes of co-ordination by voluntary committees and by political or economic hierarchies (David and Greenstein, 1990; Schmidt and Werle, 1992). However, they all usually co-ordinate standards by some form of consultative, consensus process and most have some other policy overtones. Unfortunately, in either case, the process does not always work as well as intended. There are inherent difficulties of using committees and official standards bodies to make decisions for new technology. The variables are numerous and fast changing, and the outcomes are crucial to the firms' commercial interests, so that it is not surprising that consensus is hard to achieve. In practice official standards also bring their own set of problems. There are a number of reasons why involving an official standards body in the standardization process is not costless. These are in five areas, as follows.

(a) Difficulty reaching agreement

It is hard to get agreement by committee. Even if reached it may not be upheld unless backed up by market forces. Vital commercial interests are involved and standards may be too important to the future of the firms to be settled purely by committee negotiations. Firms are bound to compete in product development and possibly to try to pre-empt the decision by launching products on the market. If a decision goes against them they may attempt to bypass the official standard in the market. Thus the agreement may be of little value unless it is backed up by market forces. Where members are under pressure to generate agreement, consensus may ostensibly be achieved but without full commitment. Such standards are often worded ambiguously, and effective standards may still have to be determined *de facto* by market competition. This is especially so if the process is slow and the conditions which led to the original agreement change over time. The difficulty in obtaining agreement is partly to do with the organizational design of the committee. Historically standards bodies have been mainly interested in quality standards, such as for British Standards Institute (BSI) safety standards. These focus on common standards for existing products where the commercial interests are already settled and the issues are primarily technical. However, the processes of consultation and consensus which work well with quality standards are not so effective for interface standards for new technology, where more complex commercial interests are involved.

(b) Technical bias

Official standards bodies tend to concentrate on technical rather than commercial aspects and so use too narrow criteria. They often express surprise when the most technically advanced standard is not adopted by the market. Yet standards contests show us that the most advanced standard often does not win, and that it takes other aspects such as obtaining broad support, complementary investment, and distribution to establish a standard. This bias may be partly a response to the difficulties of obtaining commercial information. It may also be part of a historical focus of standards committees on quality standards. As an administrative body the authority may be remote from the market and not have sufficient information or indeed motivation to choose the most attractive standard. This is less likely to be an issue if the committee mainly represents a consensus of member firms. If, as is more likely, it has some independent power it may not be fully informed about commercial possibilities and will tend to concentrate more on technical performance than market criteria.

(c) Lobbying process

A basic problem is that the committee approach introduces an extra player into the game, in the form of the standards body itself. This changes the focus of competition from the product itself to influencing the standards authority. Firms' efforts are diverted into finding out what the regulator is thinking and trying to influence it in their favour, changing the game from an economic to a political process. It is often unclear what criteria are being used in the decision, which may confuse users. The merits of the product may easily get overlooked. The authority cannot have all the information, especially business information, to make the commercial judgements needed for success in the market-place. It must rely on the firms to supply this information, which apart from being at second hand may also be selective regarding the merits and costs of alternatives. The only way to fully understand the product is intimate involvement at the firm level. Yet relying on adoption by the standards authority is often a bad strategy for the firms. It was no guarantee of success for telepoint and BSB in the UK, or for the European MAC standard for HDTV.

(d) External policy agenda

An important problem for regulated standards is that the authority may bring in its own policy agenda beyond setting an efficient standard. This may influence the standard in ways which make it unacceptable in the market. It is hard to resist the temptation to use standards to promote national industry. Attempts to use standards for industrial policy aims may seem costless as the standard is sensitive to small influences one way or another in the early stages. However, this is likely to interfere seriously with standards co-ordination. Decisions are made not on the basis of setting an efficient standard but on other grounds. The success of a standard is very sensitive to its credibility in the early stages—any interference can easily destroy this and make it unacceptable to the market. Private agendas are especially likely in regulated industries, which are just the areas where official standards committees are likely to have most power and to try to use this to further exterior policy aims. Telepoint is a case where the standard was restricted to fit other policy aims to promote UK manufacturers and influence telecommunications competition, but led to an unworkable standard.

(e) Timing

The committee process is usually slow and may operate on a much longer time-scale than the market needs. Fact finding and negotiations, especially for voluntary agreements, inevitably move slowly. One of the crucial elements in setting a new standard is speed. There is a narrow window of opportunity to establish a standard. This gives a chance for a faster-moving market solution to bypass the official standard and establish itself as the *de facto* standard before the official standard appears. The process is also inflexible, so that modifications to the standard which become apparent as the product is being introduced either cannot be made or take too long.

Decision mechanisms are cumbersome and changes may not be feasible once the process is far advanced. This is especially a problem in industries where the technology and industry structure change very quickly. Committees can have difficulty keeping abreast of market developments and may only confirm what has already happened. For telepoint, vital changes to correct basic product errors by adding pagers and two-way calling took over a year to be approved and were still not introduced when the initial services failed. Delay is occasionally an advantage if it avoids premature standardization, as may be the case with HDTV in the USA, where delays in approving standards have given digital systems time to be developed. However, this effect is not predictable.

3.2 Policy choices between official or market standards

The choice between official and market standards, and the need for policy intervention, depends partly on the effectiveness of the two mechanisms in setting standards quickly and efficiently with least chance of fragmentation and the problems above. This naturally depends on the particular case. Some of the main factors in this decision are given in Fig. 3.1.

Factors in favour of markets are that they usually set standards quickly and efficiently, at least for 'private' products such as consumer electronics or computers. A sense of proportion is needed in assessing the costs. Some degree of duplication of effort, market fragmentation, user isolation, technical obsolescence, and monopoly power occur with any market process.

	Market	Committee
Favouring markets	+ Clear decision + Fast + Commercial goals + Acceptable to market + Open process + Product focus + Design variety + Global	− Agreement difficult − Slow − Technical bias − Remote from market − Covert lobbying − External policy agenda − Monolithic − Local / national
Favouring committees	− Standards wars − Duplicate development costs − Fragmented standards − Stranding − Locked in obselescence	+ Orderly process + Single launch + Unified standard + Provision for losers + Technically superior

Fig. 3.1. *Effectiveness factors for market vs. committee standards processes*

Competition and duplicated effort may be a necessary part of new technology. It is possible to overstate the risks and in many cases the market itself finds ways to minimize them. If the issues are understood from the beginning markets usually converge to a single standard. As for market power, proprietary standards seem to have become almost a rarity in a world where open standards are widely used to attract support and win contests. Markets have shown their ability to resolve the complex issues involved with rapidly moving new technology. The costs must be compared to the benefits of having a clearly defined standard and the potential costs of the policy alternatives.

Even so there are areas where the costs of chaos possible under the market are more serious. The potential problems with market standards are real enough. Markets can be harsh on the losers. The costs of being stranded may be more than an individual can bear, or may fall not on the firms making the decisions but on society as a whole. The costs, say, of replacing expensive medical equipment which no longer has maintenance support or of retraining specialized skills in a technology made obsolete by a standards war, may be beyond what individuals can afford. Confusion in the use of the radio spectrum with several transmission standards makes broadcasting difficult for everyone, not just the maverick broadcasters. There are also some standards which may be beneficial but need to be co-ordinated centrally by an authority which sees the whole picture, particularly for changes to a standard. A change in the side of the road a nation drives on clearly has to be arranged by government ruling, individuals cannot change it themselves. In cases such as these there may be a need for government intervention to co-ordinate and regulate the standards process. The government may already be involved as a regulator of the industry, as in telecommunications and broadcasting. Compared to the market the committee approach is more orderly, may avoid the standards wars and other problems of markets, and potentially makes provision for all users affected by the standard—winners and losers.

The choice also depends on the likelihood of a market contest and the importance of the public interests involved. Intervention is mainly an issue only when there is a potential contest between standards. Conflict is likely when there are strong private vested interests in leading the standard and there is a high value for common standards in terms of total market growth, i.e. when network externalities are high and the winners of a contest benefit privately from capturing these (via high margins or market share). This is shown in Fig. 3.2, which draws on a discussion in Besen and Saloner (1989). When the value to the market of common standards and private interests in leading the standard are both relatively low, setting standards will usually be left to the government. This is the typical situation for traditional quality and safety standards set by official standards bodies. When the value to the market of having compatibility standards is high, but no firm can benefit

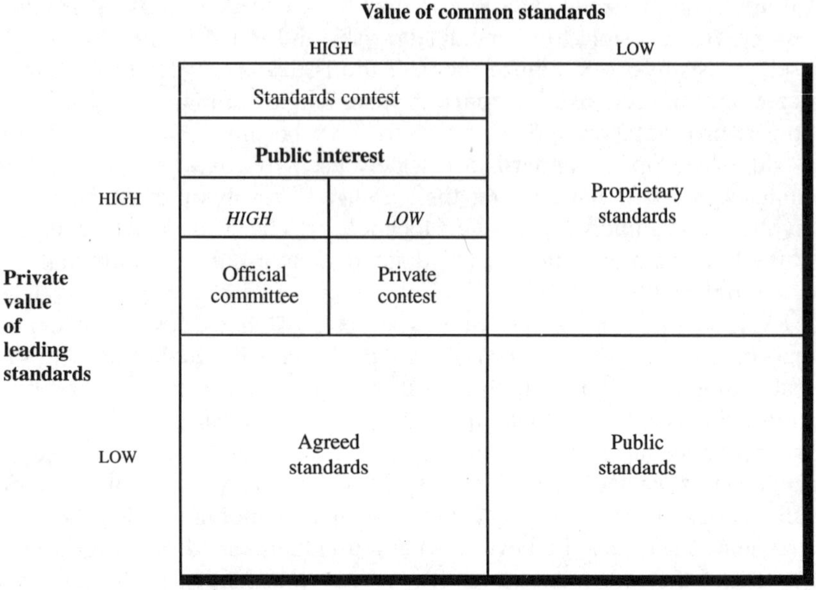

Value of common standards

	HIGH		LOW

	Standards contest		
Public interest			Proprietary standards
	HIGH	*LOW*	
	Official committee	Private contest	
	Agreed standards		Public standards

(Left axis, top to bottom: HIGH / **Private value of leading standards** / LOW)

Fig. 3.2. *Need for policy intervention in standards setting*

more than the others, then voluntary agreement is likely. These are cases of pure co-ordination, achieved via industry standards committees or *de facto* follow the leader. When there is a strong private interest in maintaining control over a standard and little to be gained by spreading its use by competitors, such as a proprietary standard in a specialized product niche, the standard is essentially a private good. The leader may be expected to make private efforts to establish the standard, such as sponsoring initial co-production and adoption, and defend its intellectual property rights. Policy may only be involved if market power is considered an issue. However, when both the value of the standard and vested interests in leading it are high, then there is likely to be a contest, in which case problems such as duplicated costs, fragmentation, and stranding may arise. If these public costs are considered high then policy intervention in the standards-setting process may be needed. If the public interests are less significant, or on balance it is thought that intervention will be detrimental to the market process, then standards may be left to the firms to decide. Thus the VCR standards contest was left to the market while HDTV and new telecommunications standards have aroused considerable policy interest.

3.3 Co-ordination as a strategic game

Further insight into policy may be given by returning to the idea of standards setting as a strategic game, in which the total returns to the industry are maximized by agreeing to common standards ahead of market entry, but firms may still fall into standards wars by seeking individual competitive advantage. The problem is that the benefits are not evenly distributed. The leader may expect higher profits by restricting access to the standard or charging high licence fees. Even if there are no net losers, some firms may gain more than others. Firms are likely to compete to have their standard adopted by the committee. The idea of standards contests as variations of a 'battle of the sexes' game has been discussed above. In this game, well known in game theory, two players both gain by agreeing to do the same thing but one gains more than the other. Unless the players are fully aware of the payoffs, they may vie with one another to be first and enter a contest, either via committee negotiations or in the market place.

The game shown in Fig. 3.3 illustrates a situation in which the joint returns to two firms are maximized by one firm agreeing to lead and the other to follow, but both firms overestimate their chances of winning a standards contest and their expected payoffs from a contest. The payoffs expected by the firms *ex ante* are shown in the table in normal type and the 'true' payoffs below these in italics. If firm A leads and B follows then A receives £7 m. and B receives £3m., making a total £10 m. for the industry. If the firms contest the standard then they each believe that their expected payoff is £4m. (this assumes they believe they both have the same chance of winning). Each firm calculates that it is better off contesting the leadership than following, making £4m. instead of £3m., even though this makes the

<table>
<tr><th></th><th></th><th colspan="2">Firm B</th></tr>
<tr><th></th><th></th><th>LEAD</th><th>FOLLOW</th></tr>
<tr><td rowspan="2">Firm A</td><td>LEAD</td><td>**(4,4)**
(2,2)</td><td>(7,3)
(7,3)</td></tr>
<tr><td>FOLLOW</td><td>(3,7)
(3,7)</td><td>(0,0)
(0,0)</td></tr>
</table>

Fig. 3.3 *Apparent and true costs in standards leadership contest*

Notes: The pay-offs expected by the firms *ex ante* from a standards contest (lead, lead) are shown in normal type, the true pay-offs are shown below these in italics. Alternatively the italicized figures may be interpreted as the modified pay-offs from a standards contest after policy intervention to charge firms the full costs of stranded users. Equilibria in the two cases are shown in bold.

industry as a whole worse off (with a total £10 m.). In fact the firms have incomplete information and overestimate their expected payoffs from a contest, and the 'true' payoffs from a contest, i.e. (lead, lead), may be only £2 m. each, shown in italics. If firms are fully informed then the equilibrium moves from a contest to agreement (lead, follow), shown in bold. Which firm is designated as the leader may depend on chance or bargaining skills, but both firms are unambiguously better off agreeing.

The tasks for the committee or policy-maker are how to uncover the true payoffs and induce the firms to chose agreement. Many of the usual ways out of this impasse do not work for compatibility standards. The regulator may try to adjudicate the decision, and the search for objective measures may be one reason for the technical bias of committees. However it will find it difficult to evaluate the conflicting claims for the many reasons given above. Similarly this cannot be a repeated game (in which case players could take turns to lead) as once the standard is set it is locked in for the duration. Deciding the outcome by hierarchy, such as following the largest firm, is also unsuitable with new technology where the market is new and leadership often changes, though it may be used after the fact once standards exist to decide which of several incompatible fragmented standards should become the common standard.

The remaining way is for the policy-maker to change the payoffs to the firms. One means of doing this has already suggested itself, to make full information available to the firms so that they form more realistic expectations of success. This indeed is one of the important roles of committees, to exchange information about different standards and the market prospects for competing designs. Beyond this a regulator may change payoffs directly and reduce the expected payoffs from a contest. It may insist that winners pay the full cost of taking care of stranded users. It may cap or tax excess profits. Thus the italicized figures in Fig. 3.3 may be interpreted as the modified payoffs after policy intervention to charge firms the full costs of the contest. The payoffs from (lead, lead) are reduced from (4, 4) to (2, 2). This moves the outcome from a contest to agreement, as above.

An alternative method is to equalize the expected payoffs to leader and follower from an agreed standard, such as by committing to equal market shares or to unrestricted access and no licence fees. The modified game is shown in Fig. 3.4, in which the payoffs to leader and follower have been redistributed to be £5 m. each, shown in italics. A firm will now prefer to follow and receive the £5 m. rather than contest the leadership and receive only £4 m. The outcome moves from a contest to agreement, shown in bold. Payoffs may be equalized by a regulator ensuring that all firms have equivalent shares of the market for supplying standard products, or by an industry association committing to open access as part of its negotiations. The success of institutions such as Unix International in agreeing open systems

Firm B

	LEAD	FOLLOW
LEAD	**(4,4)** *(4,4)*	(7,3) *(5,5)*
FOLLOW	(3,7) *(5,5)*	(0,0) *(0,0)*

Fig. 3.4. *Effect of payoff equalization policy in standards contest*

Notes: The pay-offs expected by the firms *ex ante* from a standards contest are shown in normal type. Modified pay-offs from a standards contest after policy intervention to equalize individual firm pay-offs for agreed standards, e.g. (lead, follow), are shown below these in italics. Equilibria in the two cases are shown in bold.

standards for computer software has been in large part because commitments were made by the main developer, AT&T, to keep the standard open in future.

A leadership contest may take place within a committee or in the marketplace. A way out of endless negotiations is for one or more of the players to commit to a standard by launching products on the market. The other players must then decide whether to compete in the market or follow the standard. This may be combined with continued committee negotiations to help smooth competition but once the players have decided to compete in the market the process must be followed to its conclusion. Much of the effectiveness of market standards is due to the fact that competition cannot continue for long. Costly investment decisions are made and tested against the market. Because of the high costs the process must be finite and results are decisive. It is very clear whether the market has adopted or rejected a standard and this point is usually reached after a short time. Also any changes to the standard have to be made quickly. For HDTV in Japan, the manufacturers' strategies were soon changed in response to slow consumer adoption of HDTV to introduce it in stages with enhanced definition television (EDTV). In contrast, the slower negotiation mechanism for changes to telepoint standards in the UK may have contributed to the lack of success of the initial systems.

3.4 *Other activities of standards bodies*

We have been concerned here with a standard body's role in setting new standards. Whether or not the authority is active in negotiating standards it is likely to have other traditional functions as a facilitator for new and existing standards. These are seen as valuable in their own right and are less controversial. The many aims and activities of standards bodies other than negotiating conflict are described in Sanders (1972) and Verman (1973). They include providing channels for information exchange and discussion, providing initial information about standards, and educating users. The authority may be responsible for formal drafting of standards, technical evaluation, documentation, and compliance testing. The authority may also try to correct market problems with existing standards. It may also co-ordinate the development of enhancements to existing standards. Most of these functions are strategically neutral in that they benefit the members as a whole without favouring particular firms. They have always been a major part of what standard bodies do. In the sense that more broadly dispersed information makes standards agreement more efficient, firms may be encouraged to make full use of these services and make their role in industry standards bodies an important part of their business strategy.

4. COMBINING MARKETS AND OFFICIAL STANDARDS

4.1 *Hybrid policies*

With problems with both market and official standards the question arises whether it is possible to combine the two in a superior hybrid policy. Recently there has been a great deal of interest in using market forces for standards traditionally set by regulation. In an environment of rapid technological change and global markets, official standards have become increasingly unsatisfactory. Although we may improve the committee process its basic problems of evaluation, lobbying, and external agendas remain. The trend has been towards greater use of *de facto* market standards where possible. Unfortunately market standards may have their own problems of unpredictability, cost, and fairness. For products with strong public goods aspects methods of combining markets and government authority are currently on trial.

There are two aspects to hybrid policies. First is the combination of committee negotiation with market competition as complementary ways to reach agreement. The aim is to agree standards more quickly and efficiently, without other policy considerations. Advantages are that markets are generally quick and decisive, while committees may forestall standards wars and the sunk investments which can lock the industry into fragmented standards. The standards body provides a forum for discussion and information sharing as a facilitator of an essentially market-oriented process. Second is the combination of markets with stronger direction by the regulator to address major public policy concerns. The market is used to set the details of a new standard but it is felt that policy interests are too great to be left solely to the market. The distinction is not merely the degree of official involvement. Here there is conscious regulation rather than simply using committees to improve a negotiating process. It corresponds roughly with the distinction between co-ordination via voluntary committees and via hierarchies with legal or economic power.

For the first case, committees may under certain conditions outperform the market as co-ordinating mechanisms, while hybrid systems may be better still. Farrell and Saloner (1988) compare extreme cases of standards set by committee negotiation and those set by firms which only 'communicate' by making investments in the market-place, without prior negotiation. They show that in theory a committee may be more likely to arrive at a common standard because negotiations take place before irreversible investments are made and there is less chance of choosing fragmented standards by 'mistake'. In their analysis, committee standards may be set later than pure market standards since firms delay agreement until the last moment, but the cost of delay is more than offset by the greater likelihood of agreement. Without negotiations firms try to pre-empt each other, so that 'pure market' standards are set earlier but with greater chance of fragmentation. Perhaps unexpectedly, in the hybrid system the ability to make pre-emptive investments strengthens the ability of the firms to make commitments in the negotiation process and so may be best of all.

However, this is really about co-ordination in setting *market* standards rather than about directive policy. It shows that market standards may be set more efficiently if firms are permitted to negotiate with each other. The committee itself has a purely co-ordinating role giving the firms repeated opportunities to state their preferences verbally rather than revealing them via sunk investments. This is an important lesson for standards but the value of committees as talking-shops is not controversial, as discussed above.

Problems are more likely in the second case where the regulator wants to influence the standard, either to avoid fragmentation and other market problems, or to use standards for other industrial policy aims. In practice committees are rarely neutral over which standard is preferred. It is difficult for the authority to resist using standards to pursue an external policy agenda. However, several attempts to use standards for other policy aims have not been a success. For example, the performance of telepoint in the UK shows several problems with trying to influence the market. In direct broadcasting by satellite (DBS) the unintentional combination of official and market standards in the UK resulted in the official standard being bypassed by the market standard. Standards setting is a delicate business and is easily disturbed, and other policies may better be pursued more directly. Standards are not robust enough to be general policy tools. The cases show that strong standards flow from well-managed firms, not the other way round. At an international level, policies to support national champions are probably the main reason for globally fragmented standards. Changing national attitudes may take some time.

4.2 Levels of market involvement

There are many different ways of involving the market. The questions are where to draw the boundary and how much influence the authority retains. So far hybrid policies are still experimental, and have mainly served to illustrate the difficulties of combining two very different processes. More experience is needed before any clear recommendations can be made and here we can only suggest some possible approaches.

As a first step, the authority may maintain much of its role in setting standards but truncate the selection process. Market mechanisms may improve selection while still leaving the authority to make the final decision. The authority may invite proposals from the market, setting only broad guidelines for the bids, which it then evaluates independently to decide a winner. This approach has been taken by the FCC for US HDTV standards. This differs from a straight committee process in that there are no lengthy negotiations and the time-scale is usually fixed. Having clear rules for selection may help avoid strategic game-playing. Options are to decide a winner by a date deadline, by the first to establish a clear lead, or by the first to surpass a performance threshold (Farrell and Shapiro, 1992). All have problems but the deadline method has the best chance of cutting short a to-and-fro tournament between the firms. It is important to have a fixed end to the decision process. However, there are difficulties assessing the proposals. Firms are likely to withhold some information to improve their standard's chances of selection. This is especially so for cost information, which is harder to verify than technical. As a result the regulator often chooses a technically excellent but expensive standard. One way to induce firms to reveal their true costs is by auctioning the rights to set the standard. This motivates firms to optimize the costs and features of the product. To avoid monopoly problems this should also include the condition that the final standard be licensed at 'reasonable' (low) royalties to other producers. Unfortunately a problem with this approach is that there are usually few suppliers for large systems, and there is unlikely to be an effective market bidding for the standard. The recent experience of the UK in auctioning television program franchises have not been encouraging for this kind of auction, with widely varied bids.

A second option is for the regulatory authority to set the ground rules for new standards but leave the market to design and establish the detailed standards on its own. This moves the boundary further towards the market. This is the route taken for UK telepoint. However, reconciling the very different approaches traditionally taken by official standards bodies and markets so far has made results unpredictable. Market standards need a minimum of interference while policy-makers are used to taking an overseeing role. Getting the balance right is difficult.

The third option is to use fully market-determined standards, within a minimal regulatory framework. Years of official standards setting in some industries should not make this as 'unthinkable' as we may imagine. The regulatory authorities may set out only the most basic rules for a new service, such as allocating radio spectrum bands for broadcasting or satellite transmission, and leave providers to develop whatever services and standards they can. This is the approach taken for US AM stereo radio, discussed below.

4.3 AM stereo: combining markets and regulation

One of the few examples of what can happen in turning over regulated standards to the market is AM stereo radio in the USA, described in Berg (1987). The FCC had evaluated proposals through committees for over twenty years from 1961 to 1982 without coming to a decision. Possibly because external pressure for a decision for this non-vital product was weak, the committees went round in circles trying to decide between a number of standards. This was brought to a halt in 1982, when in a surprise policy change the FCC announced that a station would be allowed to choose what standard it wished, provided it fitted within its bandwidth allocation. The first system (Kahn) was launched within two months and began recruiting local radio stations. Others followed quickly. The main competitor (Motorola C-QUAM) was introduced about six months later. This had superior technology, support, and financial backing, and overtook Kahn. AM stereo became an established service within a three-year period. Standards converged on the C-QUAM standard but left a sizeable minority stranded with Kahn, which held on to the installed base it had built up before C-QUAM entered.

The market was able to establish a standard quickly, in three years compared with the previous twenty years of fruitless negotiation, but the case also shows the problems of fragmentation. Markets are harsh on the losers and lawsuits against the FCC have been a possibility. However, the fragmentation was in part a hold-over from the previous delay. When this was unexpectedly lifted it did not give all the alternatives an equal start. Those who had been counting on FCC adoption were ready to begin broadcasting immediately, and knew their best chance against better funded rivals was to try to get in first. As the geographic coverage does not overlap very much, the costs of fragmentation for the user side may not have been excessive.

5. CONCLUSION

Many official standards institutions have evolved for historical reasons. Their traditional concerns have been to maintain quality and service standards across an industry, and the technical viability of a network. The technical approach, working through layers of committees towards consensus, is well suited to this kind of collaboration. It does not seem to work well for the fast decision making needed with compatibility standards for new technology. Co-ordinating the technologies and reconciling the various strategic interests may need market competition. The outcomes for some recent officially mediated standards have compared poorly with the successes for private standards set in the market place. Indeed standards bodies may be better equipped to deal with negotiations after standards have evolved, to move towards a common standard as painlessly as possible, than to set them in the first place.

We need to re-evaluate how market forces may be brought into the standardization process. So far attempts to combine markets and regulation have not often been successful. In some cases this may have been because attempts have not gone far enough. In telepoint, the main decisions remained with the regulator. Where the market has been allowed enough freedom, as in UK satellite television (inadvertently), and in US AM stereo, a standard has at least been set efficiently. Left to themselves, markets have shown that they will set *some* standard efficiently, and whatever its technical merits the standard has passed the important market test of user acceptability. In this the role of the authority may be to provide the conditions for the market to work and where necessary to correct excesses. If it tries to do more, and arrange the details of a new standard, it may hinder the process as much as help it.

Standards should not be seen as a simple way to implement industrial policy. Intervention may spoil a standard's chances of success. Providing information and alternatives via standards bodies is beneficial to all parties, but once the influence becomes too direct the risk is that the standard becomes unworkable. A suggested rule is to keep industrial support policies separate from the actual standards setting. Market standards cases have shown that a successful standard depends on the committed backing of strong firms, rather than the other way round. Concerns such as trade protectionism or industrial development should be dealt with directly if possible, and not made part of standards. Standards benefit support industries and users as much as manufacturing, and these are also at risk with poor standards.

4

Video Cassette Recorder:
The Value of Co-operation

SUMMARY   The introduction of the video cassette recorder (VCR) provides an excellent example of how product compatibility standards may be used to ensure the success of a new product. Despite Sony's early lead in the market, a technically superior product, and the advantage of Sony's size and reputation, the Sony Betamax was ultimately driven out of the market by JCV's VHS system. The key factor in JVC's success was its standards strategy. JVC had open standards and encouraged licensing of its format by other manufacturers. In contrast, Sony believed it could impose its proprietary standard on the industry provided it was the first on the market, and later that it could overcome VHS by product competition. Not only did JVC's strategy ensure the domination of its standard, but it gave it higher returns than if it had followed a proprietary strategy. It maintained its market share by leading further innovation within the standard. Sony would have done better had it abandoned the contest and accepted VHS much earlier than it eventually did. The contest has been revisited a decade later in the camcorder market, where Sony has had more success by first ensuring compatibility of its 8 mm standard with the cassette recorder installed base before concentrating on product competition.

1. INTRODUCTION

The introduction of the video cassette recorder (VCR) provides an excellent example of how product compatibility standards may be used to ensure the success of a new product. Despite Sony's early lead in the market, its technically superior product, and the advantage of Sony's size and reputation for innovation and quality, the Sony Betamax was ultimately driven out of the market by the VHS system from Japan Victor Corporation (JVC). How could this have happened? The key factor in JVC's success was its standards strategy compared to Sony's. JVC offered open standards and encouraged licensing of its format by other manufacturers. Sony believed it could impose its proprietary standard on the industry provided it was the first on the market, and later that it could overcome VHS by product competition. Not only did JVC's strategy ensure the domination of its standard but it gave JVC higher returns than if it had followed the same strategy as Sony. Sony would have done better to have accepted the VHS standard much earlier than it eventually did.

The case shows the power of network externalities, working via the market for complementary goods. The importance of standards for VCR is that the more recorders sold of a given format, the more pre-recorded or borrowed tapes are likely to be available, making that format more attractive to future buyers. This is a general feature of markets in which the installed base of hardware supports a secondary market in complementary software and is in turn made more valuable by it. As the market develops, the volume leader has an accumulating advantage which eventually becomes so strong that the market is typically dominated by a single standard.

JVC exploited this by using an open standard, high volume, market oriented strategy against Sony's traditional proprietary standard, high margin, technology led strategy. In combination with a product design which allowed it to get ahead of Sony in the crucial initial stage, this enabled JVC to establish itself as the volume leader, which ensured that it would be the sole survivor. Although Sony had pioneered the VCR market, its more closed approach to licensing, together with premature commitment to a design not quite ready for mass acceptance, meant that Betamax never established a significant installed base. Sony, and Philips, persisted in contesting the market for several years but were competing against increasing network effects. Convergence to the single VHS standard was inevitable. This result can not be explained in terms of conventional product introduction but only in terms of standards forces.

The study follows the introduction of the VCR, showing how standards strategy, though always important, gradually came to dominate other efforts. Section 2 traces the technical development of VCR and compares the characteristics of the two main systems. Section 3 compares the different strategies in the three main regions: Japan, USA, and Europe. Technical development took place first in Japan and competition centred on development, defining a market, and on efforts to align manufacturing and distribution. By the time VCRs were launched in the USA the product was more fully defined, and competition shifted towards distribution and the availability of software, as the standards issue became dominant. In Europe, distribution and software dominated other issues. Philips, also using a proprietary approach, could not hold on to its market share and soon converted to VHS. Finally Sony itself adopted VHS. Section 4 evaluates the profitability of the two strategies. Any other strategy for JVC would have meant much lower total earnings. Sony would have done better to have accepted VHS much earlier, when the inevitable defeat of Betamax became clear. Section 5 reviews the continuation strategies of the two firms. These include JVC's use of technical leadership to retain market share, and the extension of the VCR standards contest into the camcorder market. Sony has managed to overcome the problem of incompatibility of its 8 mm. camcorder system with the installed base of VCRs and has to some extent reversed its defeat with Betamax. Section 6 summarizes some of the lessons for standards strategy.

2. PRODUCT DEVELOPMENT AND MARKET DEFINITION

2.1 History of VCR development

VCRs are by now such a well established product that it may be hard to remember that consumer VCRs were introduced only fifteen years ago. Not only did the product have to be developed, a market had to be created. Initially it was not clear how VCRs would be used, whether for home television recording; making home movies; for 'time-shift' viewing; or for pre-recorded feature films. There was a sequence of product innovations in parallel with attempts to define the market and line up manufacturers and distributors.

The key dates in the history of VCRs are summarized in Table 4.1. The first audio-visual tape recorders were produced by the US firm Ampex in 1956. These were large expensive pieces of equipment used by television companies. Several manufacturers began working on possible consumer

Table 4.1. *Timetable of main events for VCR*

Date	Event
1956	First audio visual tape (AVT)—Ampex
1970	First prototype of consumer VCR
1974	Betamax prototype (1 hr.)—Sony
	Sony proposes that Matsushita, JVC adopt Betamax
1975	Betamax launch in Japan and USA—1 hr.
1976	Hitachi, Sharp, Mitsubishi adopt VHS
	MITI proposes JVC adopt Betamax
	VHS launch in Japan—2 hr.
1977	Matsushita adopts VHS, drops VX-2000
	Sanyo, Toshiba, Zenith adopt Betamax
	VHS launch in USA
	2 hr. Sony recorder launched—Japan and USA
1978	European launch for VHS and Betamax
	J2T agreement—JVC, Thorn, Telefunken, also Thomson
1979	Pre-recorded software reported important—1,000 Betamax titles
	Philips launches V2000 in Europe
1983	Philips starts production of VHS
1985	Miniature camcorders introduced—8 mm., VHS-C
1988	Sony starts production of VHS
1989	Sony introduces palm-sized camcorder

versions but it was 1970 before the first credible prototypes appeared. The earliest models to be introduced commercially were from Sony (U-matic) and Philips (VCR format) in 1972. These were still expensive and were aimed at the institutional market, for educational and corporate use. The main Japanese participants at this time were Sony, Matsushita, and JVC. There was a short-lived technology sharing agreement between these three in 1970, aimed to perfect the cassette mechanism ultimately used in the Sony U-matic. This gave some commonality to the basic technology. Because of competitive pressures the firms returned to independent development after 1971 (for the evolution of the VCR see Granstrand, 1984; Cusumano et al., 1990).

The first products designed for consumer markets began to appear in the mid-1970s. Although at one time there were as many as 30 manufacturers working on various formats, only three manufacturers produced viable systems as serious contenders in the market: JVC, Sony, and Philips. Betamax was launched in Japan in 1975, VHS in 1976. Philips introduced its V2000 format in 1979; its earlier models did not have the broad appeal needed for the consumer market. From the start VHS was licensed to several of the largest Japanese manufacturers. In response Sony made some less extensive manufacturing arrangements in 1977. Philips made little attempt to license the manufacturing of its format.

Sony launched Betamax in the USA in April 1975. It was not until October 1976 that JVC followed with VHS. JVC had arranged distribution of VHS machines by RCA, to be manufactured by Matsushita in Japan. RCA had no VCR of its own, having put most of its development effort into video discs. Although Sony had recently licensed Zenith to distribute Betamax in the USA this was no substitute for RCA's huge distribution network. VHS overtook Betamax in its second year. By 1981 it already had 80 per cent of the US market. Both products were introduced to Europe in 1978, this time with JVC ahead of Sony. Here the story was similar to the USA, but played through more decisively. JVC aligned Thorn-EMI, Thomson, and AEG-Telefunken to distribute VHS, leaving Sony and Philips with little alternative but to rely on their own manufacturing or existing partners. Philips dropped V2000 in favour of VHS in 1984. Sony eventually began producing to VHS standard in 1988.

2.2 Product development and technical comparison

Both VCR formats were developed from similar technology, based on cross-licensed R&D by Sony, Matsushita, and JVC in 1970. They rely on a 'helical scan' system in which the recording track is written across the tape by a rotating magnetic head. The two systems are nevertheless incompatible—tapes from one can not be read by the other. The most obvious difference is that VHS cassettes are larger than Betamax, with a longer tape. As the product was developed there were a series of incremental technical innovations, as each firm tried to improve the basic design to a point where it became a major consumer product. Competition centred on a sequence of improved features, in which each firm tried to match or leapfrog the other.

Table 4.2. *Incremental product innovations*

Feature	Year	VHS*	Betamax
Playing time	1975		1 hr.
	1976	2 hr.	
	1977	4 hr. (Matsushita)	2 hr.
	1978		3 hr.
	1979	6 hr. (Matsushita)	4.5 hr.
	1982	8 hr.	5 hr.
Programming	1977	24 hr. (RCA)	
	1978	7 day	
	1979	10 day	Programming (Toshiba)
	1982	15 day	15 day
Other features	1977	Wireless remote (Mat.)	Wireless remote
		Half speed	Half speed
	1978	Fast/slow motion	Fast/slow motion
		Portable	Portable
		Still frame	
	1979	Fast scanning	Fast scanning
			(Betascan)
		1/3 speed	1/3 speed
		Stereo record (Mat.)	
			Still frame
	1980		Stereo record
	1982		High-defin. (Betaplus)
	1983	Hi-fi	Hi-fi
	1987	High defin.	
		(Super-VHS)	
Camcorders	1982	Compact movie	
		(VHS-C)	
	1983		Camcorder (Beta-movie)
	1984	Compact camcorder	
	1985	Miniature camcorder	Miniature camcorder
			(8 mm.)
	1989		Palm-sized camcorder
	1990	Palm-sized camcorder	

* VHS innovations from JVC, Betamax from Sony, unless noted otherwise.

The sequence of product feature improvements is shown in Table 4.2. The key features were:

- Playing time
- Size
- Pre-programming
- Other features (freeze-frame, slow/fast motion, scanning, etc.)

Other aspects critical to the success of either format were:

- Image quality
- Price of recorders and tapes
- Ease of manufacture
- Ease of service

For each of the product features competition continued until any further improvement made little difference to the product. Competition then moved to another feature. For example, the most critical feature initially was playing time. The consumer breakthrough came when JVC introduced VHS with a playing time on a single tape of two hours, long enough for a feature film. Further extension to four hours gave some added advantage, but any further, to eight hours made little difference to the user. The feature had become 'saturated'. VHS systems were then introduced with automatic timers and sophisticated pre-programming. Once pre-programming could be set for a week in advance, with several different recording periods, there was no advantage in extending this facility any further.

In the early stages JVC consistently led Sony in features critical to consumer acceptance: playing time, size, pre-programming. It was also preferred on the other aspects: price, ease of manufacture, and ease of servicing. Manufacturing simplicity made it easier to license, which increased the supply and the variety of VHS products offered. Cheaper manufacturing also helped bring down prices, further enlarging the market. In the crucial stages, Betamax had only one product advantage: its slightly higher picture quality. However, this was not significant enough to be noticed by most consumers, for whom VHS was adequate. Eventually Sony matched all the VHS features and began to lead the development in some areas. It was the first to introduce high speed scanning, hi-fi sound, and 1/2 and 1/3 speed (extra long recording). It introduced a high-definition version, Betaplus, in 1983. Sony ended up with a technically 'better' product in terms of image quality and features. Unfortunately this was too late to overcome VHS's entrenched position as the industry standard. JVC in turn matched Sony's innovations, and made some advances of its own. It introduced compact VHS-C for video cameras in 1982. When it added Super-VHS, with high image quality capable of handling high definition television and equal to laser disc and Betaplus, in 1987 Betamax's last hope for VCR was gone.

The development of the product was paralleled by attempts to identify a market. Initially it was targeted at the 'technologically aware' market, which worked well at first but dried up within months. To make the transition to a mass product, JVC made a strong marketing effort in 1977 to educate and create the market. The first major sales campaigns in Japan emphasized the use of VCRs for making family movies. This created wide interest in the product. Later the emphasis moved to its more familiar uses as an accessory to the television set for time-shift viewing and pre-recorded feature films.

Sony began producing VHS VCRs in 1988, but had already begun to put more development effort into camcorders. It launched the first one-unit camcorder in 1983, followed by its miniaturized 8 mm. system in January, 1985 and a palm-sized model in 1989, in each case ahead of JVC and Matsushita. Although Sony's 8 mm. standard is now the leading contender in the camcorder market, this is not expected to impact the VCR market, whose major growth phase is over. The development of the camcorder is discussed later.

3. COMPETING STRATEGIES FOR SETTING STANDARDS

3.1 Development and introduction in Japan

The development of VCR was a simultaneous process of developing the product at the same time as defining its market. This may be the case for any other product innovation. The difference with VCR is that as the market grew new customers wanted to choose the standard which would be the eventual winner. If they chose the wrong standard they risked being stranded with a system with little software. Establishing a lead at the critical phase when customers realized that the product had 'arrived' was decisive. The standard which was accepted as the probable winner would take over the whole market. There was little hope of holding on to a market niche, as the differences in performance between the VCR standards were too slight compared with the advantage of owning the dominant system.

What we expect in such a case is that customers hold back from committing themselves until a point where the product is seen as worth buying, where the price has fallen into an acceptable range, and they can be reasonably sure they are picking the right standard. The game for the producer is to convince the customers that this is going to be the winner, and part of this is to ensure that the standard has full manufacturing and other support.

JVC achieved this by providing a system which, although second on the market, was the first to be truly acceptable to the consumer. It convinced the major section of Japanese manufacturers that VHS could command a wide market, and they adopted it as the standard. In turn this backing helped convince the market when the product was launched. JVC had planned for this from the start. VHS was designed for market appeal rather than for technological perfection, and was specifically aimed at ease of manufacture. Although well known in audio, JVC was a relatively small company, unknown in television, and knew that it would have to rely on outside manufacture and distribution in the early stages. The simpler construction made it easier for the manufacturers to adopt, while its lower cost increased its potential market penetration. JVC made the VHS standard available to other manufacturers on liberal terms with minimal restrictions. It was for the most part very open on which firms it offered its standard to. Its role as 'underdog' became an advantage—it approached manufacturers as partners, not expecting unreasonable margins, and not threatening the other firms' positions. JVC did not aim at market domination. It aimed at broad acceptance of the standard rather than trying to earn high initial rents. The returns would come over a long period once VHS was established.[1]

The Sony strategy was quite different. It had led the early development effort and was the first to market a moderately priced VCR. It felt it could establish Betamax as the leader then bring in other manufacturers on its own terms. This would be on less favourable terms than JVC offered. It expected to retain most of the manufacturing itself, as it had done successfully with televisions, and exploit its short term monopoly position with high prices and rapid technical development to keep ahead of competitors. The strategy is revealed in attempts made by Sony to align manufacturers behind its standard in 1974. Sony offered joint manufacture and marketing of Betamax systems to Matsushita and JVC, amongst others. However there was to be no collaborative development. At this time Betamax was only a few months away from launch, and Sony was offering a fixed take-it-or-leave-it package. Sony was also selective in which manufacturers it approached; there was a 'pecking order' of potential partners.[2] Sony's strategy was also aimed at high margins, intending to reduce the price gradually as the market developed. It initially held Betamax well above the VHS entry price. Only competition from the mutually independent VHS producers forced Sony prices down.

Unfortunately for Sony, although it was first, its product was not quite ready for the mass market. Its main problems were that its one hour recording time was too short, and the machine was too bulky. It failed to persuade the major manufacturers to adopt Betamax. It persisted in going ahead alone, investing heavily in manufacturing equipment and committing itself in the marketplace.[3] Being out of touch with the market is a risk with an exclusive approach, making a premature attempt to set a standard more likely. By moving too early Sony was unsuccessful in setting the standard and was also tied to an inferior system. This left JVC with time to develop a fully acceptable system which could then take over the market. If Sony had been less concerned with dominating the market by being first, it might have redesigned the format to make it more widely acceptable. As it was, the main beneficiaries of all its pioneering efforts were its competitors.

The comparison of manufacturing alliances for the different formats is shown in Table 4.3. When Betamax was introduced in 1975 it was manufactured only by Sony. Sanyo, and Toshiba introduced their own VCR, V-Code II, in 1976 but then adopted Betamax in 1977, having in effect already committed themselves to Sony in 1975. When VHS was introduced in late 1976 it was manufactured by JVC. It was soon joined by Hitachi, Sharp, and Mitsubishi, first marketing JVC machines and then manufacturing their own in late 1977. Matsushita publicly adopted VHS in January 1977 and began manufacture. It had launched its own prototype VCRs, the VX-100 in 1975 and the VX-2000 in 1976, but had been convinced of VHS's superiority following demonstrations by JVC in late 1975. JVC had greater need of second source manufacturers than Sony, since although a partly-owned subsidiary of Matsushita it was a relatively small company operating independently of its parent. It needed the manufacturing capacity and distribution network until its own capacity was built up, and this was the only way

Table 4.3. *Main manufacturers for different VCR formats*

Region	Introd. year	VHS	Betamax	V2000
Japan	1975/6	JVC Matsushita Hitachi Mitsubishi Sharp Toyo Sanyo Akai *Ricoh* *Canon*	Sony (1988)* Sanyo (1984) Toshiba (1984) NEC (1984) Aiwa (1984) *Pioneer (1984)*	—
USA	1977	*RCA* *Magnavox* *Sylvania* *GE*	*Zenith (1984)**	—
Europe	1977	*Thorn-EMI* *Thomson* *Blaupunkt* *Telefunken***	—	*Philips (1983)** *Grundig (1983)* *Siemens (1983)* *ITT (1983)* *B&O (1983)*

Notes: Primary manufacturers in normal type; distributors of OEM equipment in italics.

* (In parentheses: year adopted VHS); Sony continued to produce some Betamax after 1988; other Japanese manufacturers adopted VHS in 1984, other Europeans in 1983.

** Telefunken switched from V2000 in 1979.

to get it. Licensing gave VHS about double the capacity available to Betamax, initially mostly from Matsushita, which itself had double Sony's capacity. Indeed, Matsushita had reckoned that there was so much pent-up demand for VCRs that even Sony would not be able to supply it on its own, and would soon be overtaken. JVC's own share of VHS production was about 30 per cent of total VHS in 1978, compared with 60 per cent for Matsushita. It built up capacity as the market expanded so that by 1981 it still had 30 per cent of VHS production, which was now eight times larger, while Matsushita had 40 per cent.

Both firms approached MITI in mid 1976 for its backing, especially for the export markets. Initially MITI supported Betamax, as it was the first to appear and it did not want to confuse the market. However, following JVC's counter-arguments and the demonstration of support by other manufacturers, including Matsushita, MITI decided to accept both standards and left the market to sort out the contest. VHS soon passed Betamax. After the sales hiatus in 1977, tackled by JVC's 'educational' marketing, VHS moved rapidly ahead. Its market share in Japan rose from 40 per cent in 1977, to 67 per cent in 1980, and to 93 per cent in 1987. The effect of VHS in bringing down VCR prices is seen most clearly in the US market below.

3.2 Introduction in USA

Sony introduced Betamax in the USA in February 1976, and JVC followed with VHS in January 1977. By the time VHS arrived, VCRs were over their initial development phase. Although neither product nor market had by any means stabilized, VCRs were now more of a known entity. Thus the success of VHS was more clearly centred on the standards issue. Betamax had still not found great customer support. From the US point of view in 1977 VHS and Betamax probably started about equal. The systems were closer technically than they had been when VHS was launched in Japan. Although Betamax was still labouring with its recording time disadvantage, this was being tackled. Betamax II with two hour recording time was introduced in March 1977, answered almost simultaneously by four hour VHS systems from Matsushita. VHS had the advantage of a proven track record in Japan, backed by greater manufacturing resources. Sony was better known in the USA and had a powerful existing distribution network. Both were accepted by MITI.

The key to US success was distribution. The turning point for VHS was its adoption by RCA in mid 1977. RCA agreed to market VHS machines, manufactured in Japan by Matsushita but sold with an RCA badge. RCA did not have a VCR of its own, it had instead put most of its effort into video disc players (Selecta Vision). Magnavox also chose VHS. Sony had approached RCA to distribute Betamax in 1974, but RCA had declined. This was partly because it was not clear that Betamax was going to be the most attractive system (it was the only one on offer at that time), but also the general uncertainty about the virtues of VCR compared with video discs, or even compared with cable and satellite television, made RCA cautious. It is also possible that RCA and Sony's interests clashed in too many other areas. However, the final decision reputedly turned on Matsushita guaranteeing to deliver a four hour machine, able to record American football games, compared to the two hours of Sony.[4] Sony had already set up a marketing agreement with Zenith in March 1977, putting pressure on the VHS camp. Zenith switched to VHS in 1984.

The early sales history in the USA is shown in Fig. 4.1 and the cumulative sales in Table 4.4. Although Betamax had an earlier start, and outsold VHS in 1977, the order was reversed in 1978, the first full year of VHS sales. By 1981 VHS had 80 per cent of the US market. The installed base of VHS equalled Betamax by 1979, with 0.6 m. units each. By 1981 VHS had 2.3 m.

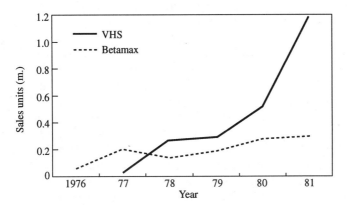

Fig. 4.1. *VCR sales, USA*

Table 4.4. *Cumulative VCR sales (USA), 1976–1981*

		1976	1977	1978	1979	1980	1981
Unit sales	Betamax	70	213	145	195	281	294
('000s)	VHS	—	38	269	293	521	1178
	Total	70	251	414	488	802	1472
Share (%)	Betamax	100	85	35	40	35	20
	VHS	—	15	65	60	65	80
Cumulative	Betamax	70	283	428	623	904	1198
units	VHS	—	38	307	600	1121	2299
	Total	70	321	735	1223	2025	3497
Cumulative	Betamax	100	88	58	51	45	34
(%)	VHS	—	12	42	49	55	66

units installed compared with 1.2 m. for Betamax, i.e. double the installed base.

Price competition was very strong. VHS undercut Betamax from the beginning. Heavy price discounting (below list) took place even though VCRs were supply constrained, as firms fought to establish their format. Product launches focused on October 1977. List prices for Betamax two hour machines from Sony, Toshiba, and Zenith were all $1300. JVC announced a full-feature two hour VHS machine at $1280. However, RCA launched a four hour VHS machine at $1000, and Magnavox a deluxe version at $1085. Sony responded by dropping the price of its Betamax to $1085 in December 1977. Discounting brought the prices down to $900 or even $800. Dealer margins at $800 were only about $50 per unit. The subsequent price history in the USA is that wholesale price fell to $470 in 1983 and to $350 in 1985. However, when Taiwanese and Korean clones arrived in 1986 they were priced as low as $200 retail.

Although the key was the distribution agreement with RCA, software became an issue in its own right for the first time as early as 1978. Initially VCRs were mainly purchased for time-shift viewing and a certain amount of (blue) movies. By 1978 the installed bases were large enough to be worth producing pre-recorded feature films, as well as the use of video clubs and private borrowing to share the tapes. Although software is the reason the leading format is more attractive, software strategy does not seem to have been very effective as a means of competition. Software supply seems to have reacted to the installed base and consequent demand, rather than having been used actively to promote one format to the exclusion of the other. Since VCRs can do many things, their usefulness does not depend solely on pre-recorded software. Also, given the ease with which titles can be pirated, software is a difficult market to control. Thus the tendency was for software to follow the hardware base, confirming the leader rather than being a critical tool against a competitor.[5]

There was some direct use of software strategy. For example, the agreement with RCA ensured that RCA/Warner movies were available on VHS, helping to make VHS attractive. However, Sony made parallel moves, and in fact initially made the greater effort. Starting in 1977 it pushed for a range of 1000 Betamax pre-recorded titles. Despite this effort the higher demand for VHS tapes eventually displaced Betamax. To begin with films were available in both formats. Now Betamax is restricted to those 'blockbuster' movies for which there is a guaranteed audience.

3.3 Expansion in Europe

Japanese VCRs were first sold in Europe in 1978, a year after their introduction in the USA. This time JVC was ahead of Sony. The basic system was now fully developed, and further improvements may be seen more as

competition between different brands rather than between different standards. The success of VHS turned almost exclusively on the standards strategy. JVC aligned three major allies in Europe to distribute its equipment:
Telefunken in Germany and Thorn-EMI in the UK (the so-called J2T
venture), as well as Thomson in France. This ensured that VHS would be
the volume leader. The arrangement with Thorn-EMI was particularly
effective as Thorn controlled most of the television rental outlets in the UK,
and rental was the main market for VCRs in the introductory stages. Some
manufacturing in Europe was started after 1982.

The European market was complicated by the presence of Philips, which
had been producing VCRs since 1972. In 1978 it still had 40 per cent of the
(very small) UK market. At that time its product was not competitive, as it
was very expensive with short playing time, but it responded to Japanese
competition by producing the V2000 system in 1979. The three systems,
VHS, Betamax, and V2000, were not very different technically, but Philips
and Sony, both with proprietary strategies, could not match JVC's high
volume approach.

The UK sales provide a good illustration of the importance of looking at
the right indicators of the competitive position in a market affected by
compatibility standards. The annual UK sales of the three standards are
shown in Fig. 4.2 and market shares in Fig. 4.3. Looking at sales figures
alone, sales were increasing for both V2000 and Betamax until 1982, and
were flat for 1983. Even when looking at market share there is more cause
for concern but mainly just for Philips, as its share dropped from 40 per cent
to 4 per cent by 1981. Even this may have been seen as recoverable once
marketing problems were resolved. Sony's share actually grew from 1977 to
1980, then was fairly stable at around 25 per cent until 1983. It may have felt
it could hold on at this level. However, in this market there could only be
one winner. The most important indicator is cumulative sales. The installed

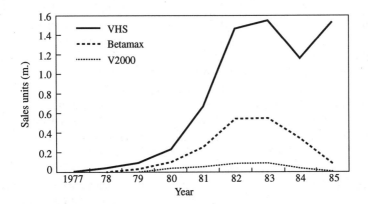

Fig. 4.2. *VCR sales, UK*

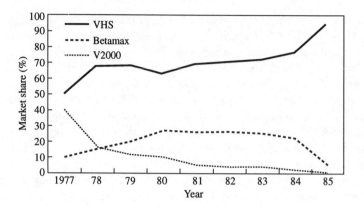

Fig. 4.3. *VCR market shares, UK*

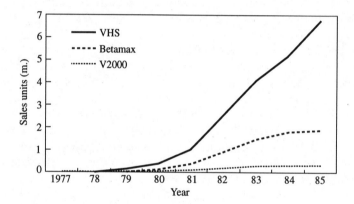

Fig. 4.4. *VCR cumulative sales, UK*

base gives the leader an ever-increasing advantage. Cumulative sales are shown in Fig. 4.4. VHS, with 75 per cent of the annual market, was building up an impressive lead, even while Sony's annual share remained constant. Despite the huge advertising which Philips and Sony put in, shown in Fig. 4.5, their efforts had no effect. Both spent heavily on R&D to introduce product innovations, again too late to have any effect.

Philips dropped V2000 and started producing VHS in 1984. This was a successful move—it now has 12 per cent of the UK market. Sony persisted with Betamax until 1988, latterly in the hope that its miniaturized camcorder could give it a base from which to maintain a niche in the VCR market. When it finally adopted VHS, Sony had less than 5 per cent of the world VCR market. It is clear from the share figures that Betamax had no chance after 1984. With an appreciation of the characteristics of standards markets the inevitability of VHS's success was clear from cumulative sales much earlier than this, perhaps as early as 1980.

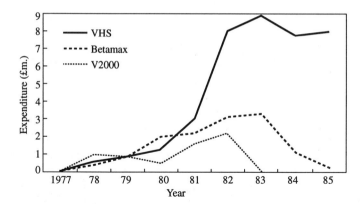

Fig. 4.5. *VCR advertising expenditure, UK*

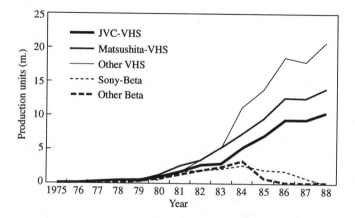

Fig. 4.6. *World VCR production: VHS and Betamax*

4. PROFITABILITY AND MEASURES OF SUCCESS

4.1 Are VHS and JVC success the same thing?

The result of the contest is that VHS eventually dominated the global market almost exclusively. Worldwide production histories for the VCR formats are given in Fig. 4.6. The shares of the different formats are given in Fig. 4.7. As JVC claimed in advertisements at the time, by 1988 of the more than 200 m. VCRs in use, 180 m. of these were VHS. There are still a few national markets in Asia, such as Indonesia and the Philippines, where Betamax is the dominant standard, having become established very early in the system's history. Elsewhere VHS dominance is total.

Although VHS eliminated Betamax as a standard this in itself need not mean that JVC's strategy was optimal, or that Sony's was a failure. We must

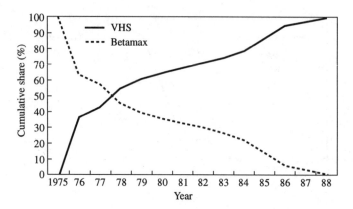

Fig. 4.7. *Cumulative VCR format shares (world unit production)*
Source: JVC.

still show that JVC, as a firm, could not have expected, *ex ante*, to earn
higher returns with any other strategy, and that Sony's result was not due to
chance. JVC's open strategy ensured the success of VHS but this was at a
cost of sharing the market with several other manufacturers. Could JVC
have earned more by adopting an exclusive standard and facing Sony
directly? Similarly, was Sony's exclusive strategy the best it could have done
in the circumstances, even though it eventually had to abandon Betamax?

For JVC the open strategy seems to have been optimal. In 1974 it was a
relatively unknown company with most of its sales in audio equipment. It
was much smaller than Sony, without its financial and manufacturing resources, or its brand reputation and distribution channels. These could have
been decisive advantages for Sony in a new market which in the first
instance had to be convinced that VCRs were a viable product. Even
though VHS was preferred to Betamax in customer acceptability and cost,
alone JVC would not have been able to establish VHS before Sony could
catch up. The open standard ensured adequate levels of manufacturing and
market acceptance, the keys to VHS's success. Further, although it licensed
many competitors, JVC managed to retain control of a large portion of the
market. It did so not by placing restrictions on its licensees but by constant
product improvement, keeping it ahead of its collaborators as well as expanding the market. Its partners left most of the technical innovation to
JVC, concentrating instead on manufacturing and marketing. This was an
impressive combination of openness and innovation leadership to maintain
its dominance of a still-growing market.

The result has been that JVC and its direct affiliates have maintained
about 20 per cent of the world market for VCRs. The largest VHS producer
is still Matsushita, which has 20–25 per cent of the market, although initially, in 1977, its production of VHS had been double that of JVC. Produc-

Table 4.5. *VCR production shares by Japanese firms, 1981–1984*

Manufacturer	Production (m.)				Market share (%)			
	1981	1982	1983	1984	1981	1982	1983	1984
VHS								
Matsushita	2.65	3.50	5.15	7.38	28	27	28	25
JVC	1.80	2.60	3.10	5.02	19	20	17	17
Hitachi	0.90	1.30	2.00	4.43	10	10	11	15
Sharp	0.65	0.95	1.50	2.66	7	7	8	9
Mitsubishi	0.30	0.40	0.65	1.18	3	3	4	4
Toyo Sanyo	0.03	0.37	0.66	1.48	—	3	4	5
Akai/Others	0.15	0.30	0.36	1.48	2	2	2	5
Subtotal	6.48	9.42	13.64	23.46	68	72	74	80
Betamax								
Sony	1.70	1.85	2.15	2.66	18	14	12	9
Sanyo	0.87	1.25	1.45	1.77	9	10	8	6
Toshiba	0.40	0.53	0.65	0.89	4	4	4	3
NEC	0.06	0.08	0.15	0.30	1	1	1	1
Aiwa	—	—	0.15	0.30	—	—	1	1
Subtotal	3.02	3.71	4.61	6.04	32	28	25	20
Total	9.50	13.13	18.24	29.50	100	100	100	100

Source: Press Reports; Granstrand, 1984.

tion share figures for all the Japanese manufacturers for the central 1981–4 period are given in Table 4.5. The sales histories for JVC and Sony for total video products are compared in Table 4.6. In 1986 JVC sold $2.3 bn. worth of VCRs, earning a estimated $250 m. In addition JVC's parent company, Matsushita, sold an equivalent amount. Its spending on R&D for VCRs is not known, but RCA estimated in 1975 that it would cost $200 m. to develop a VCR (the amount it spent on video disc). Making some very rough estimates, assuming a 10 per cent net margin an initial investment of $200 m. would have been recovered by JVC by 1981. With ongoing R&D financed out of sales, the open strategy has ensured JVC a continuing stream of earnings.

4.2 *Sony's failure to commercialize its technology*

Turning to Sony's strategy, would it have done better to have used a more open strategy for Betamax from the beginning? Similarly, should it have switched to VHS as soon as it became apparent that Betamax had little chance of surviving in the long run? If it had matched JVC by making its own standard freely available from the beginning, then with a slightly modified product it should have been able to line up as many manufacturers

Table 4.6. *Proportion of net sales from video: JVC and Sony*

	JVC			Sony		
	Net ($bn.)	VCR (%)	VCR* ($bn.)	Net ($bn.)	VCR (%)	VCR ($bn.)
1976	—	—	—	1.9	10	0.2
1977	—	—	—	2.6	14	0.4
1978	—	—	—	2.2	17	0.4
1979	1.1	29	0.3	2.7	19	0.5
1980	1.4	43	0.6	4.1	23	0.9
1981	2.0	51	1.0	4.8	35	1.7
1982	2.2	59	1.3	4.5	43	1.9
1983	2.4	68	1.6	4.7	41	2.0
1984	2.7	67	1.8	5.1	41	2.1
1985	3.5	68	2.4	6.7	36	2.4
1986	3.6	65	2.3	6.8	35	2.4

* Includes VCRs, camcorders, tapes.

Source: Annual Reports.

as JVC. This would have neutralized JVC's strategy. With Betamax and VHS competing directly it seems that given Sony's market strength Betamax could have prevailed. Sony would then have been in JVC's position, with a large share of the world market and a continuing income stream.

The question is whether this was really likely. The problem was not just that Sony's approach to licensing was one-sided, but that there was limited demand for the Betamax design as launched. Given the reservations about the recording time and equipment size, in 1974 it might have been difficult for Sony to have attracted the VHS supporters on any terms. However, it seems clear that Betamax could not have got to market in the form it did had Sony been convinced of the need for broad support. Even in 1974 there would have been ample time for product redesign before the arrival of VHS, two years later. Instead Sony thought that it could force the issue, and took a high risk strategy. It underestimated the importance of market acceptability and overestimated the importance of being first.

Some comparison of the results for Sony and JVC may be made from Table 4.5. Sony's total video earnings were only matched by JVC in 1985. However, Sony's figures include camcorders, U-matic, and tapes. In 1988 Betamax production was 150k units a month, i.e. 1.8m. per year, which would give much lower VCR revenue figures, around $0.5bn. Also Sony VCR sales were declining while JVC's were increasing, so that Sony in 1987 had only five per cent of the world market while JVC had around 20 per cent. Given Sony's strengths there is every reason for it to have done better than JVC in the same position. With the world video market now estimated at $12 bn., if Sony had 40 per cent of this its video sales would be $5 bn., enough to put it into the super-league of electronics companies occupied by Matsushita and Mitsubishi.

Once both VHS and Betamax had been developed, would Sony have been better off admitting defeat and switching to VHS earlier? There seems little doubt that the whole Japanese industry, including JVC as well as Sony, would have been better off without the costs of the standards war. Realistic decision points were at the introduction of VCRs in the USA or in Europe. Although the bulk of R&D expenditure had already been incurred over the long development period up to 1975, Sony continued to make a large effort in both R&D and advertising as it tried to overtake VHS technically and establish itself in the market. For example, the peak year for advertising for Betamax in the UK was 1983, when it was £3 m., around 5 per cent of sales. Advertising as a percentage of sales was a little higher than for VHS.[6] There was clearly no attempt to 'milk' an obsolete product. Sony continued to try for a major market share.

Some indication of the alternative had Sony switched to VHS earlier, is shown by comparing Philips' history since abandoning V2000 in favour of VHS in 1984. This required Philips to admit one of the biggest losses in its history, estimated at $300–400 m.[7] Following this decision, Philips' share of the UK market, for example, has grown from almost zero in 1983 to 12 per cent in 1986. If the R&D and promotional expenses from Betamax had been used in product competition rather than in a losing standards battle, Sony would have had every prospect of gaining a large share of the VCR market. By 1988 it was too late to have much impact on the VCR market. The main portion of VCR sales was already over, with the value of Japanese VCR production having fallen every year since 1984.

How can we explain Sony's behaviour? During the early development period Sony presumably felt it was justified in following the 'high margin' route, as it had successfully done in other consumer electronics. There were many uncertainties during the development of VCRs, so its concentration on technological development may be understandable. Why it continued with Betamax unchanged after 1974 when warnings started sounding is less clear. Sony certainly understood the importance of standards, but apparently not the best way to establish them. It also may have underestimated the all-or-nothing character of the standards issue for VCRs. The fact that it continued heavy investment in Betamax and camcorders shows that it felt there might still be a niche for a separate standard.

Sony itself gives three reasons for its difficulties. These were: (*a*) its ideas were used unfairly by JVC; (*b*) it aimed at a staged introduction via the high margin professional market, so that a one hour recording time was not seen as a restriction; and (*c*) Sony was used to leading standards and did not consider the collaborative route.[8] These correspond with the analysis here.

JVC's explanation of its own success is simpler: it managed collaboration better.

However, part of the reason for Sony's persistence with Betamax long after it had a real prospect against VHS may lie outside any single product. Adopting a competitor's technology did not fit in with Sony's image as Japan's innovation leader. After the poor results in the Japanese market in 1978, Sony chairman Morita said, 'Sometimes face is more important than profit.'[9] Since then they have been fighting against the inevitable.

5. CONTINUING COMPETITION AND NEW PRODUCTS

5.1 Maintaining market leadership

JVC maintained its leading position in the VCR market largely by continued technical innovation within the VHS standard. It has kept its share at a relatively stable level over the 15 year life of the consumer technology. From 1978 to 1984 JVC's share declined from 19 per cent to 17 per cent, to which must be added sales by direct affiliates. In comparison the share of the total market supplied by Matsushita declined more rapidly, from 36 per cent in 1978 to 25 per cent in 1984. The innovations introduced by JVC are listed in Table 4.2. Almost all of the new features after 1978 originated from JVC, and the major modifications to the central technology, such as compact VHS-C and high definition Super-VHS were also JVC developments. These continued to be licensed to other manufacturers under similar conditions to the original VHS format.

What loss of share there has been since the mid 1980s has been due to the encroachment by Korean and Taiwanese producers, who by 1986 had 13 per cent of the world market, and possibly about a quarter by 1992. This has affected the Japanese manufacturers as a whole. It has been mainly price-based competition and is a significant contributory cause of the reduction in average VCR prices since about 1986 (see below). JVC has managed to avoid some of the effects of this price competition by moving continually to more advanced features. This is helped by the market trend towards VCRs with more advanced features, as most sales are now upgrades for households which already own a first VCR. By 1991 77 per cent of US homes owned at least one VCR; in Japan 60 per cent of purchases were replacements or second machines (Depma, 1992). Matsushita, relying to a somewhat greater extent on its strengths in manufacturing, may have been more affected by price competition.

5.2 Extending the market with camcorders

One of the areas to which the Japanese VCR manufacturers have shifted is the market for camcorders. The growth of this market is shown in Fig. 4.8,

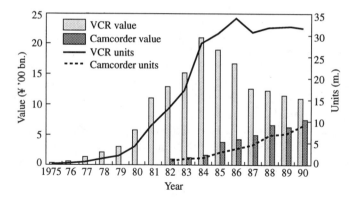

Fig. 4.8. *Japanese VCR and camcorder production*
Source: MITI.

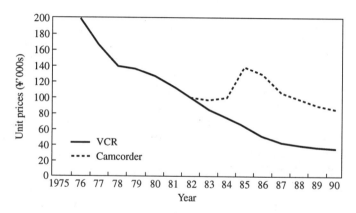

Fig. 4.9. *VCR and camcorder unit prices (Japanese production)*
Source: MITI.

which contrasts the production history of VCRs for Japanese firms with that
for camcorders. In value terms sales of camcorders by Japanese firms may
equal those of VCRs by 1993. Prices for camcorders have remained high
while those for VCR have continued to decline, as shown in Fig. 4.9. Much
of the apparent price stability is due to the rapid innovation of camcorder
product features. The first video cameras for the consumer market, developed at the same time as the VCR, were large items and did not appeal to
most VCR owners even though they used the same tapes as the VCR.
Consumers bought VCRs for time-shift television viewing or movie rentals
rather than home movies. The miniature camcorders introduced in the mid-
1980s with Sony's 8 mm. and JVC's VHS-C systems were much more portable and created a major new consumer electronics market. They have
taken over the market from the full size models, so that in 1991 they

accounted for 68 per cent of US camcorder sales, and a higher proportion in Europe and Japan (EIA, 1992).

Several aspects of the VCR story went into 'instant replay' with the camcorder, but with a different ending. Sony was again first with a miniature camcorder, the 8 mm. system, in 1984. JVC soon followed with similar sized camcorders using its compact system VHS-C. As with VCR, Sony's product is technically superior. Its various models are generally smaller than comparable VHS-C models and the picture recording quality is higher. Both use tape cassettes of about the same size, similar to an audio cassette, with VHS-C slightly larger—tape for VHS-C is a standard 12 mm. width (1/2 inch) while Sony's is 8 mm. The length of playing time is now to Sony's advantage. Used on comparable quality setting, 8 mm. tapes may last two hours to VHS-C's 20 minutes. There have been sequences of product feature innovations, led by Sony. After JVC matched the original miniature camcorder, Sony introduced a palm-sized model, the CCD-TR55, in 1989, weighing 790 g., less than 2 lbs. JVC launched a comparable product a year later, by which time Sony had added other features, such as stereo sound and better zoom, and then reduced the weight further. There have also been high definition versions, High Band 8 mm. (Hi-8) and Super VHS-C.

Despite 8 mm.'s product advantages, VHS-C seemed at first to have a massive network advantage in that it uses a version of the VHS standard which may be played on existing VCRs. In contrast, tapes of 8 mm. are incompatible with both Betamax and VHS. However, both systems achieve compatibility with the VCR installed base by using adapters, though in very different ways. Sony's 8 mm. camcorder contains its own internal VCR player mechanism and circuitry, so that it can connect directly into the input socket of a television set to play back movies, or into a VCR input to make edited copies on VHS tape. VHS-C relies on the tapes, which are the standard VHS width, being playable on a VCR machine provided they are first loaded into a 'transporter box', the same size as a normal VHS cassette. Competition between the two systems has focused on these different methods and whether it is more convenient to be able to play the movie directly into any television set (with 8 mm.) or through any VCR (with VHS-C). An advantage for VHS-C is that tapes can be mailed to a friend, who is more likely to have a VCR than a camcorder, without needing to be rerecorded. Part of the network disadvantage for 8 mm. is that it must include many of the features that would normally be part of the VCR, such as fast scanning or hi-fi sound reproduction, built into the camcorder. Yet Sony has achieved this without adding greatly to size or cost. It has also been more successful than it was with Betamax in recruiting other manufacturers to adopt its standard.

So far the systems have shared the market, both with significant market shares, but with 8 mm. much the more successful. In 1989 Sony alone had 40 per cent of the 7 m. unit global market.[10] This was due to increase to 45 per cent in 1990, with other manufacturers of 8 mm. (Sanyo, Canon, Ricoh, and Hitachi) accounting for another 35 per cent. It appears that the product superiority of Sony's 8 mm. has been enough to outweigh any network inconvenience from having to use the camcorder as its own adapter rather than playing the tapes directly into a VCR. The relative importance of small size has already been shown by the displacement of full size camcorders by the miniatures, despite the fact that the older models use full length tapes which can be replayed on a VCR without an adapter. Having found an acceptable way to stay compatible with the VCR and television installed base, Sony was free to design the 8 mm. format without being restricted to the VHS format, and could develop a superior system. With equivalent access to the installed base, the two formats have competed via product features and technological innovation, which has favoured Sony.

6. LESSONS FOR BUSINESS STRATEGY

This study provides some lessons in how to recognize products influenced by compatibility standards. VCRs depend for their usefulness on a complementary product, taped software, which may only be used with products designed to a given technical format. The larger the installed base of hardware on this format, the greater the variety of software produced. This adds to the attraction of the standard. Such markets converge on a single standard if the market is still developing, buyers are well informed and the competing standards are fairly close equivalents. Unless differences in performance are large enough to outweigh the advantage of owning the dominant standard there will be no niches serving specialist tastes. This also implies that conventional competition via technical development and product features will not have much effect once the installed base effect takes over. The dynamics of market development are that although they may be aware of the new product, customers postpone purchase until expectations about its further development are clear. They wait until the product, price, and standards dominance are perceived as 'right'. Once common expectations are formed there is a rapid increase in sales, as if a barrier has been passed. Firms may guide these expectations by coordinating their manufacturing, distribution, R&D, promotion and software strategies. Attempts to force a standard prematurely, before the product has been developed to a point at which it can be accepted by the market, are likely to fail. A main lesson from the case is how an open standards, market penetration strategy may win against a proprietary standard, high margin approach. This applies when a firm has a good product but cannot risk taking on a stronger opponent on its own. Once one standard has established a clear lead, it may be better for the opposing sponsor to switch its position and join the dominant standard. This gives it access to a larger, expanding market in which it may still compete in various ways, rather than fighting for a standard against ever increasing odds. The case also shows that the true picture of the competitive position is given by cumulative sales rather than absolute sales or market share. Sales and share may both be growing but still leave the leader with a faster growing installed base. Additional strategies include directly influencing the software market to make complementary software available, in this case pre-recorded movie tapes. For VCR this was probably less important than for some other products. Home taping and time-shift viewing mean that a base of VCRs may build up independently of the pre-recorded market. Thus pre-recorded software tended to follow the hardware market, confirming leadership rather than promoting it.

NOTES

1. According to JVC's Takano, a leader of the VHS project, 'Our basic policy was to spread the information as well as to spread the technology and the format. The market is large enough to hold everybody. Japan does not have to monopolize the video market or video production. One single company does not have to monopolize the whole profit', (Nayak and Ketteringham, 1986).
2. For example, Sony had approached RCA before Matsushita and JVC in late 1974.
3. When Matsushita representatives visited the Betamax facilities in 1975, they were reported to be 'dismayed' that Sony had committed itself to the one-hour limitation without consulting them (Nayak and Ketteringham, 1986).
4. Related by the chief executive of Matsushita in Yamashita (1989), 34.
5. This may be contrasted with video disc, where it is crucial that software and hardware strategies be co-ordinated as there is no secondary use for a disc player.
6. Philips advertising was even more out of line with sales. It peaked in the UK in 1982 at £2.5 m., with sales of about £2 m.
7. Granstrand (1984).
8. Comments reported in interviews by Granstrand (1984).
9. *Sunday Times*, 22 Jan. 1978. Akio Morita has also said that he regards Sony as only a 'venture business' for the Morita family, whose main interests remain in the food industry.
10. *The Economist*, 30 June 1990.

5

Compact Disc and Digital Audio Tape: *The Importance of Timing*

SUMMARY   The contest for digital audio illustrates the importance of timing and complementary support in establishing new standards. It shows some of the conflicts involved in using industry standards committees, and in trying to sponsor two standards at the same time. Although the compact disc (CD) has been successful in replacing the long playing record, it was for some time threatened by an even newer standard, digital audio tape (DAT). DAT failed even though it was arguably a superior system and CD was far from established when DAT arrived. The problem was that DAT was delayed. It was opposed by the recording companies, who were concerned about its ability to make high quality recordings of copyright music. The deciding factor was that the manufacturers themselves postponed DAT, so as not to confuse the market, but hoped that both standards could eventually be successful. This was not possible, and DAT now seems limited to specialist recording niches. The result is that instead of DAT being potentially the single audio standard there may be as many as three, for home, portable, and recording use, with the attendant inefficiencies of fragmented standards. Other digital technologies, digital compact cassette, and minidisc, are now contesting the portable market, with uncertain prospects. The main beneficiaries of the new technology may have been the producers of complementary goods, the recording companies. Leading manufacturers have integrated into this market to capture the full value of the innovation.

1. INTRODUCTION

The apparently sudden success of the compact disc (CD) in displacing the long playing record (LP) is typical of the rapid takeover observed with a new standard. In 1990 twice as many CDs were sold as LPs in the UK, reversing the figures of only two years earlier. Once it became clear that LP was doomed its support fell off precipitately. By 1993 almost no LPs were being produced or sold, and CDs were on course to equal the record for LP unit sales set in 1976. Yet for several years it was not clear than CD would succeed. Its main challenger was not the old LP standard but an even newer one, digital audio tape (DAT). Until this threat was resolved the expansion of the CD market was limited. DAT's challenge failed although it was in many ways a more attractive product. It never appeared on the mass consumer market and is now limited to a specialist market niche for high quality recording.

The contest between CD and DAT shows the crucial importance of timing and complementary support in establishing new standards. It shows some of the problems of using industry standards committees, and of trying to sponsor two standards at the same time. DAT arrived later than CD, which was already beginning to build up customer acceptance, and DAT could not establish a base quickly enough. Equally important, DAT was opposed strongly by the recording companies, who blocked its launch by refusing to supply pre-recorded music and by legal challenges. After initially being lukewarm to CD as a replacement for LP, they had begun to appreciate its commercial value and particularly its immunity from digital copying. DAT threatened this highly profitable market as it could make perfect digital copies. Under pressure, the Japanese manufacturers delayed DAT, which gave CD time to build its installed base and establish the standard. The manufacturers were also worried about confusing the market with two digital standards arriving at the same time, while the debate between analog and digital sound reproduction was at its height. However, they continued to hope that DAT could be introduced once CD was safely established. Given the strength of the CD standard by then, this proved to be impossible.

An attraction of DAT is that it offers the possibility of a single standard for all applications, replacing LP and audio cassette, as well as CD. DAT can do most of the things that CD can do, and has the advantage of high quality recording capability and greater suitability for portable stereos. The advantages of a single standard are that it avoids duplication of personal music libraries and makes it easier for users to share tapes. A larger market allows economies of scale and competition in the production of pre-recorded tapes and accessories, which reduces costs.

The probable outcome of the contest is that rather than a single audio standard there may be at least three, for home, portable, and recording use. CD has the in-home market, DAT is likely to be limited to the professional recording market, while the portable market is currently the subject of a third contest—between Philips's digital compact cassette (DCC) and Sony's minidisc (MD)—although it still clings to audio cassette. This outcome involves the usual inefficiencies of fragmented standards, with smaller individual markets, duplicated development, and higher costs for equipment and software. This may be less than optimal for everyone, except perhaps the recording companies. Users are unhappy about the high prices of CD discs facilitated by the standard and still have reservations about the system's attractiveness. Manufacturers are unhappy that the high disc prices hold back expansion of the audio markets, and that the bulk of the profits from CD are going not to the firms which developed the technology but to the music producers. For the recording companies CD has been a boon, removing the threat of large scale copying of copyright material and putting them in a strong market position. However, the total audio market is probably smaller than with a single standard. The main CD manufacturers, Sony and Philips, have attempted to gain more strategic freedom by vertically integrating into music production, though so far these have been left to manage themselves.

In this chapter, Section 2 gives the history and description of the two systems. Section 3 discusses the standards strategies used by manufacturers of the two systems, including timing issues and the role of industry committees. Section 4 discusses the profitability concerns for the manufacturers in promoting both CD and DAT at the same time. Section 5 compares the digital audio contest with that between video disc (VD) and video cassette recorder (VCR), ten years earlier, in which the arrival times of tape and disc were reversed. Section 6 looks at extensions of the standards in products such as CD video and CD-ROM, and at the current contest for a portable digital standard between DCC and minidisc. Section 7 draws some general conclusions.

2. PRODUCT BACKGROUND

2.1 History of digital audio

(a) Compact disc

The key dates for CD and DAT are listed in Table 5.1, which also compares the schedule for digital audio introduction with that for the video contest between VD and VCR, a few years previously. CD was developed from the video disc technology of the mid-1970s. This was combined with digital recording techniques, used for tape mastering since 1972 and the professional industry standard for audio processing (using video cassette tapes) since 1979. In October 1979 Sony and Philips pooled efforts on CD, with Philips contributing its capabilities in laser technology (developed for its VLP Laservision system) and Sony its capabilities in pulsed digital coding and electronics technology. As a merger of two existing technologies the alliance was very successful. Development was rapid. CD was launched in Japan in October 1982, and in the rest of the world soon after. It was launched in the UK in March 1983.

CD Players: Japanese production history for CD players is shown in Fig. 5.1, together with DAT production. Demand for CD faltered in 1987 and again in 1989, as marketing and standards issues were resolved, but has since grown steadily. CD's success only came after a period of great uncertainty about its prospects during its first five years or so. Annual production of CD players in 1991 in Japan was about 10.5 m. units.

Looking specifically at the UK market, the early sales history for CD players is shown in Fig. 5.2. After a slow start during the first three years,

Table 5.1. *Timetable for introduction of VCR, VD, CD, and DAT*

	Video		Digital audio	
	VCR*	VD**	CD	DAT
Basic technology	1956	1965	1972	1972
Research start	1971	1972	1979	1981
Standard prototype	1974	1978	1981	1985
Product launch:				
Japan	1975	1983	1982	1987
USA	1975	1979	1984	1988
Europe	1978	1981	1983	1987†

* Betamax.
** Philips Laservision, VLP.
† France, Germany (countries with tape levies); UK launch 1988.

there was a steady increase in player sales since 1985, with 1 m. players sold for the first time in 1987. This growth has been accompanied by price falls, shown in Fig. 5.3. Market penetration in 1988 was still relatively low, with only 10 per cent of UK potential owners having a CD player. In Japan the figure in 1988 was 20 per cent and in the US 8 per cent. Prices of players have come down sharply, with a basic player in the UK falling from £480 in 1983 to £130 in 1987 and to below £100 in 1990. The lowest priced portable CD players are now also around £100.

Discs: The sales of recorded music on CD increased steadily after 1985, with the real breakthrough happening from 1988 onwards. Worldwide, CD has now almost totally displaced LP and is on the way to eclipsing audio cassette as well. Current world market sales by segment (for USA, Japan,

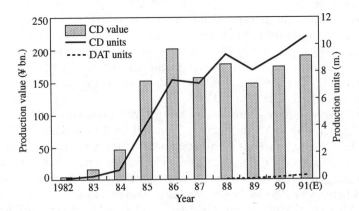

Fig. 5.1. *Japanese CD and DAT production*
Source: MITI.

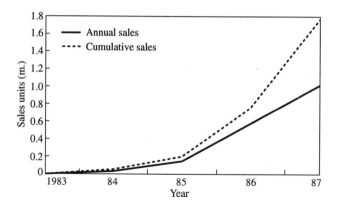

Fig. 5.2. *CD player sales, UK*
Source: BPI.

and Europe) are shown in Table 5.2. Annual CD disc sales in 1991 were about $13 bn., compared to $6 bn. for analog audio cassettes and less than $1 bn. for LP. Unit sales of CD and audio cassettes are closer, since CD disc prices are much higher than those of cassettes.

   Details of UK unit sales of recorded music for CD, LP, and audio cassette are compared in Fig. 5.4. Sales by value are shown in Fig. 5.5. LP sales had been declining for years as the audio cassette market grew but since 1983 had been fairly constant. In 1988 LP sold 52 m. units in the UK compared with 40 m. CD discs. By 1990 this picture had reversed. LP sales were down to 24 m. and CD discs were at 50 m. Audio cassette had increased a little from 65 m. to 74 m. CD disc sales exceeded LP by value in 1988 and by units in 1990. By 1993 sales of LPs were almost zero, with total CD sales of £410 m. and audio cassette sales of £140 m. CD unit sales were on course to

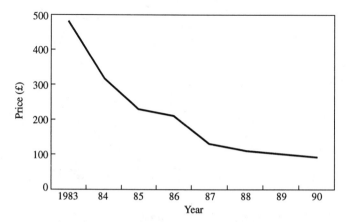

Fig. 5.3. *CD player base price, UK*
Source: BPI.

Table 5.2. *World audio market segments (USA, Japan, Europe)*

	CD ($bn.)	Cassette ($bn.)	LP ($bn.)
1988	5.9	6.5	2.5
1991	13.3	5.8	0.9
1995 (fcst.)	18.6	2.6	0.2

Source: BIS.

Table 5.3. *CD disc catalogue size (UK)*

Year	Titles
1983	200
1984	450
1985	3,000
1986	8,000
1987	18,000

Source: BPI.

equal the record for LP sales achieved in 1976, when 92 m. vinyl LPs were bought in the UK.[1]

CD's breakthrough in pre-recorded music is also indicated by the number of record titles on CD, with 18,000 at the end of 1987, after only 3,000 in 1985, shown in Table 5.3. CD has now exceeded the highest level of 30,000 titles on LP, and 20,000 on audio cassette. About 20,000 new CD titles are

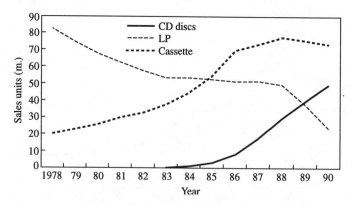

Fig. 5.4. *CD, LP, and cassette sales, UK—(units)*
Source: BPI.

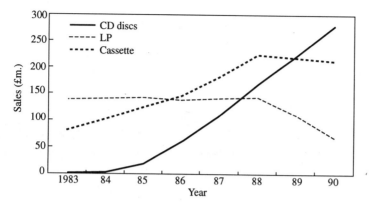

Fig. 5.5. *CD, LP, and cassette sales, UK—(value)*
Source: BPI.

now issued a year worldwide. After 1988 the recording companies started issuing much of their music, especially classical, on CD and audio cassette only, so the number of titles available on LP is falling quickly. CD disc sales are now increasing largely because of bigger software libraries, which in 1988 were averaging only 17 discs per player in the UK.

To establish itself over LP, the new CD standard had to present some clear advantage. For CD the main one was that it was seen as indestructible, advertised as 'perfect sound forever'. Although this turned out to be only partly true, as CDs may deteriorate over time, the absence of surface noise was a major product advantage. CD discs were also smaller than LPs, were more convenient to use, and had random access play. There were initial difficulties convincing audiophiles that the quality of digital sound reproduction was preferable to analog, but the other features eventually outweighed the doubts. CD found its route into the market via the classical music market. This was partly because classical enthusiasts were prepared to pay more for unimpeded sound, but also because the existing huge catalogue of classical music could be transferred to CD easily, providing a ready-made installed base of recorded music. CDs only became the main recording medium for popular music in the late 1980s.[2]

It is not clear whether the sudden disappearance of the LP in the late 1980s was due to collapsing demand and pressure from the music retailers, who refused to stock three separate formats, or to decisions by the recording companies, who decided that profit margins were too low on LP to keep both formats in production. Decisions by the recording companies coincided with the takeover of some of the major recording companies by equipment manufacturers (Polygram by Philips in 1985, CBS Records by Sony in 1987, MCA by Matsushita in 1990), who were intent on rationalizing their hardware and software strategies for CD and DAT.

Disc prices: Despite the success of CD, prices of discs have remained high, and in the UK have actually increased. In 1991, UK retail prices for full priced pop discs were £10.99, and full priced classical £11.99, compared with £8.99 in 1983. By 1993 pop discs had been increased to £11.99 and classical to £12.99, and to as much as £14.49 in some cases. The history of disc prices is shown in Fig. 5.6. Mid-price and Budget ranges were introduced in 1986, priced at around £7 and £3–4 (now £8 and £4–5). Full price LP and audio cassette cost £7–8. Rising CD disc prices may only be a feature of the UK market. In other countries, disc prices have also remained high but have generally followed a downward trend. Disc prices in the US are currently about $14 for full priced discs. Sales and price history for players and discs in the US market for 1983–90 are shown in Fig. 5.7.[3]

Initially high prices may have been explained by a shortage of pressing capacity, with only six plants worldwide up until 1986. There are now over 40, shown in Table 5.4. The first CD production came from two pressing plants built and operated by the equipment manufacturers, Sony and Philips. The next plants were mostly joint ventures between manufacturers and recording companies. It was only in 1986 that recording companies and independents began operating their own plants. For a long time CD disc manufacturing costs were higher than LP, with lower manufacturing yields (reportedly 80 per cent but sometimes lower). In 1990, disc manufacturing costs were reported at around £1 compared to 40p for LP. With large-plant economies, CD costs have fallen further since then. According to US data, CD pressing costs may now be lower than LP, though there are still higher packaging costs. Manufacturing costs are a small proportion of the final price, and hardly explain the £4–5 difference in selling prices between LP and CD.

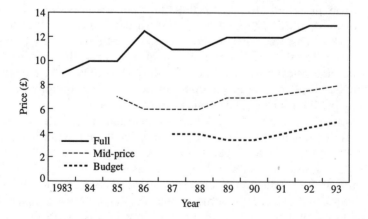

Fig. 5.6. *CD disc prices, UK*
Source: Consumers' Association.

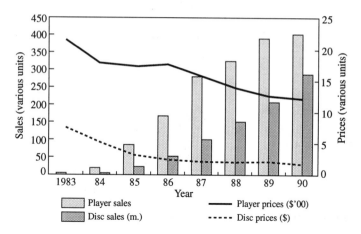

Fig. 5.7. *US CD players and discs—sales and prices*
Source: RIAA.

Breakdowns of CD disc costs compared with audio cassette and LP, as of 1990, are given in Table 5.5. As most of the costs in this breakdown are accounting allocations based on sales price, with more detailed figures not released by the recording companies, the profit contribution from CD is probably much higher than shown. Dealer margins are also considered high. CD profit levels have variously been called, from different viewpoints, 'tremendous value' or 'obscene'.[4]

(b) Digital audio tape

DAT uses the same digital coding techniques as CD, combined with minia-turized VCR technology. The tape technology is a modification of that developed for 8 mm. camcorder by Sony. The use of tapes for digital audio for professional recording predates CD, as noted above. VCR had been on sale since the mid-1970s, and digital audio processors, based on VCR and Sony's digital coding system, were in wide use by 1979. Development efforts

Table 5.4. *World-wide CD disc production capacity*

	Plants	Capacity (m. units/year)
1983	2	4
1984	5	15
1985	6	56
1986	13	137
1987	49	570

Source: Press reports.

Table 5.5. *Cost breakdown for LP, audio cassette, and CD (1990)*

	LP	Cassette	CD
Retail Price (£)	6.99	6.99	11.49
Costs			
Manufacture	0.42	0.45	1.05
Other costs	0.36	0.36	0.48
Advertising/promotion	0.42	0.42	0.42
Overhead contribution	0.78	0.78	1.13
Artist royalty	0.85	0.85	1.32
Mechanical royalty	0.38	0.38	0.59
Design/packaging	0.30	0.15	0.23
Distribution/discounts	0.84	0.84	1.12
VAT	0.91	0.91	1.50
Dealer margin	1.44	1.44	2.70
Recording company profit	0.29	0.41	0.95

Source: Consumers' Association.

for consumer DAT only began in about 1981. DAT prototypes were ready by late 1985, but the launch was postponed, critically, for strategic reasons until February 1987, in Japan. It was made available in the UK in March 1988. Only 30,000 DAT machines had been sold worldwide by the end of 1987, mostly for professional recording use. The growth of DAT production has been slow, especially compared with CD. About 300,000 units were manufactured in Japan (the only producer) in 1991, versus 10.5 m. CD players in Japan alone (see Fig. 5.1).

The introduction prices of DAT players were high, at around £800–1500, though by 1991 these had come down to £500. Aiwa launched a Walkman sized portable DAT player in the UK in 1990 at £100 and Sony launched a combined CD/DAT player in 1991 at £900.[5] Prices have come down further since then but even in the USA DAT players are still about $500, probably above the level at which DAT could become widely acceptable. Given DAT's greater mechanical complexity (70–80 per cent of the parts are similar to VCR), manufacturers estimate that player prices will remain at least 50 per cent higher than for CD players. Pre-recorded tapes were introduced in the UK at £20, though producers are confident that this can be brought down to the cost of CD. Pre-recorded DAT tapes may remain relatively costly, for similar reasons to CD.[6]

Development of DAT was not as rapid as CD, as there were technical problems to overcome in miniaturizing tape cassette technology. However, the main delays were strategic, concerning attempts to obtain agreement upon common standards. Whereas CD was defined by a closely held set of patents owned by Sony and Philips, and could be offered ready-made to other manufacturers, DAT was based on a number of previous patents, and the standard needed to be set by some form of consensus. The first conference on common standards was held in June 1983 (eight months after the CD launch). A series of conferences and other meetings were used to try to resolve technical issues between the manufacturers, and, what proved more difficult, to obtain the support of the recording companies. Facing concerted opposition from the record producers, and not wishing to disrupt the introduction of CD with what had become a more risky product, the equipment manufacturers themselves decided to delay DAT until CD's introduction was resolved.

After much argument, inside and outside the standards bodies, agreement was only reached much later, in 1989, when a workable compromise was made on the copying issues. This is the effective launch date of DAT as a usable consumer product. The recording companies agreed to support DAT provided it included a serial management copying system (SCMS) or 'Solocopy' device to restrict copying from CD or other digital sources.[7] SCMS allows any number of DAT digital copies to be made from an original digital recording (from CD, DAT, DCC, or MD), but recognizes a copy and will not allow any subsequent digital copies from copies. Thus users may copy a CD for their personal or automobile stereo, but not start pirating in large volumes. SCMS is only intended to be included in consumer machines; 'professional decks'—defined as those costing over $1,000 in the US—are immune from this restriction. There had been much activity both behind the scenes and in public to reach this compromise. However, the agreement was probably only achieved once DAT had little chance of major consumer success.

In parallel with these developments in the equipment markets there has been significant vertical integration by the manufacturers into various forms of entertainment software, as noted above. The strategic logic of these takeovers was to gain access to movies, records, and programming that would entice consumers to buy the parent's hardware equipment. This should have allowed greater co-ordination between strategies between equipment and music production, both for CD and DAT. However, the music companies have generally been left to manage themselves. It was widely expected at the time of Sony's purchase of CBS Records in 1987 that it would release material on DAT. This did not happen, and CBS has yet to support DAT. However, the takeover signalled the end of CBS's active opposition, and probably paved the way for SCMS. Pre-recorded DAT tapes were first offered in the UK in August 1988 by the then independent producer, Chandos.

2.2 Technical description

Both CD and DAT use the same basic technique for digital sound reproduction, called pulse code modulation (PCM). This eliminates background noise and distortions introduced by the recording medium. The sound waveform is encoded as a series of digits, stored as 'dots and dashes' rather than as a direct analog representation of the original sound. The digits give the strength of the waveform measured at a high sampling frequency (44.1 Khz for CD and 48 Khz for DAT). When played the digital coding is converted back to an analog waveform. The method includes correction techniques which mask errors in reading, such as those due to scratches or dust, by smoothing out short gaps in the reconstructed waveform.

In CD the digital coding is written as pits on the surface of a disc, to be read using a laser. The 12 cm. diameter plastic disc is made by pressing from a master disc. The playing surface is vacuum coated with aluminium to reflect the laser beam, and then sealed with a lacquer coating for protection. In use this is read from beneath, from the centre outward, with the disc rotating at 200–500 r.p.m. Recording time is up to 74 minutes. Tracking has to be very accurate and the laser beam is kept centred on the recording track by automatic control. CD originally had no recording capability, and although techniques for recording, if not erasing, with CD have now been developed the technology does not lend itself easily to this.[8]

In DAT the coding is stored on magnetic tape, using a 'helical scan' system similar to that for VCR. This wraps the tape, on a skew, around a rotating head (a 3 cm. diameter drum, rotating at 2000 r.p.m.), which reads and writes the track diagonally across the tape. Linear tape speed is less than 1 cm./sec.[9] The cassettes are small (7.5 × 5.4 × 1 cm.), about the size of a credit card. Recording capacity is up to two hours, with a four-hour version from JVC. Players have complete play, record, and erase facilities.

The different sampling frequency for DAT from CD had been used from the start by the manufacturers (at MITI insistence) to limit DAT copying and try to keep the two products separate. The digital signals could not be copied directly from CD to DAT without going through a decoding stage. The effectiveness of this separation is only partial, as DAT will play back on either frequency, and it should be relatively straightforward for an audio enthusiast or pirate to design a module to bypass the feature blocking DAT copying on CD frequency. Also copies may be made from the decoded CD output, which should still be of high quality.

This was not considered enough by the recording companies, who proposed a 'Copycode' placed at intervals within the digital coding which would disable any copying of CD or DAT. This would have made it impossible to copy from CD by programming the DAT player to recognize the codes and switch itself off. This particular suggestion was technically inept, as the range of audio frequencies reproduced had to be reduced to allow room for the code. It also required changes to CD. Copycode was eventually rejected by all parties. The disagreement was finally resolved in 1989 with the addition of the SCMS device, which allowed limited copying from originals. This does not require changes to CD but works by adding a code to the DAT copy. SCMS has minimal effect on the reproduction quality, as Copycode would have done.

2.3 Product comparison

A comparison of product features is given in Table 5.6. In most dimensions, the two systems are equivalent, either performing equally well or with advantages and disadvantages in balance. *Reproduction* quality for the two systems is equal, as they use the same PCM technique. *Durability* is equivalent, though there are differences. For *hardware durability*, DAT is mechanically more complex than CD but may not need such careful adjustment. Both are based on tried technologies (VCR and Laservision). *Software durability* is qualitatively different for each system but the end result is that both are relatively long-lived and on balance probably equivalent. Although CD discs were initially portrayed as virtually indestructible, they will fail if large areas of the disc are spoiled. Also, it has become clear that unless manufactured to high quality standards, and stored carefully ever after, the disc may eventually fail on its own, due to corrosion of the aluminium film. Manufacturers' estimates of the average life of a CD disc are about eight to ten years, depending on how they are manufactured and stored. Failure tends to be absolute, with the CD unusable, rather than the gradual deterioration with analog systems. By now most CD users are familiar with the strange pranks they get up to.[10] The magnetic tape used in DAT is probably longer lived than CD. The main threats to DAT are tape snags and buckling, as with VCR. There is gradual deterioration as the magnetic film wears, though the manufacturers claim this is negligible. DAT should play about 600 passes before any degradation becomes noticeable or cannot be masked by the electronics. Thus CDs may fail over time, used or not, whereas DAT tapes wear out with use.

Hardware prices are likely to remain higher for DAT than CD, probably at around double, even with large volume production. *Software prices* depend on the pricing policy of the producers as much as the production costs. The major expense in either system is software, which for CD may be 10 per cent of the player cost for each disc. In the near term CD has a cost advantage but this could disappear over time. Although recording a tape sequentially is inherently more expensive than pressing a plastic disc, mass recording techniques for DAT have been developed. Quality and yield requirements for CD discs may make it difficult to bring down CD manufacturing costs much further. Also DAT has a greater recording capacity, so per unit costs could eventually be equivalent to CD.

Capacity gives DAT an advantage. DAT offers cassettes with 80 or 120 minute playing time, and on up to four hours. The maximum playing time of a CD is 74 minutes (reputedly chosen by Sony to contain the whole of Beethoven's Ninth symphony on one disc). Capacity is probably more

Table 5.6. *Product feature comparison*

Feature		CD	DAT
Reproduction		Digital (PCM)	Digital (PCM)
Durability	(h/w)	Good; laser cheap (£10); 7,000 hrs. life	Good; playing-head expensive (£40); needs cleaning
	(s/w)	'Indestructible' in use; deteriorates over time (7 years)	Hard-wearing; liable to tape-snagging; head wear
Production cost	(h/w)	Cheap, mainly mechanical cost; continual reductions	Higher than CD (double); electronic and mechanical
	(s/w)	Initially expensive (£1–2); now cheap	Moderate (similar to VCR)
Price	(h/w)	Introduction £480; now £100 or less	Introduction £800–1300; now £500; finally £200 (as VCR)
	(s/w)	Initially £10 per disc; now £13, £8, £4–5	Introduction £20; blanks £6; estimated same as CD
Size	(h/w)	Medium; limit 12cm. disc	Medium; potentially small; limit 7 cm. cassette 7.5 × 5.4 × 1 cm. cassette
	(s/w)	12/8cm. disc	
Capacity		12 cm.: 75 min.; 8 cm.: 23 min.	80/120 min. (JVC 4 hr.)
Recording		Available (write once); prototype erasability	Full recording, erase, play; features equal to recording studio
Portability		No 'joggable' CD player, easily 'skates'; high power use	Robust; good for auto/personal stereo; high power use
Power use		Medium-high (rotate disc)	Medium-high (rotate head)
Cueing		Programmable; rapid direct access: 0–2 sec. access	Programmable; moderate direct access; 0–20 sec. access
Future development		CD-ROM; CDV; CD-I; LD; Multimedia	Computer, data storage; VCR/camcorder links (8 mm.)

important for recording than for pre-recorded music, especially with multiple play machines. Nearly 90 per cent of the market is pop and few albums are likely to last two hours. DAT capacity may be more attractive for classical music as it can contain a complete opera on one tape. *Equipment size* for an in-home player is about the same. DAT portable players are currently larger than CD but potentially could be smaller, limited mainly by the tiny cassettes. Software size slightly favours DAT, which has small, credit card sized cassettes compared with the 12 cm. CD discs. These are more convenient and also do not require such careful handling.[11]

Beyond this, DAT can do two important things which CD cannot. First, DAT has full *recording capability*. It can record, erase, and edit from sources such as LP, CD, DAT, radio, digital satellite broadcasts, and live recording. If not disabled it may record digital signals from CD or DAT directly without going through an analog stage. It is particularly attractive for professional recording because of the quality and various editing features. In contrast CD has only playback facilities. Recordable and erasable CD has now been developed, but still does not look as though it will lead to commercial products, despite hopes. Recording capability increases the usefulness of DAT to consumers in the same way that VCR is more useful than VD. It allows copies from various sources onto a common medium and shared software with other users. The sound quality and suitability for personal/automobile stereos mean that in theory DAT could replace both older systems, LP and audio cassette, as well as CD, with a single set of software, with ensuing economies of needing only one library.

Second, DAT has superior *portability* for applications such as personal and automobile stereos, to which CD is not overly suited. Though there are many portable CD players on the market they are susceptible to vibration and easily jump tracks when bumped. This lack of a 'joggable' CD contrasts with DAT where the tape is in close contact with the head and is not affected by moderate vibrations. The potentially smaller size of the players also favours DAT for portable use, and the tiny tapes are ideal for carrying. DAT players are the size of a large personal stereo. They could eventually be made smaller. Miniature CD players with small 8 cm. discs have not been a success, offering only 23 minutes playing time. Also CD discs have to be handled more carefully than tapes. However, both systems have relatively high *power consumption*, for CD to rotate the disc at high speed and for DAT to rotate the head (which is in contact with the tape). Thus both are likely to need heavy batteries or frequent battery charges, providing some problems for personal stereos.

However, CD has an advantage of its own, with superior *cueing* facilities for track identification and programming, to search and play particular tracks. Both systems have random access but CD is faster. It takes only about two seconds to access a given CD track, where DAT takes an average of around 20 seconds to do the same task (DAT fast-searches a tape at 400 times normal speed). DAT supporters argue that the difference in access speeds is not significant.

Development potential for the technology and links with other systems favour CD at this point, though are probably comparable for both over the long term. CD is making important progress as a bulk data distribution medium with CD-ROM. Major development work is going ahead largely around CD for multimedia uses involving computers, video, audio, and telecommunications. The unknown lifetime of CD discs is a reason for concern about its use for data archiving. In home entertainment CD audio and video are combined in products such as CD video, interactive CD and laser disc. Surprisingly, DAT may have as much promise, at least in the computer and multimedia areas. It has read/write capability, greater data capacity (at 1200 megabytes this is already double that of CD), low cost (a tenth that of data optical disc) and the known long-life characteristics of magnetic tape. It also has a form of random access. These make it an excellent medium for bulk data storage.[12] There is already a large market for DAT as a computer backup system. These other applications need not affect the audio market directly, but imply continuing product and cost improvements to come.

3. STRATEGIES FOR ESTABLISHING STANDARDS

3.1 Timing and the 'window of opportunity'

As a product DAT offers more to consumers than CD. Both systems provide significant improvement in quality, durability, and convenience over LP at reasonable cost. But DAT is able to record as well as play and is probably more suitable for portable stereos. Where CD is essentially a replacement for LP, the more versatile DAT could replace LP, audio cassette, and CD. Unfortunately for DAT, standards are not decided on straight product comparisons. CD had formidable strategic advantages. It was first on the market, by some years, and had the support of the recording companies. Together these were sufficient to overcome any technical advantages of DAT. The four year lead that CD had in the market was decisive. It allowed it to present a more or less proven product with a proven installed base. If these were not 'systems products' we might expect a significant share of the market for the DAT format. Instead it was shut out of the main consumer market and has only slowly established itself in specialist recording niches, where compatibility is less important.

The dynamics of standards are that if one system can establish itself as the leader, it becomes the natural choice for new buyers, who are assured access to a larger range of recorded music. The greater the installed base of equipment using a given standard, the more complementary goods, such as recorded music, are produced for it. Getting an acceptable product to the market first gives a product like CD a strong advantage as it begins to build up its base of users and starts the 'bandwagon' process. These demand-side advantages are compounded by conventional learning curve effects, allowing the leading standard to reduce prices and consolidate its advantage. In the case of CD and DAT, the complementary product is especially important, as the software (music) market eventually becomes much larger than the hardware (equipment) market.

DAT technology only became available to consumers after CD had been launched. By the time DAT was finally released CD had a significant and rapidly growing installed base. CD had a large range of available titles and, equally, the expectation that it would continue to be supported with software. New users deciding which standard to buy saw a risk with DAT of being stranded without support. Music producers made the same calculation of whether it was worth investing in production for the new standard. Judging by the tiny sales of DAT, most users decided that the standards advantages of CD, with available music and a known product, outweighed the product features of DAT. DAT had to be bought on faith. The opposition of the recording companies at that time was very great, and added to the risk. The high price of DAT players completed the problem. At the same time many of the DAT manufacturers restricted the scale of their production and sales effort. This was partly a response to technical restrictions placed on DAT by MITI to placate the recording companies, so that makers felt that the final system lacked the real appeal of DAT, as well as to the daunting prospect of competing with CD by this stage.

Yet, when DAT was first available in 1985, CD was still not established, and there was a 'window of opportunity' for either standard to establish itself. A critical point for any standard is when the installed base becomes large enough to sustain a separate software industry. CD had reached that point by 1987 but probably not in 1985. For example, there were only six disc pressing plants in 1985, compared with over 40 in 1987. By 1987, when DAT was eventually launched, the bandwagon effects were already working strongly for CD, and it only needed a further delay of a few years to ensure that the window was permanently closed against DAT in this market.

Some of the delay in presenting DAT to the market was due to the manufacturers themselves, who had difficulty with some joint technical decisions, possibly reflecting indecision over what to do with the product. However, the crucial delays took place in the negotiations in standards committees and elsewhere to get DAT accepted by the music industry. This may have been wasted effort, as the music companies probably did not want DAT under any conditions, seeing the success they were beginning to have with CD. The various delays associated with the committee process, as well as legal challenges, are discussed below. Intentionally or not, these served the interests of the opponents, since by the time a standard had been agreed in 1989 the market had lost interest in DAT.

Since the contest took place before DAT was launched, the relative credibility of the two standards was also important. As one standard was already on the market and the other only being proposed, the advantage was very much with CD. It had already got over most of its credibility problems by this time, though many of these were generic to digital audio compared with analog. When CD was first introduced there had been long debates about the sound quality. These had been resolved by the mid-1980s. CD was accepted by large sections of the public and they were convinced of its advantages.[13] Although DAT did not have to overcome these particular credibility problems, it had others. DAT was a new product and users were not sure what it could do, how much it would cost or whether it would be supported in future. It had taken a long time coming to market, which looked hesitant. There was no foreseeable way in which the recording companies were going to support it. Not only did DAT look risky to the public but the manufacturers were themselves not convinced.

Part of the users' hesitancy was that the manufacturers also had interests in both CD and DAT, and once CD began to succeed against LP they did not want to disrupt it at a sensitive stage. DAT could have been launched soon after the prototypes were displayed at the October 1985 Tokyo hi-fi show. The launch was postponed reportedly due to arguments by the Japanese big stores that in 1985–86 DAT would confuse the consumer market and stop the newly emerging CD from getting established. When DAT finally arrived in 1987, it was introduced at high prices to test the market. Given the obstacles, this is an understandable approach, but it also ensured that DAT could not build up an installed base quickly enough. As users were not reassured on any of these points DAT was left to professional recording users, a segment of the market which was less concerned with cost of pre-recorded music, and is more concerned with DAT's excellent recording capabilities.

3.2 Standards committees and recording company opposition

It has become conventional to blame the recording companies for the failure of DAT. They were the authors of many of the difficulties, but it is going too far to say that they are solely to blame. They would probably not have opposed DAT without the strong alternative in the form of CD. When the idea of digital tape was first suggested as a consumer product at the beginning of the 1980s, well before CD became a significant product, the music companies were acquiescent and saw DAT as essentially an update to analog audio cassette. It was only after CD was on the way to establishing itself, and had proven its profitability, that opposition to DAT crystallized. It did this by biasing market forces rather than leading them. Given the large markets opening up with CD, the music companies were as much responding to demand as influencing it. Also, it should be remembered that the recording companies had at first not embraced CD, and had only started to support it after extreme efforts by the manufacturers.

Digital audio's problems with the recording companies are extreme examples of coordination problems, of ensuring that core and complementary products are available at the same time. For both CD and DAT, nobody wanted to move first. The recording companies did not want to promote the new standard without sufficient users to provide a market, while users would not buy players until there was some software. In both cases cross-industry standards committees were used, but with little direct effect. To convince the co-producers the manufacturers had to make a strong commitment in the market. For CD the impasse was resolved by the manufacturers producing the initial complementary goods themselves until the market became self-sustaining. For DAT the opposition was more active, and the impasse remained in place until DAT was no threat.

(a) Compact disc

For CD the manufacturers, Sony and Philips, made great efforts to encourage the music companies to produce CD discs, including the use of industry standards bodies to obtain agreement on the new standard. Encouragement was not enough and the manufacturers eventually had to provide the initial supply of discs themselves. The investment needed was large, at $10–20 m. per disc pressing plant, and the recording companies were not ready to support such a risky venture, especially given their large investments in LP pressing plants. For the first CD discs the manufacturers built two disc plants of their own. Several of the next disc plants were joint ventures between the manufacturers and the music firms. Manufacturers continued to make efforts to gain support, licensing the standard at low cost to music companies and other equipment manufacturers to ensure its wide use. Even so CD disc capacity was initially severely limited. It was 1986, three years after the launch, before the recording companies and independents accepted CD's potential and invested in major disc-making capacity.

The importance of recorded music, and the larger size of the music market relative to the equipment market, may have helped shift the balance of bargaining power towards the recording companies. The liberal licensing terms and sponsorship of disc production needed to encourage music company support, may also have helped determine which group has gained most from the new technology. CD margins have been much higher on music than equipment. Gross margins on consumer electronics are usually no more than about 2 per cent. Earnings on CD discs are reported at about 10 per cent (copyright payments excluded), a figure which is probably understated due to company cost allocations. High disc prices, which are partly a consequence of the coordination problem, continue to limit market growth. The CD market has always grown steadily rather than with wild enthusiasm.

(b) Digital audio tape

With DAT the coordination problems have been greater. The recording companies not only boycotted DAT because of its ability to make perfect copies of copyright material, they also attempted, ultimately successfully, to prevent the introduction of DAT machines with unrestricted copying capability. Without the large record producers, none of the smaller companies would take the risk of entering alone. This blocked the acceptance of DAT. It entered the market with no prerecorded music, and not surprisingly hardly any players were sold in the consumer market. Even in Japan only a handful of Sony recordings were available for the initial machines. The manufacturers had tried from the beginning to placate the recording companies by making CD and DAT not directly compatible. At the insistence of MITI, different sampling frequencies had been used for the two systems, so that music could not be copied directly from CD to DAT. The intention was to separate CD and DAT, which would then compete independently. On this theory, expansion of DAT would not directly hurt CD sales and any software opposition to DAT would not feed back to CD. This was not enough for the recording companies, who essentially preferred no DAT copying at any price, whether from CD or other DAT players.

Using the market to resolve the standards issue was not a realistic option for DAT, given the determined opposition of the record producers, as well as the conflicting interests of many of the manufacturers. The DAT conflicts had to be resolved before launch, which meant by committee negotiation. There were a series of standards conferences, beginning in June 1983 and involving up to 84 firms (21 non-Japanese), representing the consumer electronics and music industries.

This collaboration was not successful. At one level, the standards bodies attempted to resolve basic technical standards for the system. Even here negotiations were not effective, possibly because there was no market in sight to support any decision. For example, it was July 1985, after five major meetings and numerous smaller ones, before basic specifications were completed for the two competing DAT technologies: R-DAT (rotating head) and S-DAT (stationary head). Sub-committees of the DAT Conference were still attempting in 1988 to finalize the sub-code standards. There is still no definitive standard, as there remain some minor points of incompatibility between different machines.

At the level of inter-industry coordination between equipment and music interests, later conferences in particular may have provided a forum for dissent, rather than have helped resolve the differences. These conferences focused on copyright issues, for which it seemed that basic differences of approach left the two sides unable to appreciate the other's viewpoint.

Apart from disagreements in the standards committees, this spilled over into international trade issues. The US trade representative and the EC committee on trade expressed concern over the potential infringement of copyright by DAT. In response MITI gave written instructions to 27 makers of DAT in February 1987 requesting them not to commercialize the consumer use of DAT machines which permitted the direct digital copying of CD (Depma, 1992).

The style of negotiation is illustrated by Copycode, proposed by the record producers in 1986 as a way around the copyright issue. Technically this made nonsense of DAT, a system whose main attraction is high quality recording, and did not appeal to the manufacturers. It distorted the sound quality in a system sold on its near perfect reproduction, and could never have been acceptable to the users. It would also have been quite simple to bypass by modifying the recorder. It was clearly not a feasible solution, and was rejected by the National Bureau of Standards in the USA in May 1988. Yet it helped distract the industry for two crucial years, and to confuse potential customers, postponing the acceptance of DAT while CD built up a lead.

The alternative copy restriction system, SCMS/Solocopy, proposed later by the manufacturers, was accepted by the International Federation of Phonogram and Videogram Producers in May 1989.[14] They agreed to allow DAT to go ahead without a ban on supplying music. Subsequent national legislation such as the US Audio Home Recording Rights Act of October 1992 set royalty levels on digital recordings and blank media.[15] SCMS may have unblocked DAT but came too late to make a difference. By then the music companies may have been more willing to settle the issue. CD was well established so that DAT was little threat. Also by this time recordable CD had become a distinct possibility, a threat to CD which the producers liked even less than DAT—since recording does not need a second system. SCMS will be part of DCC and minidisc, which seem destined to carry the portable digital audio flag.

This shows the difficulties of co-ordinating standards via committees when there are major conflicts of interest involved. In retrospect, it is not clear why so much faith was placed by the manufacturers on this route, rather than on private coalitions. Possibly Sony felt it had to attempt the cooperative route, after its problems with Betamax VCR, and the lack of clear proprietorship over DAT.[16] Eventually the manufacturers internalized the interests of the two groups by integrating into music production.

4. PROFITABILITY AND STRATEGIC INTEGRATION

4.1 Overlapping interests in CD and DAT

CD surprised both manufacturers and record producers by the scale of its success. At the beginning few people seem to have expected CD to have made such inroads into the market, or to have lasted so long. Even Sony expected CD to be more successful for computer data storage than as an audio product. Most surprising was probably the speed with which CD displaced LP once it had achieved a critical level of market acceptance. Much of the rapidity was due to the overlapping interests of the music producers of the two standards, who could earn more by issuing a single format. Music retailers also rebelled against stocking both formats, in addition to audio cassette. The deciding factor was the integration of the leading electronics manufacturers into the music business, which apparently triggered the industry decision to drop the LP. While rapid adoption of a standard, or 'tipping', is typical for a successful standard, it was not widely predicted.

The unexpectedness of CD's success may help excuse some of the manufacturers' ambivalence to DAT. Similar strategic calculations to those which established CD so rapidly when LPs were dropped, also worked against DAT. The manufacturers wanted to avoid cannibalizing sales of CD by promoting DAT at a sensitive moment. The same firms were involved in CD and DAT, and the two leaders, Sony and Philips, also now had interests in software. The object was to maximize joint returns on hardware and software, rather than allow a straight CD/DAT contest. Though the manufacturers supported DAT, it always took second position to CD. The initial DAT specifications were modified to avoid direct confrontation with CD, years were spent trying to negotiate standards with record producers committed to CD, and the DAT launch was delayed for nearly two years until CD was established. Various copy restrictions were proposed and eventually adopted, which stopped DAT doing the thing it did best.

Standards theory tells us that commitment is vital for the success of a standard. This double thinking meant that DAT had little chance against CD, if the intent was to contest the same market. And if DAT was intended for a secondary market in portable stereos, it was too sophisticated. What is perhaps surprising is that a strategy with these contradictions continued for so long. DAT has now found a specialist niche which it could have had from the beginning.

The original strategy of the manufacturers was to promote CD and DAT separately with a space of a few years between them. DAT would be held back until CD was well into its life cycle, then take over as CD sales started to fall.[17] This kind of product sequencing, which may work for conventional products, does not work with standards. Once network effects and software took over, the CD standard became unassailable. What may have originally been seen as an interim product assumed a life of its own.

Although CD is now reckoned a success, this may not have been an optimal outcome for the manufacturers. They expended a great deal of time and money to establish CD, yet the result is that the audio market is still fragmented into at least two standards, for the in-house and portable markets, and probably more. Each sub-market is only partially supported with equipment and software. The prospect is that users have two or three new layers to add to their stereo systems (CD, DAT, and DCC/MD), making, with LP and audio cassette, a strange collection of four or five partially supported systems for audio alone. Conceivably these could all have been replaced by a single DAT system. Even if the manufacturers still manage to sell two systems not one, they may have missed an even larger single market. And the bulk of the earnings have gone to the music producers.[18]

4.2 Vertical integration

The basic problem for the manufacturers was that they and the recording companies had conflicting interests. Much of what happened was outside the manufacturers' control. Once the CD market was growing strongly it could not easily be disrupted by DAT. Most of the gains were going to the music producers, whose high price of discs was restricting growth of CD and whose software ban had blocked DAT. But the Japanese manufacturers could not easily oppose the music producers head on.

To cope with these dilemmas called for an integrated hardware and software strategy. It was an attempt to internalize these conflicts that led Sony to purchase CBS Records in late 1987. Philips was already the world's largest CD producer, with Polygram. At one step this promised to reduce the two restrictions on Sony's freedom of action.[19] A measure of the pressure on Sony is the high price paid, $2 bn. At the time Wall Street estimates of the market value of the CBS Records division was around £1.25 bn., so that Sony paid a premium of $750 m., or 60 per cent.[20] The premium indicates the value Sony placed on being able to coordinate its hardware and software strategies for CD and DAT over time. Maximizing joint profits for hardware and software in introducing the new technology implies a different set of strategies than if both players maximize profits independently. This recalls traditional arguments for vertical integration due to incomplete contracts and transactions costs, but put in a dynamic context.

In the event, neither Sony nor Philips have made fewer changes to the music companies that at first expected. Sony has left CBS operations to manage themselves, acknowledging the difficulties of managing two very different industries.[21] However, appearances may deceive. The main value of integration may not be so much in active cross-promotion but in removing opposition to new products and creating favourable conditions for the combined industries. The merger removed the basic conflict between the manufacturers and the recording companies over technology. CBS dropped its vocal opposition to DAT, and the SCMS agreement followed in the next year. Even so, Sony did not rush to issue DAT titles. The software interests in CD and DAT were internalized by Sony, which in fact may have made it less willing to disrupt the CD standard and helped take DAT out of the contest.

In this case it also imposes a long term view on both sides. Though there may not be been an obvious link between CBS and Sony hardware sales, it has allowed Sony to introduce products such as minidisc as it wished. Similarly with Philips' introduction of DCC. Also the increased influence of the manufacturers as a group over the music industry has had an effect on the CD market. In addition to their contribution to the decision to halt production of vinyl LP records, they have initiated the more active marketing of CD titles (such as the boxed set reissues of archive collections), which has made CD players more attractive. Such links are likely to become more important with the new products being developed for the home entertainment market.

4.3 Recording company profits

Although the recording companies have done well from CD, it is still an open question whether they were wise to oppose DAT. CD has been profitable, and the inability to copy CD helps support the value of copyright material. However, DAT prices of pre-recorded music were also expected to be high and this could have been a larger market than CD. The ability to make home copies makes DAT attractive to users, and the market expansion could outweigh the loss of original sales. For example, this seems to have been the case for audio cassette; despite ongoing worries about pirating, audio cassette has been a great success for the recording companies, and still provides 40 per cent of their revenues. Admittedly, copying is more of a threat with DAT, as there is no loss in quality between generations of copies. Even so, had CD not been developed first, the recording companies might have accepted DAT as an alternative, high-quality cassette, and not have opposed it so strongly.

The manufacturers have argued that the music companies confuse home copying, which may expand the market, with large scale pirating, which takes away market share and may threaten prices. The threat of pirating from DAT may have been overestimated. For one thing it needs a large investment and a determined pirate. There were already technical reasons, due to the different frequencies used, why direct copying, at least from CD, was not straightforward. The recording companies clearly did not believe that market expansion with DAT could offset the higher losses from pirating. They may naturally take a shorter term view of the market and be more concerned about maintaining property rights over their material, than in the potential long term size of the combined market. It took the integration of the electronics manufacturers into the entertainment business to try to change this.

5. PARALLELS WITH VIDEO STANDARDS

An indication of what might have happened had the order of arrival of CD and DAT been reversed is given by the contest between VCR and VD, played out ten years earlier. The contrast helps emphasize the importance of timing compared with other product differences. In the video case the tape system was introduced first and it was the disc which was excluded. The introduction dates for the four systems are given in Table 4.1, above. When the main VD contender, Philips's Laservision, was launched in the USA in 1979, it faced an installed base of VCRs which had been growing for three or four years and already was over a million units. The same happened in Japan and Europe. Video disc was rejected and it was a decade before it could gain a market for high quality movie videos, now called laser disc.

VCR had many of the product advantages seen with DAT. It had recording capability and higher capacity than VD. Recording made it more versatile as it could record from TV for 'time-shift' viewing as well as play pre-recorded tapes. As Keiichi Takeoka, president of Matsushita USA, said in 1981, 'I personally think the video disc business should not be in a great hurry. Video cassette can do so much more'.[22] In comparison VD had higher picture quality and potentially lower hardware and software costs, using simpler manufacturing processes. However these depended on volume to bring down costs and the lower capacity of discs countered any software advantage. Thanks to economies of scale VCR has always been cheaper than VD. VCR was easier to introduce as home TV recording made the scarcity of initial software less of a problem, whereas VD depended fully on recorded discs.[23] The main advantage that VCR had, and DAT did not, was that is was about four years ahead of VD. By the time the VD was launched VCR was well established, and any advantages the disc players had were insufficient even to find a niche market. A large market for pre-recorded VCR tapes had built up. VCR market penetration was only 8 per cent when VD arrived but this was sufficient to keep VD out. Roy Pollack, RCA vice-president for video disc development, said in 1984, 'Our mistake was we were late. Five years earlier it would have been a great success'.[24]

In digital audio the product features of tape and disc are also mostly equivalent except that the tape system 'can do more'. As with VCR, DAT's main advantage over disc is its recording capability, though as this still needs digital input to be fully useful (from other tapes, as this is not generally available on radio) pre-recorded software plays a more critical role in audio than video. However, DAT has an added advantage for portable stereos. The strategic difference is that for audio the disc system was first on the market. It had established a base of players and discs and was supported by the recording companies. It also represented a major investment already made by the manufacturers. The sequence of events was enough to reverse the video result.

6. CONTINUING DEVELOPMENT

6.1 Extensions to other technologies

The technologies used in both CD and DAT have potential applications in other fields, primarily in the video and computer markets. In consumer electronics the laser beam technology used in the CD is the same as in laser disc (LD). CD technology has been extended to develop video systems such as CD video (CDV) and interactive CD (CD-I), listed in Table 5.7. The coding standards in each of these cases are different, and LD uses analog video, but combination players which play any CD, CDV, CD-I, and LD, whatever the size or format, are now common. There are demand side cross-benefits between the different consumer products. The combination players make the individual standards more valuable, by creating an installed base which accepts any standard. The installed base of players increases demand for CD and other discs while the CD disc base has made it easier to establish CD/CDV/LD products. In Japan 10 per cent of households already had LD players in 1993, most of which also play CD and CDV, and the market for CD-only players had reportedly disappeared. In the USA there are 1 m. LD players in use. The prices of LD players and discs are now approaching VCR prices, at £399 per player and £25 per disc in the UK.

In computers, CD-ROM, which uses the same laser technology but different coding standards, has now become a major storage medium and component for multimedia systems. These related technologies provide a larger manufacturing base for CD-like discs, but any influence this might have on bringing down CD costs comes too late to affect CD itself. Recently technological benefits have been in the other direction, as consumer development of CD must have helped bring down initial CDV and CD-ROM production costs. Sony is a major manufacturer of CD-ROM drives, using technical skills built up in CD.

DAT has a similar set of technological links, the mechanism having been developed as a spinoff from VCR and 8 mm. camcorder, with the same digital audio as hi-fi VCR. It has many applications for data storage in computers. On the supply side there could be some benefits to DAT from innovations and reduced manufacturing costs due to an increase in production for the computer market. However, on the demand side these applications are probably too dissimilar for there to be any network effects between the installed base in one area and users in the other (such as using the same unit for data storage and music reproduction).

Table 5.7. *Digital optical disc technologies*

Standard	Name	Year	Description
VD	Video disc (analog)	1978	Analog video, analog audio
CD-DA	Compact disc	1982	Digital audio CD
CD-ROM	CD read only memory	1983	Data storage for PC
LD	Laser disc (analog)	1985	Improved VD, digital audio
CD-ROM XA	CD-ROM extended architecture	1988	Extension of CD-ROM to CD-I
DVI	Digital video interactive	1987	Full PC video from CD-ROM
CD-I	CD interactive	1988	Video and audio, moving image
Photo CD	CD photograph	1990	Colour still photographs
CDTV	Compact dynamic total vision	1991	Video and audio on CD

6.2 Current contest for portable digital audio: DCC and minidisc

Although DAT is capable of serving the market for portable digital audio it is probably too expensive a technology for the portable market alone. The two simpler technologies which have now been developed for portable stereos are digital compact cassette (DCC) and minidisc (MD). These are currently involved in a contest to establish a portable standard. This plays out the tape versus disc contest for at least the third time, after VCR/VD and CD/DAT.

DCC, developed by Philips, was unveiled as an alternative to DAT for portable stereos in mid-1991. It was launched worldwide in November 1992. However, portable models were not demonstrated until June 1992 in Japan and only launched worldwide in September 1993. It is simpler than DAT, with a static recording head. It uses the same size cassette as the current audio cassette, but with digital sound recording. An advantage is that it will also play existing analog cassettes though not with digital sound. It is highly suitable for portable stereos, with most of the size, stability, and power consumption characteristics of audio cassette. Players are priced below DAT, at about £300 for a portable and £300–450 for an in-car model. Teac has produced a combined DAT/DCC player priced in the USA at $599. Blank tapes are about the same as DAT, at £6 for a 90 minute tape. Pre-recorded tapes will probably be priced as high as CD. The system has been accepted by the major manufacturers. It includes the SCMS/Solocopy re-strictions accepted for DAT.

Sony's minidisc, originally the 'audio discorder', is closer to CD but using an opto-magnetic medium which allows recording. It uses a 6.4 cm. minidisc similar to a computer diskette. It was announced in May 1991. The first products were launched worldwide in November 1992, followed by a second generation, 50 per cent smaller than the first, in October 1993. The current machines are still larger than a typical personal stereo, though there seems no reason why they should not eventually be as small as other personal stereos. To overcome the 'joggability' problems of CD portable stereos it includes memory buffers which store up to four seconds of play so that if jogged the machine has time to recover automatically without a break in the music. Playing time is about two hours. Machines are still expensive, priced at £340 for a playback only model and £500 for playback and record. Blank discs are expected to be £10 for a 60 minute disc. MD also includes SCMS. Sony agreed in late 1991 to support the Philips DCC standard but continued with its own MD standard as well.

The products are more alike than might appear. MD and DCC both have full recording, erase and play facility. Both use a modification of the digital coding used in CD and DAT, but compress the signal to save recording space, so that the sound quality is not quite equal to CD or DAT. It is claimed that for most listeners, especially for a portable system used outdoors, the quality will be indistinguishable to CD and superior to audio cassette. As a disc, MD has the advantage of faster random access.

Sony seems to have made a better start in the contest than Philips. Largely as a result of Sony's greater promotion efforts, MD has reportedly outsold DCC by two to one, though neither are performing particularly well. By mid-1993 about 300,000 MD players had been sold worldwide, with equal shares in Japan, USA, and Europe. Philips admitted that it had been slow to bring out portable models; instead it concentrated first on easier to manufacture in-home models, giving the image of an up-market product and missing the point that DCC's only attraction is as a portable system. In contrast Sony has moved very quickly to miniaturize MD.[25]

From the standards viewpoint a main feature is that DCC is compatible with the installed base of analog cassettes, with the same size cassette and able to play, but not record, in either format. Users will be able to switch from audio cassette to DCC without needing to discard or re-record their existing audio cassette tape collection. As a backwards compatible standard, it can access the existing installed base and avoid the worst of the coordination problem of providing an initial library of software, or at least as large a library as MD. Users may build up a new DCC software collection at their own pace. In contrast MD is a radical standard, and users must buy a new collection of discs, or at least re-record their old music collection. Sony says that 1,200 titles are available for MD (compared with 17,600 CD titles issued in Japan alone in 1992). So far DCC seems to have recruited more manufacturers to support it. Both systems are open standards.

Whether compatibility with audio cassette is an important advantage to DCC depends on how strong the network effects are for personal stereo standards. Sony believes that most MD buyers are not concerned about last year's music tapes and will buy MD for the higher quality sound and playback features compared with audio cassette. Philips believes the opposite. The opinion of some press commentators in late 1993 was that DCC's relatively poor performance so far may have been due to Philips's failure to convey the compatibility point strongly enough to the market. In theory either standard could play the role of a single standard for in-house and portable stereos, which DAT failed to do. DCC at least offers the prospect of replacing the audio cassette deck rather than adding another component. However, for either system the reproduction quality is probably not good enough to challenge CD, especially given the huge installed base of CD players and discs, and the lack of clear cost/feature advantages. At best this may add yet another standard to the audio stable, with further fragmentation problems of duplicate investment in hardware and software.

So far few consumers have been prepared to make the new investment. None of the digital systems, which include portable CD as well as DCC and MD, have dented the personal stereo market, which remains overwhelmingly analog audio cassette. There has been limited adoption of automobile CD. The reason may be that a satisfactory portable digital system has not yet been developed, but it may also be that the portable market, on its own, does not justify a high quality system. Portable applications do not need the high fidelity of a home system, and if home copying is needed then an audio cassette copy of a CD is probably acceptable. The market also may not justify the high prices of the digital systems, which may remain well over £100, compared with the £10 or so for the cheapest personal cassette player. The portable digital market seems destined to remain unresolved for some time yet.

7. CONCLUSION

CD has been successful in establishing itself against the existing LP standard as a result of the large effort and investment made by the manufacturers, predominantly Sony and Philips. Once this investment had been made it was perhaps inevitable that DAT would be delayed, as much by the manufacturers' need for a return on their investment as by the opposition of the recording companies. CD was a greater success than anticipated and DAT took second place. Because of the dynamics of standards this became not merely a postponement, as the manufacturers seem to have hoped, but the permanent exclusion of DAT from the main market. This was despite its attraction as a product. DAT is now liable to be left with small market niches for high quality recording, while the portable market is either split between two digital standards, or permanently wedded to audio cassette. Yet this outcome may have been as much due to the timing at which different CD and DAT technologies became available as conscious strategy.

This puts the opposition of the recording industry in context. It is rare for a complementary industry to have as much influence on a core product as it does here, with a complementary market which is much larger than the core market. The music companies added significantly to the delays which blocked DAT. However, it is possible that this on its own would not have been effective had the manufacturers been more determined. The music companies' initial scepticism about CD had been overcome by strong sponsorship, and something similar could have worked for DAT, had the manufacturers not held back. That the manufacturers did so was because they eventually realized that only one standard could be successful, and they chose CD. There may have been another reason the opposition was effective—the concern of the Japanese electronics manufacturers not to upset trade arrangements with the USA and Europe for such a relatively unimportant market as audio components. This has been a political issue as well as an economic one.

NOTES

1. British Phonographic Industry (BPI) figures, reported in the *Guardian*, 27 Nov. 1993.
2. A contributing reason for this was that classical music does not involve overdubbing or multi-track recording, so that existing digital classical masters could be transcribed without modification to CD, to get the full benefit of digital audio (DDD recordings). Digital multi-tracking, used for popular music, was only developed in the late 1980s. Thanks to Edward Sherry for noting this.
3. Data from RIAA (1990).
4. *Observer*, 25 Feb. 1990; Consumers' Association (1990). However, an investigation by the UK Monopolies and Mergers Commission, completed in 1994, cleared UK recording companies of charging too much for CD disks (*Guardian Weekly*, 3 July 1994).
5. *Financial Times*, 18 Aug. 1990; *Guardian*, 29 May 1991.
6. Manufacturing costs may remain higher than CD because tapes have to be recorded sequentially, which even with multiple copying machines—which have been developed—is more expensive than pressing discs. Audio cassette and VCR have similar tape production problems.

7. *Financial Times*, 25 July 1989.
8. For an evaluation of recordable CD see *New Scientist*, 22 July 1989.
9. For some time it was not clear whether it was best to use rotating head technology as in VCR (R-DAT) or a stationary head, similar to multi-track recorders (S-DAT). This was one of the technical issues considered by the international standards committees (Nakajima and Kosaka, 1986).
10. CDs are made from a layer of metal film containing the musical information sandwiched between a plastic disc and a protective layer of lacquer. The lacquer is likely to fail over time and the metal foil then corrodes, ruining the disc (*New Scientist*, 7 July 1988). As the oldest discs are still only about ten years old and most are only a few years old, the extent of the problem is not yet apparent. However, large numbers of discs manufactured as recently as 1989 have already become unuseable. CDs are unlikely to become collector's items (*Guardian*, 23 Nov. 1993).
11. It has been suggested that at some point miniaturization may become a handicap, for keeping track of the tiny DAT cassettes (*Guardian*, 5 May 1990).
12. *New Scientist*, 2 Sept. 1987.
13. Many audiophiles still maintain that CD gives a sound which is inferior to LP. Pioneer recently developed a hi-fi CD which reproduces extra inaudible frequencies to give a fuller sound (*Financial Times*, 15 Nov. 1991).
14. *New Scientist*, 22 July 1989. The proposals for SCMS/Solocopy were reportedly led by Philips.
15. *Electronic Business*, Dec. 1992.
16. The intransigence of the negotiating positions and the international grouping, broadly between Japanese manufacturers, US and European software producers and one of two large European manufacturers, are reminiscent of those in HDTV. Some similar problems with standards bodies are seen with telepoint, discussed in Chapter 9. General issues in using committees for standards are investigated in Farrell and Saloner (1988).
17. Talking about CD technology in 1988, Jan Timmer, now chief executive of Philips, said, 'the timing and spacing of introducing products are crucial to their success'. A Marantz executive believed that 'the investment in CD is so big the electronics industry itself will put DAT on hold' (Reuters, 9 Jan. 1989).
18. A comparison is with VCR, which has been a huge success with a single standard. It is hard to imagine that the video market would have been so successful if shared between VCR and VD. CD has had nowhere near the market impact of VCR.
19. In November 1987, Sony bought CBS Records, both a leading producer of CDs and the main opponent of DAT, for $2 bn. It bought the rest of CBS, Columbia Pictures Entertainment, in January 1988 for $3.4 bn. This followed Philips, which increased its ownership of its record producing subsidiary, Polygram, from 50% to 90% in 1985. Philips and Sony are now the world's first and second largest CD producers. Matsushita, not to be left out, bought the US entertainments company MCA in October 1990 to $6.7 bn.
20. This estimate is borne out by the gain of £866 m. recorded by CBS Inc. for the sale. Sony had offered $1.25 bn. the previous year, but had been rejected not because the price was too low but because CBS considered its records division too central to its business.

21. CBS announced some small reductions in CD prices in March 1988 (by $2). The joint company has used some CBS/Sony artists to promote electronics products but there has been no clear link to Sony hardware sales as a result of the merger.
22. *Fortune*, 2 Nov. 1981, quoted in Graham (1986). Matsushita and JVC had interests in both VCR and VD and had chosen to pursue VCR most strongly. VD was pursued later.
23. Availability of VD discs was initially delayed by problems in deciding on royalty rates and prices for VDs, and by movie companies' lack of knowledge of how to set prices for home viewing.
24. *Electronics*, 19 Apr. 1984, quoted in Graham (1986). There may be some wishful thinking here, given the many problems RCA had developing SelectaVision. It also underestimates the difficulty selling a system (SelectaVision) based on a mechanical pickup in an era which was moving towards lasers and magnetic tape, with sophisticated electronic control. However, it is interesting to think what the video market would have looked like had RCA developed an acceptable system.
25. *Wall Street Journal*, 19 Aug. 1993; *Financial Times*, 5 Oct. 1993.

6

Personal Computers:
The Power of Open Standards

SUMMARY   The introduction of the personal computer (PC) is a paramount example of the ability of open standards to focus new technology and create a new
industry. The IBM PC defined the product at a critical time, and became the *de facto*
standard for other manufacturers and co-producers. It came as the market was
ready for a credible standard on which to focus hardware and software development. Other producers and users followed it because they recognized the PC as an
acceptable combination of available technologies, and, as an open standard, they
could look forward to wide support and unrestricted access. The open architecture
made entry into manufacture easy, as components makers did not need to produce
an entire system. Only Apple, with an existing installed based, held on to a separate
standard in a specialist market niche. The problem for IBM was that although the
open standard had given it leadership of a huge, fast-growing market, it gradually
lost share as it failed to keep ahead in developing the standard. Instead it tried
unsuccessfully to reassert control with a proprietary standard. The case shows the
strengths and weaknesses of an open standards strategy, and the trade-offs between
market size and share. In continuing competition, trying to 'reclose' the standard
may be a futile effort. Other strategies based on evolutionary technological development of the standard may be more successful, as shown by other PC makers,
and by the leading microprocessor manufacturer (Intel) and software producer
(Microsoft).

1. INTRODUCTION

The introduction of the personal computer (PC) is an astonishing story of
market growth and changing fortunes. A decade ago the microcomputer
market hardly existed. It is now the largest segment of the computer equipment market, with annual sales over \$60 bn., and has played a major role in
restructuring the whole computer industry. IBM helped create the market
and led it for several years. It developed the PC, which became the *de facto*
standard for the industry. Although not the first on the market, the PC came
at a critical time, as producers were ready for a credible standard on which
to focus hardware and software development. Other manufacturers and co-
producers adopted the design because it was recognized as an acceptable
combination of available technologies, it had IBM approval, and, as an
open standard, promised wide support and unrestricted access. The PC's

open architecture made entry into the industry easy, as specialized components producers did not need to manufacture an entire system, and PC manufacturers could assemble parts from a proliferation of suppliers. This provided a ready market for software producers. New complementary industries in packaged PC software, add-in boards, and peripherals were created, comparable in size to the PC industry itself.

Subsequent market development has been as impressive as the initial success. The PC has been subject to intense competition. Although IBM's sales continued to grow, it gradually lost market share, and profit margins as new firms swarmed into the industry. Having developed the PC as an open standard, it attempted to reassert control by introducing a new, proprietary, range of PCs, the PS/2. Far from being a sweeping success, these were coolly received and IBM lost share faster than before. Other firms, competing more effectively both on price and quality, and on technological innovation, have increased their market share and grown quickly. Many of today's leaders are firms which, like the PC, did not exist a decade ago. This process has continued. IBM, though still the largest supplier, no longer has a special claim on the PC market. Competition continues to become more acute as the architecture becomes still more standardized, though the market is still growing rapidly. In all, this is a very different story from the one-firm dominance typical of computer markets in the past. It underlines the changing nature of the computer industry, as microprocessors and external software become the defining technologies.

There have been three phases to the PC introduction: the rapid development of the personal computer market around the open PC standard; the erosion of the leader's market share and profitability as new firms entered the market; and the continuing attempts by different firms to maintain market share in the face of the intense competition. The key to the success of the PC was that, by necessity as much as by design, it was an open standard. This allowed the PC to be developed quickly and ensured wide support. The strategy of rapid product development based on outside sources, with open standards to encourage complementary support, is a model for leading market development from a late entry position. However it also involved open competition. The leader's response was to try to 'reclose' the standard and link the PC to other proprietary computer markets. This was notably unsuccessful. It was an expensive effort and only attracted corporate users committed to IBM mainframes. Other firms relying on technical innovations within the standard increased their market share. The other main beneficiaries of the standard have been the co-producers, especially the leading microprocessor developer, Intel, and the leading software producer, Microsoft.

Lessons for strategy are the effectiveness of an open standard in establishing a product quickly in a disorganized new market; the profit trade-offs involved in an open standard; and the great difficulty of trying to assert proprietary control over an established open standard, especially when not backed by significant product innovation. There are more effective ways to maintain position within an open standard, building on the standard rather than trying to change it.

The PC is now fully of age. There were about 140 m. microcomputers in use in 1993, 90 per cent of which were PC compatible. Only Apple, with a following before the PC arrived and the subsequent development of a highly differentiated product, the Macintosh, was able to maintain a separate standard, a position which is only now being threatened. The PC now overlaps with workstation and mainframe computer markets, and is likely to be a central part of developments in networked computing and the integration of telecommunications, computing and video technologies, now underway. The complementary markets for software applications, peripheral devices, and networks are gradually placing the computer within an extended system in which it is no longer easy to separate core and complementary goods. These are areas with their own standards issues.

The chapter looks at the establishment of the PC, and the changes as the market has developed. Section 2 outlines the history of the PC. Section 3 studies the IBM strategy to establish the PC and the implications of the decision to use an open standard. Section 4 looks at the profitability trade-offs facing the standards leader, between a growing market and declining share and margin, and IBM's attempt to impose a 'retrospective' proprietary standard. Section 5 contrasts this with continuation strategies followed by other PC manufacturers, and by the microprocessor and software producers. It also revisits Apple's niche strategy in the light of recent developments, further highlighting the trade-offs between open and proprietary strategies. Section 6 makes some concluding remarks.

2. CREATION OF AN INDUSTRY

2.1 History of the PC introduction

It is sometimes hard to remember that PCs have been generally available for only a little more than a decade. The first microcomputers, based on the newly invented microprocessor, appeared in the mid-1970s, with the first general machines in about 1978.[1] Sales expanded rapidly, but only took off after 1981, the year IBM introduced the PC. The growth in the world-wide market, and the IBM share, are shown in Fig. 6.1. The world-wide PC market grew from $2 bn. in 1981 to $31 bn. in 1987, and to $60 bn. in 1992. Precise figures for the total market are difficult to obtain as many of the PC manufacturers are small companies, making it hard to collect complete statistics. PC revenues for the top 100 information systems (IS) corporations world-wide in 1992 were $45.5 bn., and total world PC sales are

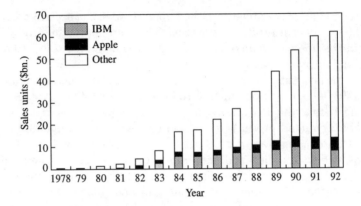

Fig. 6.1. *World-wide PC sales*
Source: Datamation.

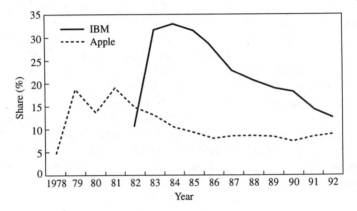

Fig. 6.2. *World-wide PC market shares by value*
Source: Datamation.

generally believed to be 30–40 per cent above this.[2] Estimates of the current total world PC market are over $60 bn. The average annual growth rate for the first six years, 1981–87, was 53 per cent. It was 16 per cent from 1987–92 and 36 per cent for the full eleven years, 1981–92. Over the same period unit sales increased from about 0.2 m. units world-wide in 1979 to 1.5 m. in 1981, 16 m. in 1984, 25 m. in 1987, and about 40 m. in 1992. The changing market shares of the two major manufacturers, IBM and Apple, are shown in Fig. 6.2. The world market shares are now about 13 per cent for IBM and 9 per cent for Apple, from highs of 33 per cent and 20 per cent respectively.

PC prices have fallen rapidly during this time but the real gains have been in price/performance measures. The first IBM PC was introduced in the USA in 1981 at a list price of $12,000. This had fallen to about $4,000 by

1983, with a clone machine priced at perhaps half this. The next generation PC, the AT, was also priced at about the same level when it was introduced in 1984, but this offered a great increase in computing power. Thus although average unit prices appear to have been relatively steady overall (dividing total revenues by unit sales) this masks the great increase in performance over the period. PCs have progressed from simple machines running computer games to personal computers with the power of some mainframes. While unit prices have remained in a range around $2,000 the cost of PC computing power has continued to fall. The cost per million instructions per second (mips) capability of a PC has fallen enormously, from $3,000 in 1987 to $300 in 1992.[3] The fall in unit prices in the central period 1983–87 is shown by the UK list prices for comparable microcomputers in Fig. 6.3. The first model IBM PC in the UK was listed at £4,400 in 1983. Its price had fallen to £1,400 by 1986, when the basic IBM PC was withdrawn. A basic PC clone in 1987 listed at about £400.

The changing world market leadership is shown in Table 6.1. Most of the pioneer firms, such as MITS (Altair) and IMSAI, soon disappeared, and others, such as Atari and Commodore, gradually declined, other than Apple. These were replaced partly by traditional computer manufacturers, but on the whole these have been unsuccessful. Firms which have tried and failed in the PC market include most of the major computer manufacturers, such as DEC, Hewlett Packard, NCR, AT&T, and ICL. The main growth has been by newer firms such as Compaq, Dell, AST, and Gateway 2000. There have also been many other clone manufacturers, often very small. The current top ten PC manufacturers are given in Table 6.2. Dell was the fastest growing company in the computer industry in 1992. The difficulties being experienced currently by the more established older firms in the

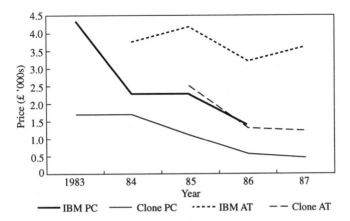

Fig. 6.3. *PC price history, UK*
Source: Which Computer.

Table 6.1.   *Changing market leadership and share*

1975	1978	1981	1984	1987	1992
MITS (25)*	Tandy (50)	Apple (20)	IBM (33)	IBM (23)	IBM (13)
IMSAI (18)	Commodore (12)	Tandy (15)	Apple (11)	Apple (8)	Apple (9)
Proc Tec (8)	Apple (10)	H-P (12)	Commodore (6)	Compaq (5)	Compaq (7)
		Commodore (7)	Tandy (4)	Olivetti (4)	NEC (7)
		Gould (7)	Sperry (3)	Tandy (4)	Fujitsu (4)
		Cado (3)	H-P (3)	Unisys (4)	Toshiba (3)

* In parenthesis: share (%) of estimated world PC revenues.

Table 6.2.   *Top ten PC manufacturers world-wide, 1992*

Company	Revenue ($bn.)		Change (%) 1991–2	Share (%)* 1992
	1992	1991		
1 IBM	7.7	8.5	−10.0	12.8
2 Apple	5.4	4.0	10.4	9.0
3 Compaq	4.1	3.3	25.3	6.8
4 NEC	4.0	4.1	−3.6	6.7
5 Fujitsu	2.6	2.3	12.9	4.4
6 Toshiba	1.9	2.1	−6.9	3.2
7 Dell	1.8	0.7	171.6	3.0
8 Olivetti	1.3	1.6	−15.0	2.2
9 AST	1.1	0.8	42.4	1.9
10 Gateway 2000	1.1	0.6	76.6	1.8

* Share (%) of estimated $60bn. world PC market.

Source: Company revenues, *Datamation*.

computer industry, IBM, NEC, and Toshiba, are apparent from PC revenues which actually declined in 1992.

IBM launched the IBM PC in the USA in August 1981. This was only a year after the project to develop the PC was begun, using a specially formed small design team.[4] Needing to move as quickly as possible, IBM decided to buy-in assorted parts from other companies. This included commissioning the operating system, PC-DOS, from Microsoft, and adopting the Intel 8086 microprocessor. The resources which IBM would normally have utilized in developing a proprietary standard were not made available, and the long-term strategy for the standard was probably little considered. IBM was unwilling to allocate large resources to the still unproven micro market. The risk involved was probably an important factor given the failure of two previous attempts (the 5100 in 1975 and the 5110 a year later). An 'off-the-shelf' model reduced the risk of a repeat.

With most parts bought in, the PC was easy to manufacture, and copy. The key decisions were the use of Microsoft's DOS operating system and the Intel chip, and both companies were willing to sell to anyone. Other important choices were the basic layout of the PC, including the keyboard layout, the (single) 5¼ in. floppy disk drive, the 16-bit operation, and the logical architecture of the machine. These defined what a PC would look like and what it could do. The only IBM parts were the keyboard and the basic input/output system (BIOS) chip, both of which could be, and were, easily invented around. No significant patents were taken out by IBM, or indeed probably could have been easily enforced. The BIOS chip was soon cloned (e.g. by Phoenix Systems), using clean-room reverse engineering to avoid legal problems. Other versions of the DOS operating system were developed.[5] No licensing fees were paid to IBM by clone manufacturers at this stage.

Whilst IBM has increased the in-house content with each new model, the open availability of components, and the simple manufacture help explain why clone makers have been able to copy the basic design. One of the most important features of the PC was its use of an open architecture, in which components were assembled on boards connected by an internal communications bus. This modular layout would be natural for mainframe designers, but contrasted with other microcomputers which were designed as a unit. This made improvements to the PC easy, since specialist suppliers could enter the market with add-ins (such as video cards from Hercules, disc drives from Teac, hard drives from Seagate), without having to enter the entire business. This in turn made entry as a clone producer easy, as this was primarily an assembly operation.[6] Manufacturers such as Dell, AST, and Gateway 2000 began as simple assembly operations, relying mainly on innovative marketing strategies. There were also clear advantages to users of being able to upgrade components as they wished, and tailor systems to their needs.

A further key factor in the take-off of PC sales was the supply of applications software from third-party vendors. Initially software houses had to be encouraged to produce packages for the DOS operating system. This was done by a mixture of commissioned software and various forms of collaboration. Industry lore is that each major product generation needs a new software 'killer' application—a major advance which will not run on the previous generation—to establish the product in the market. For the Apple II, in 1978, this had been the Visicalc spreadsheet. This had shown that the microcomputer could be a serious business machine. Also it had shown that third party software vendors could supply the low priced applications packages that were needed to make the machine useful, creating a precedent for IBM's decision to rely on outside development of PC software. The critical applications packages for the PC were probably the Lotus 1-2-3 spreadsheet and the Wordstar word-processor, which took the microcomputer fully into the office.[7] Once the initial supply of hardware and software existed, the complementary markets continued to grow on their own, as producers of software, add-ins, and peripherals clustered around the PC and the DOS operating system. The increasing library of software packages made the PC more attractive to users and other manufacturers.

With this combination of support, the PC was an instant success. The market grew rapidly, with IBM having a major share. Other manufacturers soon adopted compatible designs and new firms entered the market by producing clones.

2.2 Standards and computers

Standards are particularly important in the computer industry because ultimately most of the cost of a computer system is in software. Compatibility standards add value to the computer mainly by making software less expensive. They increase the size of the *complementary market* for software and add-ins, which can be developed for a larger hardware installed base. This includes training in how to operate the computer and to write software for it. Standards also increase the *portability* of software between machines from different manufacturers and different technological generations, and increase the *connectivity* with computer networks and peripherals. Portability reduces the switching costs when moving to new equipment, and so retains the value of software investment, and saves expensive reprogramming and retraining. It also allows more competition in the computer market, as users can no longer be 'locked-in' to a particular supplier, and can 'mix and match' components. These network effects depend on the amount of support the standard has with other manufacturers and complementary producers, which in turn depends on the installed base of computers. Since development takes time, when other players are choosing whether to support a given standard, their expectations of its prospects may be decisive factors.

There are also supply side influences on standards, if products all use the same basic technology. Here the new generation of computers are designed around the same microprocessors from a few independent suppliers. The PC uses the (Intel) ×86 series of microprocessors. This does not necessarily mean that all products must use the same compatibility standards, which are primarily software decisions. But it does imply some commonality in design, depending on how closely the software is married to the internal workings of the chip, contained in the chip microcode. For example, this defines which instructions are performed inside the chip and which must be written into the external software, in what form data inputs are expected, and the timing specifications for different functions. Thus the standard is a combination of the overall PC architecture and the chip architecture. It also includes the design of the operating system, which runs the computer hardware and interfaces between the applications software and the central processor. For similar reasons to those for the microprocessor, the operating system also helps define the compatibility standard for how the PC interfaces with the applications. Thus the PC standard is a combination of PC, microprocessor and operating system architectures, and could be referred to as the PC/DOS/×86 standard.

A standard may also be reinforced by economies of scale and learning effects in production, by the PC, microprocessor and software firms, as it becomes more widespread. However, the more conventional learning effects are usually exhausted at relatively low production volume, whereas the demand side effects continue to increase with volume.

For traditional mainframe computers the key components and software were produced in-house by the individual computer manufacturers. In contrast, for the PC each may be produced by a separate specialized industry. This has brought the costs of development down enormously, and it has also meant a very different structure for the industry. The specialized components producers have made entry to the PC industry much easier, as noted above, Similarly, this makes it more difficult for the PC maker to protect a proprietary design. Any attempt to make a design proprietary may be foiled by competitors using the same components. Thus the common component technology has strengthened open standards at the PC assembly level. Some proprietary control over the design may be shifted to the microprocessor and software developers, in this case to Intel as the leading producer of the ×86 series microprocessors for the PC and Microsoft as the leading operating systems supplier. The extent of this control is not considered in this study, since the main microprocessor and software producers supply PC manufacturers on equal terms.

2.3 Latent demand for standards

The market for microcomputers in 1981 was disorganized. The product was just coming out of its initial development stage, during which time they were primarily limited to hobbyists. Machines were beginning to be produced with the power to move beyond simple game applications at reasonable cost, but it was still not clear how the product would be designed or who would use it. However, the market was growing, and two makers, Apple and Tandy, were beginning to take significant market positions.

Into this market came the PC. Technologically this was by no means a breakthrough. It was a composite of existing components from outside vendors, packaged into a workable machine capable of being taken seriously by the business user. The strength of the PC was that it focused the demand which was building up as microcomputer power was going up and prices were coming down, but was held back from expressing itself by general market confusion. IBM's sponsorship of the PC put a seal of approval on the market. The arrival of the PC, with IBM's imprimatur, convinced the market that the microcomputer was a valid business tool—useful, reliable and reasonably priced.[8] The PC confirmed the demand and defined what the product would look like. Backed by IBM, this was going to be the standard if anything was. The fact that it was less than revolutionary may have been an advantage, as an advanced machine could have added to the confusion rather than have cleared it up.

The PC also focused the activities of the complementary producers, and allowed the manufacturers access to these resources to present a complete hardware and software system to the market (Teece, 1986). The users accepted the PC almost immediately, and soon began buying in large numbers as the software producers began producing large volumes of packages for the PC. Producers of peripherals and add-in cards also switched to the PC.[9] Other manufacturers began to produce PC compatible machines almost as quickly as they could readjust, including existing manufacturers and new entrants. This created a virtuous cycle of support for the PC, in what has been called a 'tidal wave' of growth. The strength of the standardization forces is shown by the totality of the conversion to the PC and the rapid growth around the standard. Within four years, by 1984, the IBM PC had a third of the market, its highest share, and about 30 per cent of the rest of the market was already PC compatible. By 1987 over 80 per cent of the market was PC compatible and by 1993 it was 90 per cent compatible. The non-compatible market is now almost all associated with Apple.

3. STRATEGIES TO ESTABLISH THE PC

3.1 IBM's open standards strategy

Although the demand for a standard was strong, the success of the PC standard would probably not have been possible without IBM's use of an open standards strategy. The open architecture permitted copying by other manufacturers of computers, peripherals, and add-in cards. Together with the lack of clear intellectual property rights over the PC, this made entry by other PC manufacturers easy, expanding the market. Much of the technical growth of the standard came from the niche components suppliers. IBM also encouraged the production of a large library of software for the PC by making the technical specifications of the machine easily available; by using loose partnerships with software firms, soliciting certain packages through an IBM publishing house to be sold alongside the PC; and by directly commissioning some software. This combination convinced both software houses and manufacturers that there would be an adequate market for their efforts, and convinced users that the PC would be fully provided with software and other support. IBM strategies in its traditional markets have been firmly based around proprietary standards, so we need to understand why an open strategy was used here.

IBM was essentially forced to use an open standard for three reasons. First was speed. It was the only way that IBM could play a leading role in the growing microcomputer market which would get the PC produced and accepted quickly enough. IBM was coming in late in a market which was already beginning to take-off, and in which leaders, in particular Apple, were beginning to emerge. Timing is critical in new markets once the product reaches basic acceptance. It has been estimated that if this had all been produced within IBM this could have taken another two years, by which time IBM would have been locked out.

Second, outside sourcing of both the basic PC and the associated software and add-ins was a cheap and low risk way to enter the market. It was still not clear even to IBM how large the market could become. Indeed, the impetus for the PC had come from a 'maverick' group inside IBM, who did not have the resources to develop a proprietary system. Probably fortunately for the PC, the PC only became integrated into IBM corporate strategy several years later, after it had proved its potential.

Third, being mainly sourced from the outside, the standard would have been very difficult to protect. There was very little of the PC which IBM could call proprietary even if it had wanted to. IBM's dilemma was that it might have been technically feasible to protect the PC, but it would have required a considerable effort and taken too long. IBM did attempt to make the BIOS chip design proprietary, but imitators soon invented around this. Paradoxically, the limited legal protection against a reverse-engineered BIOS chip was a key factor in allowing the PC market to explode. Being intrinsically unprotectable made the open standard more attractive to the compatible manufacturers, and added to the long term credibility of the PC. This is similar to the 'strength in weakness' strategy, a feature of some negotiation games, in which a commitment by a weak player is more believable because it has few alternatives.

However, it may be repeated that IBM also actively sponsored the PC. It commissioned the operating system from Microsoft. It worked closely with Intel to develop versions of the 8080 microprocessor, and later took a large stake in the company, in 1983, investing $400 m. to support Intel when it was in difficulty in its memory business.

3.2 Profitability of the PC

It is difficult to separate out the profitability of the PC to IBM from the question of whether it could have been established with anything but an open standard. Following IBM's loss of PC market share and its other major difficulties in the computer market, it is often suggested that IBM made a mistake by allowing the PC to benefit the industry as a whole rather than making it proprietary from the start. This overlooks the considerable profits IBM has earned from the PC and the fact that it had little option but to make the PC an open standard. Margins may not have been at the levels experienced with mainframes but volumes have been very high. The PC has been one of IBM's largest selling product lines and a strong contributor to profits. Its PC revenues are now almost as large as its mainframe equipment business (though not after including related software and peripherals). In 1992, even after IBM had been losing market share for nine years and absolute PC revenues had been declining for two years, PC sales accounted for 12 per cent of total IBM revenues. At their highest point in 1990, IBM PC revenues were $9.6bn., or 14 per cent of its total revenues. Also, if IBM's PC margins were lower than in mainframes, they were still the highest in the microcomputer industry, excluding Apple. For many years IBM prices were above the rest of the industry, and its manufacturing costs, because of economies of scale, were reputed to be the lowest in the industry.

If IBM had realized how great the PC market was to become, would it have used a more proprietary strategy? Given the timing issue and the use of outside technology, the open strategy was probably the best it could have done. Also, this ascribes more prescience and speed than IBM had shown so far in microcomputers, having tried unsuccessfully to enter the market twice before. It is most significant that the PC was developed by a small group of employees working outside the normal R&D process. In many ways IBM was playing a classic follower strategy with the PC. It waited until the product was over the initial development stages then took over the market with a well positioned entrant. The problem was that in this case IBM nearly waited too long! There is only a narrow window of opportunity to affect standards dominated markets. When it became time for IBM to move, only a crash programme was possible, a fact that was apparently only realized by the maverick group. Given the real possibility that IBM could have been only a minor player in the PC market, its open strategy must be counted a great success; indeed, it was almost a stroke of fortune.

3.3 Apple's proprietary niche

The only major hold-out to the PC standard was Apple, which now accounts for almost all the non-compatible market. Though the PC took the major part of the spoils, the microcomputer market was more accurately created by Apple. Founded in 1976 by Steven Jobs and Stephen Wozniak, its first computer, the Apple I launched that year, had taken the home microcomputer from being an enthusiast's machine assembled from kits to a recognizable computer that non-technical users would feel comfortable with. It set the basic configuration with desktop computer, keyboard and screen. The Apple II in 1978 was the first machine to attract third party software producers. In particular, the Visicalc spreadsheet was the first application to take the microcomputer from a toy to a valuable business tool.

Following the failure of the Apple III and Lisa in 1983, Apple launched the Macintosh in 1984. This took the computer a step further in usability with the graphical user interface (GUI), using a mouse to position a pointer on the screen, icons to identify functions, and overlapping screen images for different applications. In 1986 it moved into the office market with the Mac Plus and the Laserwriter printer. The PowerBook notebook computer was introduced in 1992, though manufactured by Sony. In 1990, citing the strategic importance of software (on which margins were higher than hardware) it reversed its decision to spin off its software subsidiary, Claris.[10]

Apple products had been developed before the PC and had used a different internal architecture based on a different microprocessor, the Motorola 68000 series. Apple developed its own operating system and some other software. As a pioneer, with most of the design and software developed in-house, Apple could and did keep its standard proprietary. This continued with the Apple II and Macintosh. Apple systems had an installed base before the PC emerged. It had its own system of support and a group of dedicated users, who were to some extent locked-in. When the PC arrived, for Apple machines to have become PC compatible would have needed a complete redesign, probably including a switch to Intel microprocessors and abandoning much of the software, which was the main attraction. In 1981, Apple systems were still ahead of the competition and were very profitable. It probably felt it had little choice but to remain incompatible, even had it wanted to change.

With the Macintosh, Apple had a system which because of the GUI had especially strong customer appeal. It was also liked by systems developers, who tended to produce applications on the Macintosh first. In all, the installed base, the highly differentiated product, and the supply of applications software, permitted it to continue as a proprietary niche standard, at a time when other manufacturers were switching to the PC. If this meant that Apple could not easily grow beyond its niche, it was certainly a very profitable business. Apple had the highest producer margins in the industry for several years, around 50 per cent. The downside of the strategy was the mirror image of IBM's. Apple had all of its niche, but the niche was limited in total size, and was vulnerable once the niche was no longer unique. To keep its position, Apple did not license its design or its software to any other manufacturers. Thus it stayed at around 10 per cent share of the total microcomputer market. Though John Sculley, Apple's president and chief executive officer from 1983–93, expressed the hope of reaching a 20 per cent share, the cumulative PC installed base stayed massively larger. In the late 1980s, Apple decided that to continue to grow into the corporate market it had to have access to the PC installed base. It began to develop PC-compatible applications for the Macintosh II. It eventually formed links with IBM itself, in July 1991, for joint systems development, based ironically on a proprietary chip design, the PowerPC. The increased pressure on the Apple standard once Microsoft's Windows software for the PC matched the features of the Macintosh user interface after 1990 is discussed below.

4. PROFITABILITY AND EROSION OF LEADERSHIP

4.1 Loss of margin and market share

An open standard is very effective in establishing a product, but eventually secondary producers take a larger and larger share, reducing prices and margins as competition grows. This is not a problem initially, so long as the market is growing and the leader has a substantial time advantage. It becomes a problem after the compatible manufacturers have caught up and the rate of market growth stabilizes. This is what had happened to the PC. The market continued to expand, and IBM sales still grew, but after 1984 it began losing market share. Its share had declined from a peak of about 33 per cent of the 'top 100' PC market in 1984 to about 23 per cent in 1987. Other complementary markets, such as add-in cards, had also grown, with very little IBM participation. Profit margins on PCs had never reached the high levels IBM was used to in other segments, and they continued to fall over time.

By now the PC had been brought within IBM's corporate strategy, and was being managed in a very different way from that in which it had been developed. The original development team had dispersed soon after the PC was launched. The first response to the competition was to compete on quality and price. Quality and service are usually to IBM's advantage, as the volume leader with various economies of scale. However, users learned by experience that quality was not necessarily worse for the clones, and seemed to bear little relation to price. They knew that many of the components were the same whoever was the final manufacturer. Also service was hard to provide for such a low price machine, except for large customers. IBM was forced to compete more and more on price. It was an effective price competitor but this reduced margins.

The second strategy was to try to keep ahead technically, using the emulation lead over competitors to protect market share. The leader may offer improved features and increased power, which can only be copied after a lag. IBM increased the memory size, data storage capacity and processing speed of different versions of the PC. Subsequent versions of the PC were introduced with higher power, with the XT in 1983 and the AT in 1984. Attempts at new market segments, such as the PCjr in 1983, were unsuccessful.[11] The XT and AT necessarily retained the same architecture as the PC, making innovations easy for other manufacturers to copy, and the emulation lags became shorter with each step. Significantly, IBM also did not develop any exceptional products in the areas of peripherals, especially printers, or network systems. Hewlett Packard led the printer market, Compaq and others led in portable PCs, and software producer Novell led in office network systems.

A worse problem was that other manufacturers soon showed that they were as well fitted as IBM to make new innovations within the standard. New products came in large numbers, in a wide variety of shapes and sizes for computers, add-ins and peripherals. IBM seemed unable to innovate PC products at a comparable rate, tending to rely instead on manufacturing and marketing skills.[12] The new firms also had more flexibility to introduce new designs without alienating users who already owned older models and cannibalizing their own sales of existing products—an interesting example of *diseconomies* of scope. Although IBM managed to maintain leadership up until the AT it was outmatched as more powerful PCs and workstations began to appear. Makers such as Compaq took over the initiative in PCs, and there were already some threatened overlaps from the workstation market by firms such as Apollo and Sun.

The third option was to find some way to lock in users to a proprietary standard, so that their base of software, peripherals, and training would only work on one manufacturer's equipment. The proprietary approach was more in line with the strategies which had traditionally worked for IBM in the mainframe market. To do this some way had to be found to add a key proprietary component to the open standard, a 'gateway' technology to give control over the standard. This was where the PS/2 and its Microchannel Architecture (MCA) entered the story, intended as the 'clone-killer'.

4.2 IBM's attempt to 'reclose' the standard

In an attempt to deal with the problem of low margins and declining market share, IBM made a major policy move by introducing the PS/2 to replace its PC range in 1987. This was linked with a new operating system, OS/2, which amongst other things was intended to be compatible with other ranges of IBM computers as part of its attempt to develop a common Systems Applications Architecture (SAA) across all its computers. It also included a Windows-type user interface. Although the PS/2 include some technical advances, the main intent was to establish a proprietary design. This was 'reclosing' the open PC standard. Anyone wishing to copy the PS/2 could only do so on IBM's terms, and anyone wishing to buy a personal computer from IBM had to buy the PS/2. A number of manufacturers took licences to produce PS/2 standard machines, though few went into production. Licence fees were high, reportedly set at about 5 per cent of sales.

Yet the PS/2 was slow to be accepted. Its main successes were confined to corporate niches where its ability to link into other IBM machines had some value. The operating system OS/2 had development problems of its own; it was delayed and would only run on high powered machines, so that most of the PS/2 range has continued to run the DOS operating system. There was also very little third-party software written for the PS/2, apart from OS/2 which was a joint effort between Microsoft and IBM. Against initial expectations, the bulk of the PC market paid little attention to the PS/2. Faced with disappointing sales, IBM eventually reintroduced models which were virtually identical to the PC AT models that were supposed to have been replaced. Within about two years PS/2 licences were being offered at little or no licensing fees. Even so there been no attempt specifically to clone the PS/2. Instead the PS/2 has been reabsorbed into the PC standard, as IBM's offering in the market. Together with the OS/2 operating system, the PS/2 was expensive to develop and promote, and ended by losing IBM market share faster than before.

To convince users to switch to a new standard calls for significantly improved performance. The new standard must either run existing software faster or offer new applications. A replacement standard not only has to be good enough to justify a new investment, it has also to be incrementally better than staying with the existing standard, with its advantage of an installed base of users and software. The problems are fewer if software may be migrated forward to the new system, as it could for the PS/2, but to justify the expense the new system really calls for new software (the 'killer' application). In this case overcoming the hurdles was even harder, as IBM was trying to impose a proprietary standard over an open one. Proprietary standards limit second-sourcing of hardware and make it harder to get software support. Users were reluctant to tie themselves to a single supplier, having got used to the lower prices under open competition. Also software developers were unwilling to supply for a proprietary product without assured markets and guarantees of future behaviour. In theory a proprietary standard may have offsetting advantages in that the sponsor has an incentive to develop and promote the standard in expectation of profits to come. However, the PC already had a single standard.

The PS/2 did not offer sufficient advantages to overcome these problems. The technical differences introduced with the PS/2 were very small and many of the changes (more powerful microprocessors and new software) were inevitable upgrades which all PC makers were making. The main hardware advance was the MCA bus, which provided for more powerful communications than the AT. The need for communications was only growing slowly and at that time most users did not need anything as sophisticated as MCA. One commentator likened selling PS/2 on the strength of

MCA to 'trying to sell an automobile on the strength of a new camshaft'. IBM also hoped that users would buy the PS/2 as this was the only way to get IBM quality. Unfortunately, quality was less important than previously, as the clones had proved reliable, and this appealed only to corporate users who might expect IBM service (which IBM did not deliver for the PS/2). It included new software capabilities, such as windows and graphics, but these were soon developed by Microsoft and others for use on DOS machines too. The value of the IBM logo had its limits.

A further problem was that when a new standard attempts to take over from the existing one, the old standard is likely to fight back by increasing its rate of innovation. The existing DOS standard proved quite capable of matching any of PS/2 technical advances. The technical leadership passed to Compaq, which soon introduced a DOS-based micro using an Intel 386 microprocessor, fully compatible with its PC predecessors and with performance equal to the top end PS/2. The industry also formed a consortium which successfully developed an open-standard alternative to MCA, the EISA bus. The first PCs with the EISA bus appeared in 1989.

In any case the users had moved on. Having got used to open standards, they were not willing to tie themselves to a single supplier, especially users new to computing. The proprietary approach seemed out of place in the new market conditions. The remaining hope for PS/2 was that as part of IBM's grand plan for computer networks, SAA, it could share software with other IBM computers, including mainframes. This linkage could add value to the PS/2 and provide the initial installed base of software for the PS/2. Unfortunately, this has proved too long term and too dependent on SAA's mixed fortunes to have had any effect.

5. ALTERNATIVE CONTINUATION STRATEGIES

5.1 Technology leadership and extending standards

Other firms have competed more successfully in the PC market by combining conventional price, quality and service strategies with technological innovation within the standard, without changing the openness of the standards regime. The list of leading firms in the PC industry is scarcely recognizable from that of a decade ago. Of the top ten PC manufacturers world-wide listed in Table 6.2, four have only grown up since the PC was developed (Compaq, Dell, AST, Gateway 2000). Each of these began by producing PC compatibles and building sales by offering reliable machines at lower prices than the leader, together with distribution and maintenance. Most have continued to rely on marketing, while staying abreast of the technology, and their position from year to year is precarious. However, to some extent each has gone further by developing enhancements to the PC, with new features and higher performance. They have been in the forefront in introducing new generations of PC incorporating new microprocessors and other components as they were developed. These enhancements maintained full compatibility with the existing installed base of equipment and software. Many of these performance features have gone on to be incorporated in the *de facto* PC standard, without changing the basically open regime. Some of the enhancements, such as the EISA bus, have been more formally included in the standard by agreement between industry members.

The technological leader is currently reckoned to be Compaq, which was the first to bring in 386-based PCs in 1987. Founded in Houston, Texas in 1982, Compaq has grown to PC sales of $4.1bn. in 1992, in third position after IBM and Apple. Compaq began as one of the first developers of portable PCs, then moved to desktops, so has always been a technically advanced company. It became a major supplier in the corporate market with the Desk Pro and System Pro lines, where it developed a reputation for product reliability and service. Its 1991 R&D spending was 6.0 per cent of sales, hardly that of a clone maker (as a benchmark, Apple, one of the highest R&D spenders, spent 9.2 per cent of sales on R&D in 1991). Of the new firms, it is followed by Dell Computer, of Austin, Texas, founded in 1984 and now seventh in the market with sales of $1.8bn. Dell has relied more strongly on developing complementary assets, by introducing direct response telemarketing and distribution systems and a phone-in maintenance service. Other manufacturers, including IBM, have started to imitate the Dell direct marketing approach and Dell itself has started to put more emphasis on technological innovation. R&D is now 4.9 per cent of sales.[13] Of the other newcomers, AST was founded in 1980 and Gateway 2000 in 1985. All four companies have experienced performance problems recently.

5.2 Marketing changes

As the design of subsequent generations of PC have become even more standardized, with components taking a larger share of the architectural design away from the individual PC manufacturer, differences between manufacturers have decreased further, and prices for the top tier machines such as IBM, Compaq, and Dell, have had to be brought down closer to the clones. Rounds of price reductions in 1992, and again in 1994, brought prices down by about 30 per cent in a few weeks. Whereas US dealer margins on the first IBM PCs in 1981 were 48 per cent, they were down to about 20 per cent on a compatible PC in 1987 and are now about 6 per cent. This has put more pressure on firms to look for new more sophisticated applications for the PC, at the same time that it puts more stress on prices and pure marketing.

This has been accompanied by changes in the nature of marketing for the PC. In the 1970s, the microcomputer was primarily a hobbyist machine, assembled from kits. The second phase, in the early 1980s, came with the Apple II, Macintosh, and the PC, which were sold mainly through specialist computer stores and value added retailers (VARs). Later the computer stores were replaced by superstores, which sell complete systems and components in high volume. The PC is now in its mass marketing phase, with many sold as a commodity item by mail order or discount stores. Systems are more likely to be in standard configurations, with most components already on a single board, to take advantage of manufacturing economies in an era where most consumers are unlikely to change a component themselves.

The PC divisions of IBM, following corporate reorganizations in 1992–3, are behaving more like the 'newcomers'. IBM divided its PC activity between three separate divisions for the PS/2, lower priced machines, and PC motherboards for other manufactures.[14] These operate with more autonomy than previously and may compete with other IBM divisions. Much of IBM's effort is now with low price, high volume, industry standard PCs. These have standard ISA expansion buses, SVGA graphics, and Microsoft DOS and Windows operating systems, a far cry from the 'strategic' technologies that were part of the PS/2 effort, i.e. the MCA bus, XGA graphics, and OS/2 operating system. However, there also has been an increase in IBM's development effort, specifically in high performance chip making, aimed at the PC and workstation markets, such as its 'Blue Lightning' version of Intel's 486 microprocessor and the IBM/Motorola/Apple joint venture to develop the PowerPC chip.[15] To what extent this signals a move away from a 'proprietary-defensive' strategy to a technology-led 'standards-enhancing' strategy remains to be seen. However, the new chips are intended to be sold to other manufacturers, so that the openness of the PC standard may remain largely intact.

5.3 Continuation strategies by co-producers

Some parallels with the microprocessor and software industries supporting the PC may help make the point. The greatest individual beneficiaries from the PC standard have turned out to be the microprocessor manufacturer, Intel, and the software producer, Microsoft. With products which are included in the major proportion of all PCs shipped, their revenues have increased along with the total market. The stock market valuations of these companies have risen at the same as IBM's has fallen—by a coincidence both equalled IBM's capitalization in the same year, at about $22 bn. each in 1993. Intel became the world's largest semiconductor firm in 1992, with total revenues of $5.8 bn. and earnings of $1.1 bn. Microsoft is now the world's largest independent software producer, with 1992 revenues of $3.3 bn. and earnings of $0.9 bn. To keep their share of their respective markets both have relied to a large extent on a combination of competitive pricing (sometimes by necessity) and continual innovation of performance and features. These enhancements have been kept forward-compatible with the existing standards (i.e. old software written for PC/DOS/×86 standards can be run by the new generations of microprocessors and operating systems). They have also extended the features in ways which usually have become incorporated in the *de facto* standards. Some of these enhancements may have a proprietary content, so that the producers' control over access by imitators may at least be kept constant, if not actually increased. However, the main protection may be the emulation lag as imitators try to catch up.

(*a*) *Intel*

Intel was chosen by IBM to supply the original microprocessor chip for the PC and has kept its leadership position in this market through five generations of the ×86 series of microprocessors. The progression of generations and their performance are shown in Table 6.3. Having invented the microprocessor with the 4004 in 1971, Intel developed the second generation 8080 in 1974 and the third generation 8086 in 1978. The 8086 (or the similar 8088) was chosen by IBM for the first PC in 1981. This marked the beginning of generations of microprocessors associated mainly with the PC, the ×86 series. The 80286 was launched in 1982 as the basis for the PC-AT, followed by the 80386 in 1985, the 80486 in 1989 and the Pentium in 1993. As noted above, 90 per cent of the PCs in use in the world today are based on ×86 chips. Though the original design is due to Intel, there are several other competing producers of ×86 chips, licensed or unlicensed. Of the $49.6 bn.

Table 6.3. *PC microprocessor generations*

Gen.	Year	Intel MPU	Trans/chip ('000s)	Performance (m.i.p.s.)*	Word size (bits)
1	1971	4004	2.3	0.06	4
	1972	8008	—	—	8
2	1974	8080	10	0.2	8
3	1978	8086	29	0.8	16
4	1982	80286	130	2.6	16
5	1985	80386	275	11.4	32
6	1989	80486	1,200	41.0	32
7	1993	Pentium	3,100	100.0	32/64

* m.i.p.s.: million instructions per second.
Source: Intel.

market for 32-bit microprocessors in 1992 (not all of which are used in PCs), Intel had a 64 per cent share, with revenues of \$3.2 bn.[16] AMD, its nearest competitor for ×86 chips, had 7 per cent. There are increasing threats to Intel's dominance with new generations of reduced instruction set computing (RISC) microprocessors aimed at the high performance PC and workstation markets. These include Sun's Sparc chip, DEC's Alpha, the PowerPC chip from IBM, Apple and Motorola, and several others. Some of the implications of these developments are discussed in the chapter on open systems.

(b) Microsoft

Microsoft was founded in 1975 by Bill Gates and Paul Allen to adapt and sell a version of the Basic programming language to MITS for the Altair PC. Microsoft's great opportunity came when it was chosen by IBM as the supplier of the DOS operating system for the PC in 1981. This gave it the basis for growth, but its subsequent performance has depended on continual development of the original products. Since 1981 it has brought out improved versions of the DOS system, having reached versions 6.2 by 1994. It was also involved in the major two year effort with IBM to develop the OS/2 operating system, and in developing its own Windows operating system, both of which included a graphical user interface similar to Apple's. Microsoft launched Windows version 1.0 in 1987. When initial OS/2 sales proved disappointing the relationship with IBM cooled and in late 1989 Microsoft began to concentrate on Windows (Carroll, 1993). It launched the much improved Windows version 3.0 in 1990. It has also developed successful applications software packages for the PC, notably its Word word-processor, Excel spreadsheet and Access database. Microsoft is the overwhelming leader in the PC operating systems market, with almost all the PCs sold in the world, other than Apple machines, coming with Microsoft DOS already installed. This trend is now applying to Windows as well. Operating systems account for about 40 per cent of Microsoft revenues.

Microsoft has maintained its dominant position and high profitability in operating systems by a combination of pricing and technological advance. It has kept the price of DOS relatively low, so that margins are not high enough for other producers to want to copy the product or for users to pay to switch to another standard. There have been several competing versions of DOS over the years, but these have failed to make an impact.[17] The combination of high volumes and moderate margins has made Microsoft one of the most profitable firms in the IT industry. Microsoft has also persistently encouraged other software producers to write programs to run on DOS and Windows. It has also developed its own applications packages to run on Windows (e.g. World, Excel, PowerPoint) and has been a leader in bringing down package prices. However, its main protection from competition has been the rapid development of improved versions of operating systems and applications as the power of microprocessors has grown. These enhanced versions have been kept backwards compatible with all earlier versions so that users have not needed to scrap their old software when upgrading. In the software industry, most products can usually be imitated and improved on by competitors, and new potential applications are arising constantly. Microsoft has shown itself to be a highly capable innovator and has kept ahead of trends.

5.4 Erosion of Apple's proprietary standard

Apple made a fateful decision in 1987, the same year Microsoft launched the first version of Windows, to continue with the proprietary strategy it had used against the PC. At least two companies, Sony and Tandy, asked Apple to license the Macintosh graphical user interface (GUI) and the OS operating system to run on other hardware platforms. Had Apple done so the Macintosh GUI could conceivably have become the interface standard for the PC instead of Windows. Apple did so because it saw itself as a hardware company and believed that its proprietary software was the best way to sell its computers. However, Apple computers were limited to a niche, for the reasons given above. With the installed base of the PC secure, Microsoft had five years to get Windows right. The result has been that with Windows 3.0, launched in 1990, there was a GUI for the PC which was no longer appreciably different to the Mac. Not only had Windows been improved but PC power had been greatly increased so that it could now run Windows adequately. Instead of sponsoring the Macintosh GUI and OS as the software standard, pre-empting Windows, Apple attempted to block Windows in the courts, an effort which diverted much energy and ultimately failed.[18]

Although proponents of the Macintosh defend the 'look and feel' of the system, which has been designed around the needs of the graphical interface rather than having it engineered onto the existing DOS operating system designed for data manipulation, it is no longer sufficiently different from what is offered on the humble PC. The installed base of Windows systems has rapidly overtaken the Macintosh. The number of copies of Windows 3.0/3.1 sold since 1990 reached 40 million by the end of 1993, with sales running at 1.5 million copies a month. Almost all new PCs sold, including many from IBM, now have Windows pre-installed on them by the manufacturers. In contrast 10 million Macintoshes have been sold since 1984. Perhaps more significant is the fact that sales of Windows applications are increasing rapidly—these exceeded $2bn. for the first six months of 1993 and in Europe reached a level of 74 per cent of all application sales.[19] This reversal of the installed base advantage as the leading GUI has been a critical point for Apple, whose position in the microcomputer market has quite suddenly come under pressure. With less to differentiate them, demand for its products has fallen. Apple has been forced to cut prices dramatically to maintain sales volume, halving its profits in 1993 even though sales are rising. Apple's stock market value was halved within a few weeks in mid-1993 and John Sculley was replaced as company president. Apple may have to continue to bring its prices down in line with its competitors in the PC market, many of whom are themselves reducing prices to compete with clones.

Apple is now closer to the typical position for a minority standard, which for years it avoided by its specialist appeal as a 'small-based', but not 'minority', niche standard. Applications had often been developed first on the Macintosh, with PC versions brought out later. Once the Windows base became larger than Apple's there was less reason to develop applications on the Macintosh, when the main market was to be on the PC anyway. The rapidity of its fall from grace is associated with the credibility issues surrounding standards, once users and co-producers realize that the standard may have a limited future. It seems clear that the proprietary strategy has finally come up against its natural limits, and unless Apple now moves to become part of a broader standard the firm's prospects are restricted. It is probably too late to hope to get the Macintosh GUI accepted as a standard for the PC. It may not be too late to incorporate some of its aspects in future systems, such as the PowerPC for the next PC generation.[20] Apple has already moved towards some degree of PC compatibility for its systems. From now on probably every new application may need to be designed to work also on the PC.

It is hard to argue with Apple's success for so many years in terms of high profits and its maintained market share. However, its position was bound eventually to be challenged. Keeping its system proprietary would always hinder the company from becoming a dominant player. It may have misread the lessons of IBM's loss of PC market share. The size of the PC market and volume of development effort it generated gave the PC too much of an advantage in the long term. Given the technological lead that Apple had for so long it should have been possible to have taken a much greater share of the microcomputer market using a more open approach to licensing, without compromising its profit position. This needed to be done some years ago, instead of focusing on immediate profit margins.

6. CONCLUSION

The introduction of the PC shows the strengths and weaknesses of an open standards strategy. It was used by IBM to create and lead a market in which previously no common standard existed, and where there was no time to develop and establish a proprietary standard. It allowed the market to grow rapidly. However, this also required opening up the market to strong competition; the market was too large for a single firm to control. In these conditions further innovations are soon imitated and can only give temporary market power. The attempt to change radically the standards regime and claim control of the standard by introducing 'gateway' proprietary features, as IBM tried with the PS/2, contained basic flaws. It tended to isolate the new product from the installed base, its main source of value. It could only take effect if the new product genuinely represented a major technological step. Even then there were limits to how far it could move away from the existing standard. A better strategy may have been incremental innovation around the open standard, gradually building up market strength, as some other firms have done.

Yet IBM's introduction of the PC is one of the great success stories, for IBM as well as the industry it created. Despite the fact that IBM gradually lost its original lead, it remained a major player in a market in which it could easily have had only a small role. Witness the other traditional computer firms who tried and failed in the PC market. Weaknesses were more apparent in IBM's continuation strategy. It failed to keep the technological lead and allowed newer firms to play this role. The organization IBM used to run its PC business once it became a major product line was very different from the one it had used to create the PC. The original development took place outside the normal management structure of IBM. Perversely, this helped ensure its success. Once IBM tried to bring the PC within a proprietary regime it began to fail. The PS/2 was not a response to technology or shifting demand but was introduced for strategic reasons. This implies that the proprietary standards approach which had been part of the computer mainframe market does not work well in the new computer markets. By linking the PS/2 with plans for large networks IBM attempted to bring the personal computer into the realm of the large-system market which it had dominated in the past. However, the market for personal computers is different. The advantages of open standards, with multiple core and complementary suppliers, rapid technological change, and product variety, cannot be matched by one firm.

NOTES

1. For the technical development of the microcomputer and market development prior to 1980 see Gupta and Toong (1988).
2. *Datamation*, 15 July 1993.
3. Estimates from Dataquest, quoted in Manasian (1993). This compares with an estimated $25,000 per mips for the original PC in 1981.
4. The history of the PC project is given in Rodgers (1986) and Chposky (1989).
5. The concept of an isolated set of 'basic I/O routines', containing all the system-

specific hardware interfaces, had been developed earlier by Digital Research, for the CP/M operating system for 8-bit microcomputers. This introduced the concept of machine independent applications programs. Digital Research also developed CP/M-86, and later DR-DOS, which competed with MS-DOS as a PC operating system (Wharton, 1994).

6. The basic board architecture in the PC consisted of a mother board (microprocessor and memory), and boards for the disc controller, graphics controller, and input/output, connected by a communications bus. Thanks to Edward Sherry for pointing out the influence of the open architecture on entry.

7. Lotus 1-2-3 was designed as a spreadsheet, database, and graphics system in one. For the Macintosh, in 1984, the key application was to be the graphic user interface (GUI).

8. The business value of the microcomputer had already been demonstrated with the Apple II and Visicalc, but it took the PC to spread this awareness throughout the business community.

9. In contrast, this never happened with the Apple IIc or the IBM PCjr, both of which were closed architectures, and both failures.

10. For the history of Apple see Butcher (1988); Sculley (1988).

11. The PCjr is considered one of IBM's major product failures. It was an unattractive product, whose performance was deliberately limited, and it was seen as not taking the home market seriously. Among its deficiencies was the problem that the PCjr was made incompatible with the PC.

12. See the views of a competitor, Sun Microsystems, in McKenna (1989).

13. Dell patents have grown from zero with 10 pending in 1988, when Dell made its initial public offering, to 11 with 69 pending in 1992.

14. These were called the Personal Systems, Ambra, and Alaris divisions, respectively, although the names were later dropped. Much of IBM's divisional reorganization, aiming to break it up into a dozen competing 'Baby Blues', introduced by chief executive John Akers after 1988, was reversed by Louis Gerstner, who became the chief in 1992. Part of the reason for marketing complete motherboards was due to the terms of IBM's licence to produce Intel ×86 microprocessors, for use in systems but not for individual sale.

15. *The Economist*, 17 July 1993; *Electronic News*, 2 Aug. 1993; *Financial Times*, 26 Aug. 1993.

16. *Financial Times*, 26 Aug. 1993.

17. A leading alternative was DR-DOS from Digital Research (now owned by Novell). PC-DOS was IBM's name for Microsoft's MS-DOS as sold by IBM.

18. Bajarin (1993). Some commentators have suggested that Apple would do better to concentrate entirely on software, though this seems to miss the strategic value of integrated capabilities (Rappaport and Halevi, 1991).

19. Software Publishers Association, quoted in *Guardian*, 2 Dec. 1993. Wordperfect Corporation announced that it was shifting its attention from OS/2 to the Windows market in late 1993.

20. The first Apple PowerMac machines with the PowerPC chip were introduced in early 1994. These run existing Macintosh applications and PC applications in emulation mode, though not at high performance.

7

Open Computer Systems:
A Standards Revolution

SUMMARY   The introduction of open systems in the 'mainstream' computer industry shows how open standards may be used to replace an entrenched proprietary
standard, and how changes in basic industry technology may create conditions for a
new standards regime. However, the form of the standards depends on firms'
strategies, including the use of new markets as a route to build an installed base and
shifting coalitions to overcome standards coordination problems. Fundamental
changes are underway in the industry. These are focused on compatibility standards,
and contests between open and proprietary systems, with software in the central
role. There have been three phases. The first has been a long battle to establish the
concept of open systems, based on the Unix operating system, after decades of
proprietary computer architectures. This phase is essentially over and major adoption of open systems is underway. Second, interleaved with this, firms have competed over the degree of openness within 'open' systems. Attempts to introduce
quasi-proprietary versions of Unix via industry consortia have been repulsed by
competing groups, committed to fully open standards. The contest has now moved
on to a third phase, of interoperable systems, in which other architectures are
competing for open systems leadership. These further separate operating systems
from the hardware design. Competing in this new industry is very different from that
in the past. Firms which have been most successful in continuing competition are
those which have accepted open standards as fully as possible and worked within the
new conditions.

1. INTRODUCTION

The computer industry is in the midst of its most significant changes since its
inception, over 40 years ago. The industry, one of the largest in the world,
has long been dominated by one firm, IBM, which defined the market and
was the *de facto* standard. Other firms were described in relation to this
standard. Now what for years was unthinkable is happening. The information systems (IS) market is changing rapidly and in each segment there
are many competitors. Trends which began in personal computers (PCs)
and workstations, with low priced machines based on microprocessors and
open standards, are spreading through the industry. IBM itself is a troubled
company, still tied to mainframes in an industry which has shifted to small

computers and integrated networks. IBM and other previous leaders have few special strengths in these new markets. It has yet to adjust to the new conditions and has suffered three years of huge losses. Other 'traditional' manufacturers tied to proprietary technologies are in similar difficulties while firms promoting open standards are growing strongly. Some of the strongest sectoral growth has been in software to run on the new open standard machines.[1]

Competition for this new world turns on the issue of compatibility standards, allowing computers and components from different manufacturers to be used together. The contest between different standards may be the single most important factor determining the future of the industry. Pressures for open standards have built up as microprocessor technology has lowered unit costs, increasing pressure for low cost software and reducing entry barriers into manufacturing. Industry structure is changing from a single-producer model with vertically integrated manufacturers to a multi-layered model, in which the production of microprocessors, computers, peripherals, operating systems, and applications software may be performed by different firms. Competition and specialization at each level, as well as the technology itself, have reduced systems costs enormously. The problem for producers and users is integrating products from the different sources, making standards crucial.

The introduction of open systems has taken place in two phases. The first has been to establish the concept of open systems in a industry dominated for decades by proprietary standards. The defining contest has been between the industry consortium X/Open, and the proprietary Systems Applications Architecture (SAA) from IBM. Both aimed to define system architectures (the layout of the hardware and software) which would allow equipment from different sources to run common software and be connected in networks. X/Open chose the Unix operating system and aimed to facilitate links between computers from different manufacturers. SAA was based on the proprietary OS/2 operating system and stressed the integration of the wide range of existing and future IBM equipment. The outcome has been surprising. Demand for integration has proved so strong that broad-based systems are well on the way to displacing proprietary architectures. Major adoption of open systems is underway and even the traditional proprietary advocates are having to restructure their product lines. SAA failed to lock in IBM customers and is no longer a factor in the market.

The second phase has been continued competition within open systems. Interleaved with the contest to establish open systems, efforts have been made by some manufacturers to introduce quasi-proprietary versions of Unix, as in the old industry model. These were opposed by groups committed to fully open standards. The contest took place via a series of alliances promoting quasi-proprietary and open versions—Open Software Foundation (OSF) and Unix International (UI). Again the outcome has been surprising. The threat to fragment Unix was averted and open versions of Unix are succeeding against proprietary versions. This was achieved by commitments to keep standard Unix fully open, first by AT&T and later by the software company Novell.

The contest has now moved on to more advanced interoperable systems. These further isolate computer architecture from software design, and some systems may not be based on Unix. Competition has focused on establishing broad support for new chip architectures, relying on coalitions with other producers and compatibility with the existing installed base. General performance attributes have also become more important. Further developments are being driven almost entirely by market competition, which is keeping standards substantially open. Firms which have been most successful in continuing competition are those which have accepted open standards as fully as possible and worked within the new conditions.

The case shows how basic technological and economic conditions may lead to a change in the standards regime, but the exact form of these standards depends on the strategies employed. Standards developed in the new markets for microcomputers have provided the route to replace the entrenched standards elsewhere in the market. A series of market-generated coalitions have been used to overcome the co-ordination problems in establishing joint standards. However, a strong common threat may have been needed to provide the motivation to reach agreement. The firms' best choice for continuing competition within open systems may be to embrace open standards as fully as possible, taking advantage of the large markets available, rather than trying to reinstate old strategies to lock in users. Firms may compete on other dimensions than standards—quality, price, user oriented development, and technological leadership. If there are policy lessons they may be that, in this type of industry, although industry standards bodies may help develop and publicize new standards in the early stages, establishing standards may best be left to market forces. Open systems built partly on ideas studied in industry standards bodies years before but which were only acted on when the market was ready for them.

In this chapter, Section 2 outlines the changes in technology and industry structure behind the new standards, and Section 3 reviews the role of standards in the computer industry. Section 4 discusses the first phase of the change: the initial contest between open and proprietary system concepts. Section 5 discusses the second phase: continuing competition within open systems. It considers the struggle between open and quasi-proprietary versions of Unix and current competition between interoperable systems. Section 6 makes some concluding remarks. A list of abbreviations is given at the end.

2. CHANGING INDUSTRY STRUCTURE

2.1 Decline of one-firm leadership

For most of its existence the computer industry has been dominated by a single firm, IBM. This leadership was established early in the industry's history. The first computers were developed during the second world war and commercial machines were introduced at the beginning of the 1950s. For the first decade several firms competed for the market but by the end of the decade IBM had emerged as the clear market leader. After competing for leadership with Remington Rand's Univac computers in the early 1950s, IBM had made a breakthrough by 1956, when it had twice as many machines in operation (87 units) as all other manufacturers together and five times as many on order (190 units).[2]

One of the most important steps in the development of the industry was the introduction of the IBM System/360 mainframes in 1964. These were the first computers to use the same internal architecture over a family of machines. This allowed users to upgrade to larger machines without rejecting existing software, but at the same time tended to lock them in to IBM. So effective was this strategy that IBM soon dominated the mainframe market. It had around 70 per cent share of mainframes until the late 1970s, with the remainder divided between smaller companies. Since then competition in mainframes has gradually increased, largely from plug-compatible manufacturers including Japanese firms, and there has been some reduction of IBM share.

In other segments IBM's touch has been progressively less sure. New competitive segments have gradually grown up, especially within the last decade. The minicomputer market grew up around systems from DEC, Data General, Hewlett Packard (HP), and others in the 1970s. IBM was slow to react, being insulated from the effects of competition by its huge market in equipment, software and services based on mainframes. The new minicomputer manufacturers were too well established to be easily challenged by the time IBM entered, and although it became a major participant it has never had the same leadership as in mainframes. The personal computer market of the 1980s has proved even more difficult to dominate by a single firm. Although IBM helped create the market and it still leads it with about 12 per cent share, the structure is very competitive, with literally thousands of manufacturers and lower profit margins than in traditional segments. This is now the largest segment of the computer hardware market, with annual sales estimated at over $60 bn. The open standard architecture of the PC has enabled the market's rapid growth, but has also meant that IBM's margins and share here have gradually fallen. It allowed technological leadership in PCs to pass to other companies.

More recently workstations, essentially very powerful microcomputers, have been developed, with power comparable with mainframes and mini-computers. The industry is very competitive with several powerful manufacturers. Like the PC these are designed around microprocessors, some of which are widely available, some not.[3] Workstations mostly use the open standard Unix operating system. This market was worth about $14 bn. in 1992. IBM had no appreciable presence in the market until 1989, though now has about 14 per cent market share, in second position after Sun Microsystems with about 17 per cent. As desk top computers such as PCs and workstations have become more powerful, and increasingly used in networks, they have started to challenge the traditional markets for large- and mid-sized systems. These traditional segments have been declining in relative importance for some years and recently have started to decline in absolute sales. This signals a shift away from industry dominance by proprietary systems producers such as IBM, DEC, Fujitsu, NEC, and the rest.

The sales growth for the world-wide top 100 corporations in the IS industry since 1980 is shown in Fig. 7.1.[4] Market segmentation and IBM shares by segment are shown in Fig. 7.2. In 1992, out of a total industry revenues of $318 bn. (top 100 firms only), IBM had sales of $64.5 bn., or 20 per cent of the total, ahead of Fujitsu with $20 bn., NEC with $15 bn., and DEC with $14 bn. (shares of the top 100 companies only; shares of the total market are lower). It is still number one in each area other than workstations and data communications, but its shares range from 29 per cent in mainframes down to around 12 per cent in data communications and peripherals. This is quite a change from the position as recently as 1980 when IBM had 70 per cent of the world mainframes market and 40 per cent of the total market, and 60 per cent of the industry's profits. Even in 1990 it

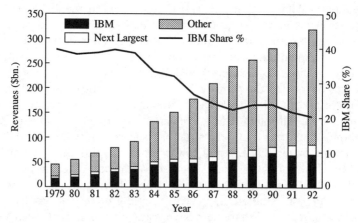

Fig. 7.1. *World-wide IS revenues (top 100 corporations)*
Source: Datamation.

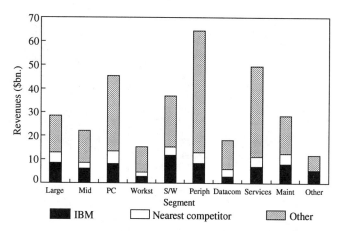

Fig. 7.2. *World-wide IS revenues by segment, 1992 (top 100 corporations)*
Source: Datamation.

had 44 per cent of the mainframe market. Since 1990 IBM has been in serious difficulties. Its total revenues have declined each year since 1990, from a high of $67 bn. in 1990 to $62.7 bn. in 1993. It has also made record losses for a US corporation in each year, of $3 bn. in 1991, $5.0 bn. in 1992, and $8.1 bn. in 1993. These losses contain huge restructuring charges, but IBM's operating profits have also declined, from $3.4 bn. in 1992 to $300 m. in 1993.[5] Significantly its revenues from mainframes are falling fast, down by a third in 1993 compared to 1992 with a further 50 per cent decline expected in 1994.[6] IBM has been down-sizing rapidly, shedding a total of 125,000 jobs in 1992 and 1993, and a further 40,000 planned by the end of 1994. This will reduce employment to 215,000, from a high of 407,000 in 1986.[7]

IBM's difficulties reflect changes going on in the make-up of the total computer market, which are equally dramatic. Changes in the revenues of different world-wide market segments from 1984 to 1992 are shown in Fig. 7.3 and changes in segment shares in Fig. 7.4. Total market size has nearly doubled from 1984 to 1992 but large scale systems (mainframe) sales have stayed virtually constant and have shrunk in relative terms from a share of 17 per cent to 9 per cent. Allowing for inflation the absolute level of mainframe sales has declined slightly. Mid-range computers (minicomputers) have also declined from 11 per cent to 7 per cent share. The major share of hardware sales are now for personal computers, which (for the larger firms' sales) have grown from a share of 10 per cent in 1984 to 14 per cent in 1992.[8] This does not mean that mainframes are no longer important, since much of the revenues in peripherals, software and maintenance depend on mainframe sales, and taken as a whole these are still reckoned to be greater than the equivalent PC market. However, the trend towards smaller computers is clear. The growth of the workstation market, from less

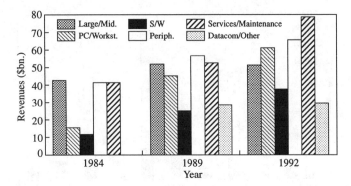

Fig. 7.3. *Changes in world IS segments, 1984–1992 (top 100 corporations)*
Source: *Datamation*.

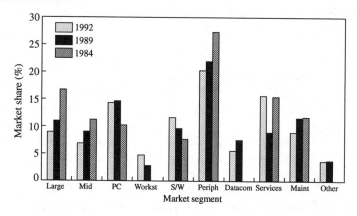

Fig. 7.4. *Changes in world IS segment shares, 1984–1992 (top 100 corporations)*
Source: *Datamation*.

than 1 per cent share in 1984 to 5 per cent in 1992, is equally significant. Apart from the shift towards smaller computers, the growth areas in the industry as a whole have shifted from equipment to the software and services sectors. These account for 12 per cent and 16 per cent of the market, up from 9 per cent and 8 per cent in 1987. Again this does not mean that the hardware sectors are unimportant, as they still account for about 37 per cent of the industry compared to 27 per cent for combined software and services. Rather it indicates the shift in emphasis from hardware products *per se* towards the applications which run on them.[9]

Changes are also apparent in the list of leading firms in the industry, which are now likely to include several of the new microcomputer manufacturers, and software and service providers. The top 20 firms world-wide in 1992 are listed in Table 7.1. These include four new firms—Apple, Compaq, and Sun in manufacturing and Microsoft in software—as well as EDS in services. The encroachment by the new areas is most apparent when considering changes in the leading US firms, as the industry technology leaders, over the period 1982–92, listed in Table 7.2. Of the top 10 firms in 1992, only five were traditional computer manufacturers, compared with all 10 in 1982. The others are the new microcomputer and software/services firms above. In 1982 the largest US based non-manufacturing firm had been General Electric (GE) in computer services, at 13th position, and the largest microcomputer firm was Tandy, at 16th.

2.2 Technological change and the new industry

To understand these changes in the computer industry we need to understand the technological changes which have taken place within the last decade. Until the advent of the personal computer in the late 1970s, all computers were large or mid-sized machines, designed and built within a single company. Developing a range of computers was a complicated pro-

Table 7.1. *Top twenty IS corporations world-wide, 1992*

Company	Revenue* 1992 ($bn.)	Growth** 1991–2 (%)
1 IBM	64.5	2.7
2 Fujitsu	20.1	4.2
3 NEC	15.4	0.5
4 DEC	14.2	−0.5
5 Hewlett Packard	12.7	19.2
6 Hitachi	11.4	10.1
7 AT&T	10.5	27.9
8 Siemens Nixdorf	8.3	14.2
9 Unisys	7.8	−2.1
10 Toshiba	7.5	45.6
11 Apple	7.2	10.4
12 Olivetti	5.8	−4.8
13 Groupe Bull	5.7	−3.6
14 Matsushita	5.1	−0.2
15 EDS	4.8	30.2
16 Canon	4.6	23.5
17 ICL	4.4	31.6
18 Compaq	4.1	25.3
19 Sun	3.8	10.9
20 Microsoft	3.3	42.9

* IS revenues only.
** Growth in IS revenues 1991–2.
Source: Datamation.

Table 7.2.   Change in top ten US IS corporations, 1982–1992

	1982			1987			1992		
	Corp.	Rev.* ($bn.)	Growth** (%)	Corp.	Rev. ($bn.)	Growth (%)	Corp.	Rev. ($bn.)	Growth (%)
1	IBM	31.5	19	IBM	47.7	3	IBM	64.5	3
2	DEC	4.0	12	DEC	10.4	21	DEC	14.2	–1
3	Burroughs	3.8	24	Unisys	8.7	19	HP	12.7	19
4	CDC	3.3	6	NCR	5.1	28	AT&T	10.5	28
5	NCR	3.2	3	HP	5.0	22	Unisys	7.8	–2
6	Sperry	2.8	1	Wang	3.0	10	Apple†	7.2	10
7	HP	2.2	18	Apple†	3.0	30	EDS††	4.8	30
8	Honeywell	1.7	25	CDC	3.0	25	Compaq†	4.1	25
9	Wang	1.3	31	Xerox	2.4	11	Sun†	3.8	11
10	Xerox	1.3	18	Hon.-Bull	2.1	4.3	Microsoft††	3.3	43

* IS revenues only.
** Growth in IS revenues over previous year.
† Microcomputer manufacturer.
†† Software/Services.
Source: Datamation.

cedure, so that even individual machines were called 'systems' and each firm developed its own unique designs. The system was designed around a specific computer architecture, defined as the combination of the physical layout of the various hardware elements and the conceptual layout of the software. The system included the basic circuitry, peripheral devices such as disc drives, printers, consoles, card readers, tape drives, and other input devices, and the software operating system to control the computer's operation. The manufacturer developed and produced all these to work together. It often also manufactured the semiconductors used for the processors and memory devices, and a large part of the applications software to run on its equipment. It provided maintenance services and usually other management support services. Finally it sold and distributed the systems through its own trained sales personnel. The industry structure was thus one of a few large vertically integrated manufacturers, providing all the design, manufacturing, and support themselves for their own machines. This vertically integrated industry structure is show schematically in Fig. 7.5.[10]

The main reason that there were few manufacturers was that developing and producing such systems required very large investments, and only relatively few designs, or manufacturers, could be supported by the market. Although the industry was large in total revenues, individual machines were very expensive and the actual numbers sold were low. A corporate user would typically own only a few machines, with mainframes used for central data processing functions and some minicomputers used for specific tasks at the departmental level. In 1980 as few as 10,000 mainframes and 105,000 minicomputers were sold world-wide each year. Thus even if IBM had not taken such a large share of the market, it was unlikely that there would have been more than a few large companies in the industry. Some specific rea-

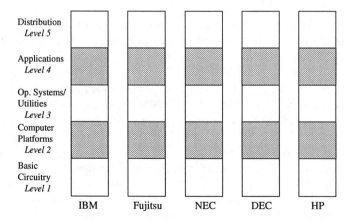

Fig. 7.5. *Traditional 'vertically integrated' computer industry structure*
Source: *The Economist*, Intel.

sons for single firm dominance, associated with standards, are discussed below.

There have been some gradual changes away from this structure over the years. Following the 'unbundling' of software and hardware sales by IBM in 1969, after which software was priced separately, an independent software industry emerged, concentrating primarily on applications software. A number of independent peripherals manufacturers also appeared. However, for the most part the vertical structure of the industry was unchanged. The main distinction was between computer manufacturers who competed for particular segments of the IBM compatible market, such as Fujitsu, Hitachi, and Amdahl, and those who developed their own designs, such as DEC, Control Data, and Hewlett Packard.[11]

The main changes have come within the last decade, following the invention of the microprocessor in 1972 and the subsequent introduction of the personal computer (PC) in 1981. The microprocessor put the basic processing functions of a computer on a single semiconductor chip. A machine could be assembled cheaply around a microprocessor from readily available components such as memory chips, input/output controllers and disc drives, and peripherals such as displays, keyboards, and printers. Many of these were already available from the consumer electronics industry and the other parts were soon developed by independent manufacturers. Computer assembly no longer required the huge development effort as the basic design is defined by the microprocessor. There was massive entry into PC manufacture, including large numbers of small firms. Only microprocessor production, where there are high development costs (and network externalities associated with a single design), has remained dominated by a few large firms. In microcomputers the dominant microprocessors have been the Intel ×86 series for the PC and the Motorola 68000 series used by Apple.

Since the new microcomputers were based on identical, widely available components, the designs of different machines were inevitably similar, and there were few technological barriers to standardizing systems architectures. The many Intel 8088-based and Motorola 68080-based systems which appeared during the early 1980s were soon abandoned—with the exception of Apple—in favour of the IBM PC standard. Standardization created large markets for developing applications software, provided there were also standardized operating systems. Operating systems need to be closely matched to a given microprocessor to run optimally, and have been dominated by a single standard—in PCs by Microsoft's DOS and Windows.[12] Operating software also includes systems for connecting networks of PCs or workstations. One of the major developments in the market has been the introduction of 'client-server' networks, in which a number of 'client' machines are connected to a central 'server' machine and may, at a fraction of the cost, do many of the functions once reserved for mainframes, such as maintaining central data files, managing the flow of information between users and allowing them to access the same files. In applications software, there has been a much wider range of products, designed to run on various operating systems, which has created a new independent software industry with large numbers of producers. Finally the distribution of inexpensive, standardized machines no longer justified specialized sales and maintenance organizations, and mass market distribution via dealers, mail order, and direct sales was more appropriate.

Similar microprocessor-based technology has spread to the workstation market and other desk top machines. These are now powerful enough to challenge the performance of mainframes. This has led to a new multi-layered structure for the computer industry shown in Fig. 7.6, with horizontal competition between suppliers at different levels of production, but few vertical links between the levels. The separation of the different levels, clearest in the PC industry, is also evident in other sectors, even though traditional computer manufacturers are trying to remain involved at several levels. The examples shown here are for the high performance PC and workstation markets. At level 1 is microprocessor production. The leading chips for workstations include Sun's Sparc series, MIPS' 4200/4400, Hewlett Packard's Precision Architecture (PA-Risc), DEC's Alpha AXP, and the Power PC being developed jointly by IBM, Apple, and Motorola.[13] Intel's Pentium, a development of the ×86 series used in PCs, is also in the high performance group. Most of these microprocessors are intended to be used in machines manufactured at level 2 by more than one firm, such as the Sun

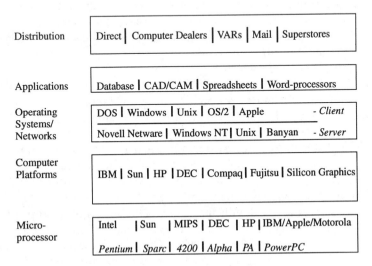

Fig. 7.6. *New 'multi-layered' computer industry structure*
Source: *The Economist*, Intel.

Sparc chip used by Fujitsu, the MIPS 4400 used by Silicon Graphics (SGI)—now MIPS' parent company—, and DEC's Alpha series, for which DEC is actively seeking licensees. The operating systems for these are produced at level 3 by software developers, who are often independent of the computer manufacturers. These include the many versions of Unix, Microsoft's Windows NT, and IBM's OS/2. In addition there are special systems designed for controlling networks, such as Novell NetWare, Windows NT (again), and the planned IBM/Apple/HP Taligent operating system.[14] It is this level which is the focus of the open systems contest. At level 4 are the applications software producers and at level 5 the many means of distributing the new systems. Other component and peripherals manufacturers may be added to the scheme, either at level 1 or level 2, and independent service providers, integrating components from various manufacturers into networks and managing facilities, might be added at level 5.

At most layers there is a high degree of competition with low entry barriers. Areas where entry is more difficult are levels which contain the basic design functions, such as the development of the microprocessors and the operating systems. At these levels a dominant standard potentially may bestow market power, which has made these the focus of the open systems contest. However, even though some market power may be achieved at each level, this is unlikely to be as strong as that of an integrated producer in the old structure, in which hardware and software standards were interlinked and had to be changed together. The trend with new generations of interoperable systems—including the examples above—is for the links between operating systems and microprocessors to be still weaker, further separating the design of software from the hardware on which it runs. This may allow for backwards compatibility, since the interfaces are designed to be compatible with as many different hardware platforms as possible. Some implications of these changes are discussed below.[15]

The forces for change which had been building for some years became critical after about 1990. Significantly, the new industry has grown up alongside the old, rather than as an outgrowth or evolutionary development, which has made it easier for new standards to be established. Also, many of the traditional manufacturers have not yet fully adjusted to the new economic model of high-volume, low-margin production. The focus for the new competition is price. Even mainframe computers are now judged for price performance by comparison with the equivalent microprocessor-based desk top computer. This price may be a tenth of that of a mainframe and is falling rapidly. Estimates are that with succeeding generations of microprocessor the cost of performance has fallen from $3,000 per million instructions per second (mips) in 1987 to $300 in 1993.[16] The mainframe in its traditional form cannot hope to keep up with this rate of progress. This does not necessarily mean that large systems are defunct. Designing computers is not just a matter of applying pure processing power. Problems of data management, security, systems complexity and applications experience, as well as the installed base of hardware and software, seem enough to assure the large system's existence in some form, if not the mainframe as such. However, the justifications for large systems are becoming more open to doubt, and given the speed of new developments no area is likely to be untouched for long.

A corollary of the dramatic reduction in hardware costs is that this has left software as a greater part of system cost; the increased importance of the software and services sectors reflects this shift. This has in turn focused attention on ways to reduce software costs in line with hardware, leading to demand for low cost packages and software which can be transferred across hardware 'boxes'. This provides an added incentive for open standards to spread development costs, and, with new types of users, to reduce training effort. Cheap hardware, as well as falling telecommunications costs, have made networks economically feasible, after decades of waiting, calling for standards to connect different equipment. The reduction in hardware prices has made software a more central part of manufacturers' strategies.

The other important change which has flowed over from the PC market is in user attitudes to computer use, in particular to costs and to open standards. After having seen the evolution of the personal computer market, users are aware of open standards and what they can offer in terms of flexibility and lower prices. A direct effect has been some shift in market power towards the users, at least for those large enough to affect the market. Governments and large corporations are beginning to specify open standards, in particular Unix, for some requirements.[17] Smaller users have less direct power, but do provide a ready market, receptive to the availability of open standards, and some users may be active in industry groups. Independent attitudes were first expressed by the 'departmental' users of minicomputers outside corporate data processing departments in the 1970s. These have been accentuated in the new structure. They are more apparent in the new users drawn into computer use via the PC who have no prior experience with the traditional industry. With about 140 m. PCs in use world-wide by 1993, there are many millions of new users, compared with the thousands who were directly involved with computers 20 years ago.[18]

3. STANDARDS AND COMPUTERS

3.1 Network externalities

Compatibility standards add value to computers by allowing the *portability* of software across computers from different manufacturers and the *connectivity* of different equipment in networks. Software portability increases the size of the market for third-party complementary software and add-ons, making them cheaper to produce and increasing their variety. It also reduces switching costs of reprogramming and retraining when moving from one computer to another. Connectivity does the same for hardware, peripherals, and other elements, allowing users to mix components and shop around for the best product. It also creates new markets for communications systems and data transfer. These 'network effects' work through the demand side, making the core product more valuable when used together with complementary products or services. To these may be added supply side effects for systems designed around the same microprocessors and other components, leading to economies of scale in production from a standard design.[19]

As networks have become more important, the needs for portability and connectivity have been extended to the concept of *interoperability*, in which complex applications may run without modification on a wide range of system configurations. This requires standard interfaces between applications software and the hardware 'platform' on which it runs, as well as standardized means of managing various hardware resources connected into a particular network. By further separating the design of the software and hardware, this tends to strengthen the effects above, by increasing the market for applications software and allowing users greater freedom to configure systems for lowest cost and highest performance.

The standard is defined by the architecture of the hardware and the operating system software. There are many other distinctions between different types of computer standards depending on the extent of the market covered by a given architecture. In the traditional industry a standard was likely to apply only to a given system design, so that it may have applied only to a range of computers from a given manufacturer, to a series of computers from the same manufacturer (multi-product standard) or to different technological generations of products (multi-vintage).

The key strategic distinction is between open standards, where adoption is not restricted and is usually encouraged, and proprietary standards, where the controlling firm may restrict adoption or charge significant royalties. In the traditional industry, tied to a single base design, the standard was usually proprietary. In the new industry, with equipment designed around common components, it is easier for an open standard to be established. It becomes easier the greater the separation of the microprocessor design from the software design, as is now occurring with reduced instruction set computing (Risc) chips and platform independent software. However, while this removes some of the critical impediments to open standards, whether they are established or not still depends on the various forces for and against open standards and the strategies of the players involved. With computers using cheap, mass-produced components it is now more difficult to protect a design. This still does not mean that all products must use the same interface standards, which are essentially software decisions. However, a common supply means that any attempt to make a design proprietary, and so lock-in users, may be relatively easily overcome by competitors using the same components.

A major concern for standards strategy is the difference between establishing a new standard and replacing an existing standard. Because of the dynamics of standardization, an existing standard may become entrenched, making it difficult to replace even by a technically superior standard. The problem is in establishing an initial installed base of hardware and software to start the process of attracting further users and software producers. This is difficult enough for a new standard but is much more so for a replacement standard, which must overcome the network advantages of the incumbent in addition to the usual coordination problems. To stand a chance of success a replacement standard needs an 'avenue of entry', to establish a base in a separate market. This provides a base from which to enter the first market. In the case of open systems this entry route has been provided by the new PC and workstation industries, which have provided the base to develop the technology and software with which to challenge the main computer markets.

3.2 Definitions of open systems

The concept of open systems was first introduced for connectivity standards for computer networks. During the 1970s and 1980s two standards, one *de jure* the other *de facto*, were generated for this purpose: the Open Systems Interconnection (OSI) reference model of the International Standards Organization (ISO) and the market-generated Transmission Control Protocol/Internet Protocol (TCP/IP) standard. Both these set out the compatibility requirements for communicating between different computer systems.[20] In different ways all of the various architectures, proprietary and open, have adopted elements of these two standards. In practice the *de facto* TCP/IP standard has become generally established as the main network standard, but elements of OSI are also in wide use.

While most of these early efforts concerned interconnectivity, the main area today is interoperability. A major impetus for this has been the spread of local area networks (LANs) and the related spread of client-server network computing. This may involve co-operative or distributed processing, in which several applications run simultaneously on different machines, often using the same database. It depends on different systems using compatible 'application architectures', the focus of the contest for open systems standards.

A problem with the term open systems is that it has been used in different contexts, often with different meanings, reflecting the fact that it has two different origins. In its 'institutional' context, an open system is a architecture that supports the full range of OSI interconnection protocols, and can therefore be interconnected and interoperated with other open systems. Applied to operating systems, the term was originally used more specifically, to describe Unix-based operating systems providing software portability, especially those promoted by X/Open. The term is now generally used for any system with a high degree of interoperability, including portability and connectivity. It does not necessarily have to be a Unix system, although up until recently most of the systems which can run on different hardware platforms have been Unix based.[21]

In open systems there are three groups of standards, competing with and complementing each other:

(a) De jure open standards, set by national and international standards bodies. These are primarily frameworks or models for standards, with some of the protocols defined in detail but with many others only provided in outline. They are essentially the 'applications layer' of the OSI standard (the other six conceptual 'layers' of OSI are mainly concerned with connectivity), including specific communications stndards such as X-400 from the International Consultative Committee for Telephone and Telegraph (CCITT).[22] These standards and their components are only guidelines, and adoption by manufacturers and users is generally voluntary, so that most of the effort in developing interoperability standards is taking place in the market, outside the official process, as below.

(b) De facto open standards, championed by industry groups such as X/Open, OSF and UI. The approach taken by X/Open has been to define the X/Open Portability Guide (XPG) for software. Now in its fourth release, the guide does not provide standard recommendations but, using an 'intercept strategy', selects the most promising existing standards solutions for establishing a Common Applications Environment (CAE). These are then included in the open standard, provided the developer accepts the terms for open access. An analogous standards proposal is the Distributed Computing Environment (DCE) developed by OSF. However, DCE sets up a 'framework' model for standards in a similar way to the OSI model, but with more detailed 'sub-layering'. Individual manufacturers may then use this model to structure their own proprietary systems. Thus, whereas X/Open selects a specific, open version of Unix for inclusion in the CAE, OSF permits each manufacturer to use its own version of Unix, provided it is compatible with the DCE model. The elements included by each manufacturer, such as the version of Unix or the detailed architecture of the microprocessor used, may or may not be proprietary, so that although the overall architecture is common to different manufacturers, there may be significant proprietary components. The distinctions between fully open and quasi-proprietary standards are reflected in the strategic differences between the consortia, discussed later.

(c) Proprietary solutions, developed by individual manufacturers and software producers. So far, the main example in this category has been IBM's SAA, which aimed to provide a common architecture for distributed processing networks capable of linking all IBM's systems, from mainframes to workstations to PCs. It included IBM's long established Systems Network Architecture (SNA) communications interface standards.[23] SAA is a highly detailed model of the interfaces needed to integrate the wide range of architectures used by existing and future equipment. It is not based on the Unix operating system but on IBM's proprietary OS/2 and MVS operating systems. Lately SAA has been largely overtaken by developments in interoperable systems, from IBM and others, seeking to become *de facto* 'quasi-proprietary' standards. A parallel example is DEC's VAX architecture, used by all its existing minicomputer range.[24]

3.3 Traditional 'lock-in' strategies

To understand the strategic importance of proprietary standards in the traditional computer industry it may help to review how these may lock-in users to a given supplier over long periods. This contributed to the one-firm dominance of the mainframe market by IBM, with similar effects for other manufacturers on a smaller scale in other segments.[25] Proprietary standards from IBM led the mainframe market. Other firms either followed with compatible equipment or accepted small market shares with non-compatible systems. Users became locked into the standard by individual joint investment in hardware and software. Overlapping hardware and software generations, each backwards compatible with the previous one, meant that users updated only one part at a time, so found it hard to switch to a totally new system, which required a complete new investment. This 'upgrade path', only capable of being provided by IBM, was the basis for the lock-in. Compatibility within IBM product lines offered users some of the advantages of common standards, but much of the value was captured by IBM. Constant updating, funded by the profits stream, kept IBM ahead of the follower firms. Followers could not stray very far from the IBM standard, and could only offer the new features after a delay and often after overcoming legal barriers. They found it hard to establish large installed bases of their own and so did not become serious threats. Once the regime was established IBM could exploit its advantage as standards leader to maintain high market share and high margins, and fund further development. With by far the largest sales volume, economies of scale in development and production gave IBM the lowest unit costs and highest margins, with ample scope for aggressive pricing strategies when needed. This completed a virtuous cycle of high volume sales, standards leadership, and low unit costs which had been a major factor in IBM's long term dominance of the industry.

The epitome of this strategy was the IBM System/360 family of mainframes, introduced in the mid-1960s, and continued with the System/370 series. The PS/2 has been a largely unsuccessful attempt to extend this strategy into the PC market. This is not solely an IBM issue. Similar situations hold with lesser effect for other manufacturers in other market segments, such as DEC's proprietary systems (PDP-11 then VAX) in minicomputers. The situation in these other areas is perhaps less one-sided as markets are more fragmented among a number of producers.

4. ESTABLISHING OPEN STANDARDS

4.1 Open vs. proprietary standards

The increasing importance of client-server networks and other changes in basic industry structure have created conditions which may favour open standards, but the actual standard regime in the new industry depends on the standards setting process. This is a function of timing and the strategies of the firms involved. The defining contest for the new standards regime has been the open systems contest between the open standard, CAE, defined by the X/Open group, and the main proprietary standard, SAA, from IBM.[26] The timetable of the main events in establishing open systems are shown in Table 7.3. The X/Open group was set up in 1984, originally as a defensive move by five European manufacturers faced with lagging technology and threatened protected markets. Unable to make adequate development investments individually they combined resources. Some previous European attempts at collaborative development of proprietary computer systems, such as Unidata in the 1970s, had failed. In such cases there had been many recriminations about non-cooperation and secrecy but the main reason may have been that the members were too weak to develop proprietary systems, even collaboratively. It may also be that there was little market interest in the consortium, since it would only have provided another proprietary alternative to IBM. X/Open was the first to include major use of outside, and open, technology. The decision for the X/Open members was between continuing to service small but limited national markets, and putting effort into common standard. Even the protected markets were doomed in the long run without new products.

The remaining decision was which common standard to use. Choosing the dominant IBM standard would have put the firms at a continuing disadvantage, and the only real hope was a new, open standard. Unix operating system was chosen as the basis for the standard partly on technical grounds, as it had been designed for interoperability. It was also readily available, was tried and tested, and had a large body of experienced users to develop and maintain it. Having been developed by AT&T, it could be

Table 7.3. *Timetable for open systems*

Date	Event
1969	Unix first developed by AT&T
1970	First minicomputers—DEC PDP series
1972	Microprocessor invented
1981	IBM launches personal computer—PC
1982	First open architecture workstations—Sun microsystems formed
1984	X-Open group formed in Europe
1986	Major US computer firms join X-Open
1987	IBM announces SAA and launches OS/2
	AT&T and Sun agree to joint development of Unix
1988	AT&T takes 20% share in Sun (Jan.)
	Open Software Foundation (OSF) group formed (May)
	Unix International (UI) group formed (Nov.)
	AT&T commits to keeping Unix open
1989	Unix 8% of world large-systems market
	OSF and UI join X-Open
1990	IBM mainframe revenues start to fall
	DEC adopts open systems strategy
	Microsoft launches Windows 3.0 operating system—PC
1991	Major IBM losses begin
1992	AT&T spins off UI to Unix Systems Laboratories (USL)
	Interoperable systems architectures appear—DEC, HP
	Taligent operating system joint venture—IBM, Apple, HP*
1993	Microsoft launches Windows NT operating system
	Novell buys USL and assigns Unix rights to X-Open
	Unix 38% of large-systems market

* HP joined Taligent in 1994.

licensed on liberal terms and there were few restrictions on its use; there seemed little likelihood at the time that the open availability of Unix would be threatened. However, its main attraction to X/Open was probably simply that it was *not* from IBM. Even if the openness of Unix became questionable later, this could not compare with the disadvantage of having to depend on following the dominant IBM standard.[27] The success of X/Open is closely linked with that of Unix. The CAE standard itself is a set of rules for systems interfaces, languages, data management, and communications. Since X/Open is so closely identified with Unix, even when not following all the CAE rules the adoption of an unrestricted version of Unix is the essential part of adopting open systems.[28]

IBM's interest in SAA also began tangentially, as a response both to problems integrating its own various computer ranges and to DEC's success in minicomputers, which used its common proprietary VAX architecture for all its systems. The initially limited aims were soon expanded into a major strategy, covering all the main systems, including minicomputers and PS/2 personal computers. This was announced as SAA in 1987. SAA is a proprietary design, suited to IBM products and backed up by proprietary hardware and software. It supports a number of IBM operating systems, including OS/2 used on the PS/2. SAA and CAE are conceptually similar in many ways and may be traced to common origins.[29] At launch, some aspects of SAA, such as user interfaces and some software, were more developed than the corresponding elements of CAE, but there was no clear lead. The components of CAE and SAA are shown in Table 7.4.

As the contest has evolved, open systems have been successful in being widely adopted in the industry. SAA has remained primarily an IBM-only standard and has not been widely accepted by other computer manufacturers or third party software producers. OS/2, associated with SAA, has not so far been accepted as an operating system outside IBM. Part of its difficulties were that OS/2 failed in its initial contest with DOS in the PC market, as discussed in chapter 6, and so SAA missed out on the leverage this could have given it as a base for adoption for other systems.[30]

The history of X/Open membership is shown in Table 7.5. Since 1984 the membership of X/Open has grown to include all the major international computer vendors. It has been both a catalyst and a vehicle for expressing support for open systems. The fact that these firms could credibly agree to anything helped validate the idea of open systems. Support for Unix has increased rapidly. By 1989, 8 per cent of the world computer market was already accounted for by systems designed around Unix, increasing to 20 per cent by 1991. By 1991, 34 per cent of technical installations and 14 per cent of business installations used Unix as the preferred operating system, proportions which were expected to increase to 50 per cent and 25 per cent within a year.[31]

Table 7.4. *Examples of open and proprietary standards, 1990*

	Open	IBM		DEC
Standard	X/Open	SAA	AIX	VAX
Architecture	CAE	SAA	AIXFD	VAX
Operating system	Unix	OS/2, OS/400, VM, MVS	AIX	VMS
Network architec.	OSI	SNA	SNA, TCP/IP	DECnet
Hardware	Open	PS/2, AS/400, S/370	PS/2, RT, S/370	VAX

Table 7.5. *X/Open members and year joined (computer vendors)*

1984	1986	1987	1988	1989
Bull	DEC	AT&T	IBM	Apollo
ICL	Ericsson	Fujitsu		Hitachi
Nixdorf	Hewlett	NCR		NEC
Olivetti	Packard	Nokia		Prime
Siemens	Philips	Sun		
	Unisys			

4.2 Strategic analysis

A question for open systems strategy was whether this was a new standard or a replacement for the existing IBM standard. As a replacement standard it had to face IBM directly, but as a new standard, developed for workstations and following many of the developments of the PC market, it had a convenient route to becoming established outside the main market before challenging it there. X/Open was created to challenge IBM in 1984, as a pure replacement standard by a group of European computer vendors. However, open systems and Unix only became serious threats with the advent of microprocessor-based systems, first in PCs and then in workstations, which began to take effect at about the same time in the mid-1980s. This not only created a market for networked systems and hence for open standards, but also developed vast amounts of software, hardware and peripherals which made adopting open systems a realistic option for users. The PC market in particular established the credibility of systems from non-traditional manufacturers, and provided a body of users willing to accept open standards and systems built on common components and to take a risk on non-integrated systems developed by non-traditional manufacturers. It also provided the initial manufacturing base for economies of scale in the design and production of components. The subsequent development of workstations encouraged the development of Unix.

The essence of a successful standards strategy is to build up a significant installed base before the opposition, and establish credibility with users that products will perform as promised and be adequately supported. In 1987, when the real open systems contest began, both standards were at similar stages. Outline standards were defined, substantial software applications were under development and both had significant user bases. Unix, created by AT&T in 1969, had been under development for 20 years, and CAE standards had an early start. However, initially X/Open could not draw on the same investment level as SAA, which channelled development from a single large wealthy corporation rather than pulling together efforts from many small organizations, and SAA soon caught up technically.

Both CAE and SAA standards had found a route over the initial installed base hurdle by using linkage with an existing base of supporting software as the starting point for the new product, as manufacturers have traditionally done when changing computer generations. Unix had a long-standing installed base in the technical community, and particularly in workstations, already a $2 bn. market by 1988 and overwhelmingly Unix-based. The workstation market was growing very rapidly and the prospects of a large Unix market meant that Unix was likely to be well supported in future, at least for technical applications. The market base of the X/Open founders was not large but included the leaders in their national markets. Unix also had an advantage of a clean start, not restricted by integration problems. In contrast SAA was designed to build on the huge installed base of S/370 systems. This was not an unmixed blessing—there are still enormous technical problems in reconciling the very different systems covered by SAA. The Unix and S/370 bases are currently about the same size, each with about 20 per cent of the total large system base in 1991, but Unix is growing much more quickly. The open systems market share was 38 per cent of the large systems market in 1993 and predicted to increase to 58 per cent worldwide by 1996.[32]

Credibility arguments should have helped IBM, but this advantage has gradually declined. Although initially X/Open was a fringe group, it was soon supported by major companies such as DEC and Hewlett Packard, by rapidly growing new firms such as Sun, and later by IBM itself, all of whom needed access to the Unix market. Unix was also a credible system, well known and with an established niche. IBM was soon suffering from some credibility problems of its own, with many observers by 1989 questioning its ability to respond to changing industry conditions.[33] These problems have continued to mount for IBM since 1991. Ironically IBM's strategies are restricted by its existing base of products, both its strength and its weakness. The old operating systems are harder to integrate than a single Unix, while the new ones such as OS/2 have to remain to some extent backwards compatible with them.

The linkage and credibility provided by secondary markets outside the mainframe market are a key reason why the current attempt to change the standards regime is succeeding where others have not. Previous attempts had been a direct attack on the IBM standard, often with great technical innovations, but starting with zero installed base. In mainframes, these could not compete with the enormous base of IBM hardware and software.[34] This time the attack is indirect via new products which set up separate bases without having to replace an existing standard. Success in the other segments has convinced users of the viability of open systems. The new products provided the 'avenue of entry' to change the entrenched standard.

As well as dealing with the internal integration problems of the IBM computer ranges, which had become a big problem for both IBM and its customers, SAA was an attempt to bring all the new classes of computers (micros, minis, workstations) into the traditional 'mainframe' pattern of standards control, described above. This strategy may have underestimated the changes in industry conditions towards open, rather than common, standards. The necessary conditions for proprietary control do not apply to the new computers. With outside components suppliers and independent software vendors there are diffuse property rights. Technological generations appear too rapidly for a single firm to keep ahead. If economies of scale exist they may be more in software than hardware, favouring open standards to ensure large software markets. Also a route for overcoming the old standards regime now exists. IBM itself helped validate and publicize the ideas of networking and common standards in supporting SAA.

Prospects for SAA declined with the fall in relative importance of mainframes, which by 1990 had been eclipsed by smaller systems. Faced with the low adoption of SAA and OS/2 outside its existing base, IBM gradually put more emphasis on Unix, at first in parallel with SAA, although the two were kept separate.[35] SAA is no longer a factor in IBM strategy but the company has not yet followed DEC, who reluctantly accepted in 1990 that it must fit its products fully to open systems and has since developed strong products for the new market.[36] Strategic alternatives for IBM revolve around how it deals with its installed base. The enormous base of S/370 users may be left as a proprietary island in an open world, or provided with the means to migrate to open systems. If migration is made simple this expands the total market for open systems but may open IBM's installed base to competitors. Remaining incompatible protects the segment but splits the market between two standards. This defensive strategy may work in the short run, but seems too isolating in the long run, relying on the ageing S/370 base while the open segment leads technological development.

X/Open has itself been overtaken by the changes it helped bring about. It introduced the concept of open systems which was then taken up by the market, as discussed below. It is now seen mainly as a 'seal of approval' for *de facto* standards developed by individual firms and private consortia. Many of the standards included within CAE may not have been sufficiently detailed for X/Open actively to shape the future of the industry, and these details are now being decided in the market.

5. COMPETITION BETWEEN 'OPEN SYSTEMS'

5.1 Continuation strategies

As open systems have become established, computer manufacturers have had to face the problem of maintaining product differentiation when users are no longer locked into a proprietary architecture. They have responded to the challenge in three ways. First, some manufacturers to try to divert the full effect of open systems by differentiating their own versions of Unix while still supporting basic X/Open standards. The hope was that they could have access to the new markets growing up around open standards but make it hard for users to switch to another Unix, in a variant of the traditional lock-in strategy. This contest between open and quasi-proprietary versions of Unix took place as open systems were being established between the two main industry coalitions, Open Software Foundation (OSF) and Unix International (UI), set up in the late 1980s.

An alternative strategy has been to embrace open systems as fully as possible, and rely on product features other than the interface standard to differentiate the firm's products. The firms using these 'super-compatibility' strategies have generally been those which supported open systems most strongly from early on, though they may now be combined with efforts to develop interoperable systems.

A third response has been to take the contest to the next generation of technology. Although the two Unix groups have come closer together, the current focus of competition is between new 'interoperable' systems, which may support operating systems other than Unix. These systems are based on Risc chips, less closely associated with a particular software architecture. Though they may have proprietary elements, they aim at open interfaces between various hardware platforms and operating systems. We look at these three aspects in turn.

5.2 Shifting alliances

The immediate problem threatening open systems was the potential fragmentation of the standard as many firms developed their own semi-compatible versions of Unix, each with some special features. Opposition to fully open Unix standards was led by a number of major manufacturers wedded to existing proprietary computer designs. Their aims were not to reject Unix absolutely; SAA had opposed open systems directly and by this time its failure was already apparent. The firms wished to maintain some proprietary control over private versions which, though broadly supporting the open standard, would be tailored to individual computer architectures and would enable firms to continue to differentiate their systems via standards. The aim was to take advantage of the pool of resources devoted to general Unix, but still maintain a proprietary hardware and software base. It was also true that converting to Unix was not easy for some of the manufacturers and it took time for them to adjust their product lines. The main variants are given in Table 7.6. Firms tried to lock-in users with 'one-way' compatibility, hoping to attract users from the general pool but make it hard to switch back. The problem, as pointed out by Rob Wilmott, former chairman of ICL and an originator of X/Open, is that this 'added value' is really 'subtracted value', as it negates the advantages of standardization and limits the potential for the market as a whole.[37] To avoid fragmentation there was a need to convince X/Open members to continue to support fully open standards.

This was combined with a second problem. From a defensive point of view the manufacturers needed to ensure that the developers of 'open' Unix did not use this to gain a competitive advantage. The risk was that the holder of the main Unix rights, AT&T, might change its position on licensing once Unix was widely used, and might exploit the other firms' dependence, treating it as a proprietary standard. When Unix was chosen by X/Open in 1984, AT&T had only just entered the computer market, licences had been granted on minimal royalty payments and existing versions of Unix were in wide use. The threat of AT&T exerting its proprietary rights was nowhere near that of IBM. However, as adoption of Unix grew, and AT&T intensified its participation in computers, there was indeed a perceptible change in AT&T's policy. Partly because it too feared the fragmentation of Unix into a group of small Unix-like standards, AT&T agreed with Sun in 1987 to develop a standard Unix with full portability between different manufacturers machines, using Sun's Sparc microprocessor. Other manufacturers, many of whom did not want to use the Sun chip, feared this would give AT&T and Sun a leadership advantage. This fear was underlined in January 1988 when AT&T insensitively announced plans to buy 20 per cent of Sun and implied higher licence fees for the latest Unix.

The aims of the different manufacturers for and against open Unix were pursued via different industry alliances, first within X/Open, then by the OSF and UI coalitions created specifically to deal with this contest. The

Table 7.6. *Variations on Unix*

Producer	Unix
AT&T(USL)	Unix System V, Release 4.0*
Bull	Spix
DEC	Ultrix
Hewlett Packard	HP-UX
IBM	AIX
Microsoft	Xenix
Novell	Unixware
Siemens	Sinix
Sun	Solaris
Univ. Calif., Berkeley	Berkeley 4.2

* Rights bought by Novell, 1993.

primary alliance has remained X/Open. This worked as a focus for efforts towards open standards. It was originally an alliance of weak suppliers, and without the threat from the existing dominant standard the firms might individually not have chosen an open standard. Later, as belief in the viability of open systems grew, stronger firms joined and support became broader.

Following the AT&T/Sun announcement, fear of AT&T grew. Though it claimed that its policy would not change, AT&T failed to convince all X/Open members that Unix would remain open as it was developed. A subgroup responded by forming a separate alliance to develop an alternative Unix, setting up OSF in May 1988. One of the motivations for setting up OSF was to remove control of the standard from a single firm, and hence attract further support for Unix (Saloner, 1990). However, a crucial aspect of OSF was the membership of IBM, playing the leading role in the alliance. Needing a credible alternative version of Unix quickly, the only available choice was to adopt AIX, IBM's standard. IBM had the resources to develop a fully portable Unix and AIX was already more developed than the other versions. However it was clear that IBM was unlikely to open up the latest releases of AIX to OSF, and that it could be designed to fit IBM hardware first, making AIX quasi-proprietary. IBM would have a considerable leadership advantage to exploit in the familiar pattern. Even so this was seen as a better alternative than having Unix turned into a proprietary standard by AT&T. Without the advantage of being open, a proprietary AT&T Unix would have been in a weak position against IBM and this would probably leave a split and weakened Unix market. These firms would rather make their own way behind IBM in a strong market than follow AT&T in a weak one.

OSF was a very credible threat. Against it AT&T had little chance of establishing a proprietary Unix and it was forced to reaffirm its commitment to open systems. It reversed its new licensing proposals and made public commitments to an open Unix. It formalized these commitments by setting up a counter group, incorporated as UI in November 1988.[38] The members of UI included those members of X/Open who had not joined OSF, as well as many other firms which had not yet joined either group. AT&T had itself been offered membership of OSF, but talks failed. The questions of whether there were to be AT&T or IBM standards, open or closed, were too important to be decided by negotiation within OSF, and OSF could only be met with an alternative market grouping. A measure of the seriousness attached to this is the funding for the two groups, initially at about $40 m. each. This contrasts the tiny sums usually spent supporting industry standards bodies.

The cross membership of the different alliances amongst the major computer vendors is shown in Fig. 7.7. More detailed lists of supporters of OSF and UI are given in Table 7.7.[39] The membership of the two alliances

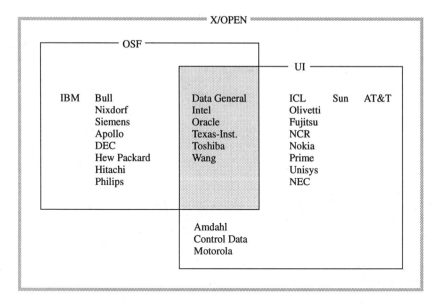

Fig. 7.7. *Alliance cross-membership, 1990*

reflected the different extent to which firms were affected by IBM or AT&T leadership. The OSF members were generally the stronger firms, led by DEC and Hewlett Packard, who were more able to survive in an IBM world or more threatened by a powerful AT&T. For example, Apollo (now part of Hewlett Packard) was particularly vulnerable if Sun, the workstation leader, dominated Unix. Those who allied with AT&T in UI had more need of open standards, either due to weak bases of their own or because of the enormous opportunities for growth offered by open systems (the Japanese firms). Firms which joined both groups, the 'fence-straddlers', may have wanted to protect their existing Unix customers who already had sundry Unix versions. OSF contained the larger information systems firms—IBM, DEC, HP, Hitachi—with a total of about 50 per cent greater information systems sales than the UI members. However UI members were more active in the Unix market, with around three times the Unix sales of OSF. Both groups also contained some software producers and users, who were thus involved in some way in the decision process.

The appearance of UI reassured the industry. More firms joined X/Open, which soon included all the major computer manufacturers. IBM's presence in the Unix market, and its willingness to join an open systems grouping, albeit as a leader, also had a strong influence in convincing the industry that open systems had arrived. The vision of IBM, DEC, and Hewlett Packard sitting down together at OSF to announce open standards marked a turning point for the industry.

Table 7.7. *Major members of OSF and UI*

Open Systems Foundation (OSF)				
Founders				
Apollo	Bull	DEC	Hewlett Packard	IBM
Nixdorf	Siemens			
Vendors				
Altos	Canon	Concurrent*	Comp. Cons*	Data General*
Hitachi	MIPS	Nat. Semic.	Norsk Data	Philips
Toshiba*	Wang*			
Semicond.				
AMD	Intel	Texas Inst.*		
Software				
Informix*	Oracle*			
Unix International (UI)				
Founders				
AT&T	Amdahl	Control Data	Fujitsu	ICL
NCR	Olivetti	Prime	Sun	Unisys
Vendors				
Alcatel	Arix	Convergent	Concurrent*	Comp. Cons*
Data Gen.*	Gould	NEC	OKI	Pyramid
Toshiba*	Wang*	Xerox		
Semicond.				
Intel*	Motorola	Texas Inst.*		
Software				
Informix*	Oracle*	Unisoft		

* Members of both OSF and UI.

Sources: OSF, UI.

This gave a clearer definition of standard Unix and reduced the possibility of breakaway into quasi-proprietary versions. Market pressures took over and the differences between versions became less important. DEC's forced conversion to fully open systems, two years after it helped form OSF, is noted above. In May 1989, UI and OSF joined X/Open, making an effective reconciliation. All the individual firms are members of X/Open, and it is conceivable that OSF and UI Unix versions may merge within X/Open standards. With agreement on basic levels of compatibility assured, the open systems market has grown steadily. Differences between versions are now minor, with switching costs probably too low to lock in users, who know that they could transfer to another supplier if they wished. In future the degree of openness is likely to depend on the market strengths of the individual players, the rate of technological development and firms' abilities to differentiate their product outside the standard. Closer collaboration between former OSF and UI members to develop common standards was announced in 1993, including a number of concessions by computer vendors. Interestingly, this move to further joint action was apparently precipitated by the threat from even newer operating systems, such as Windows NT, as well as OS/2, discussed below. Also, reassurances that Unix would remain open have recently again been necessary, this time from Novell.[40]

Shifts in strategies and allegiances have been used to convince the different firms that it is in their interests to limit fragmentation and keep Unix open. The effectiveness of these market alliances may be compared with the long efforts to promote standards such as OSI by international agreement before market pressures arose. However, the sequence of events also implies that collaboration may only be achieved in the face of a strong common threat of proprietary dominance. This underlines the argument that only an open standard has much chance of success against a strong established proprietary standard. The common threat from IBM, first with SAA and then with AIX provided much of the motivation for unity, making fragmentation an even less attractive possibility.

5.3 'Super-compatibility' strategies

Some of the most successful firms have used continuation strategies aimed at full compatibility with the interface standard, while using other product features external to the standard to differentiate their products. These include firms such as ICL, Sun, Hewlett Packard and Unisys. Features may include overall performance, cost effectiveness and quality, as well as customer service, user-oriented development and links with applications software developers.

An illustration of the approach is the UK computer maker, ICL. This firm has developed its role as a systems integrator, offering complete systems solutions. Although it remains a computer manufacturer, ICL designs systems that combine externally supplied components, mainly from its parent company Fujitsu, with its own hardware elements and a diverse array of internally developed software for systems and applications. ICL's position relies on its strengths in developing user-oriented applications and services and its ability to combine these with broad systems design. The role of the systems integrator is described by ICL as follows:

With the new products in the 1980s, computer manufacturers expanded from being suppliers of hardware and software to becoming true systems builders. ICL responded with new products—knowledge engineering, financial services, retail systems, management information systems and decision support systems. The new businesses are close to the spirit of professional services, and distinguish the true information systems (IS) firms from suppliers of 'boxes'. Today ICL sees itself not as being primarily a hardware manufacturer, but as a creator and distributor of complex information systems and professional services. This is an appropriate stance for the 1990s.[41]

Although ICL has been a major advocate of open systems, it stresses the continued importance of software and hardware links:

Yet paradoxically in the commodity-like computer market of the 1980s and 1990s, in which the user has become less and less concerned with the physical realization of IS products, success in the business will depend crucially on access to the best emerging technology. ICL is not large enough to develop this all by itself and so has gained long term access to the best semiconductor technologies from Fujitsu, and to communications technology from STC (ICL's parent corporation during 1984–91).[42]

5.4 Competition for interoperable systems

While the definition of Unix for open systems has become clearer, new competition for open systems has appeared. The main immediate threat has been the arrival of Windows NT in 1993, but there are many others.[43] This means that 'open' Unix will no longer have to compete only against IBM's OS/2 and proprietary versions of Unix, but will face a range of other systems. Like Unix, these new operating systems aim to be platform independent—they run on various hardware configurations—and claim to some degree to be open. The new systems architectures being developed will support existing proprietary operating systems as well as open ones—in the sense that DEC's Alpha AXP architecture supports its own VMS system as well as Unix and Windows NT, and Apple's PowerPC processor supports its own System 7 operating system, amongst others—so the new systems will be compatible with an existing installed base.

Competition is taking place at both the processor/architecture level and the operating system level, with continued attempts to link the two strategically. The adoption of a given architecture or operating system by other manufacturers and software developers is central to competition in the new markets. A firm controlling the technology behind an industry standard may have a highly profitable 'architectural franchise' (Ferguson and Morris, 1993). Producers hope to duplicate Microsoft's position with DOS in the PC market, and establish their system as a 'quasi-open' standard, made widely available to all users, typically at competitive licensing fees, but dominating the market. If priced correctly, this encourages the wide adoption of the standard and still allows the proprietor to earn significant monopoly rents on high volumes. The game, as it has been with DOS, is not to charge so much that users turn elsewhere or other producers have incentives to develop alternatives. Huge efforts are being made by individual firms for development and promotion. There are private alliances such as the Taligent joint venture between IBM, Apple, and Hewlett Packard to develop an 'object oriented' operating system (called Pink) for the PowerPC.[44]

These recent developments further weaken the links between operating systems and computer platforms. Interoperable operating systems—Unix, Windows NT, OS/2, Taligent—will allow the same applications software to run without modification on wide ranges of microcomputers using the latest microprocessors. Interoperability further separates the design of hardware and software, so that each can be optimized independently of the other. At the moment they are interdependent and changes to one are restricted by the need to remain compatible with the other. To take advantage of the rapidly increasing power of microprocessors the design freedom may be justified on technical grounds alone. The developments are also related to the extension of microprocessor-based systems to all segments of the computer market and to the entry of the major computer manufacturers into microprocessor design and fabrication. These players may prefer greater strategic independence from the components manufacturers and may wish to weaken the link between the software installed base and microprocessor architecture. The size of the market may now be so great that it is worth while for the manufacturers to form strategic groups to operate independently of other players with strategic power, such as Intel and Microsoft.[45]

Faced with these new threats on the horizon, it became clear by 1992 that Unix would need intense development to be able to compete effectively. It was no longer clear that AT&T had the desire or the capability to lead Unix development in such a competitive environment. As a first step to separating its interests in Unix from its other interests in the IS industry, in 1992 AT&T spun off its Unix interests into a subsidiary, Unix Systems Laboratories (USL), which absorbed UI and included the 11 other UI members as minority shareholders.

The role of leading Unix development has now been taken over by Novell, the network software company, which bought USL from AT&T in June 1993 for $320 m. The reason for Novell's move was that competition had changed since 1988 and the main threat to open systems was not proprietary Unix but the new operating system, Windows NT. This directly threatens the dominance of Novell Netware in network systems. Novell's intention was apparently to ensure that Unix would remain an alternative standard to whatever is offered by Microsoft and that adequate development efforts would be made.

However, echoing the worries following the alliance between AT&T and Sun in 1987, other producers were concerned that Novell's move would lead to a more proprietary strategy towards Unix. The potential attraction of Windows NT from a producer with a record of moderate pricing and access strategies, meant that the openness of Unix needed to be reaffirmed. In a close parallel with the formation of UI in 1988, Novell responded by committing itself to a fully open Unix. It announced in September 1993 that it was giving away its rights over Unix to X/Open and that only reasonable royalties would be charged. This reassured users concerned that a single company could control such important software. The announcement came just six weeks after Microsoft introduced Windows NT.[46] The threat of Windows NT had already caused closer cooperation between Unix supporters in early 1993, noted above.

The outcome of these new contests will not become clear until we see what impact the systems have on the market, from 1994 onwards. The advantage that Unix has with its installed base in workstations and in the integration of the large and mid-range systems may be crucial. It is also a committed open standard. However, other systems may also capitalize on compatibility with certain installed bases, such as Windows NT with the PC network market or DEC's Alpha with VAX minicomputers. The current advantage which the Unix installed base generates in the engineering and scientific workstation market may not carry over into business-oriented networks, unless business-oriented applications are developed. Microsoft, at least, has not followed strongly proprietary strategies in the past, and the openness of Windows NT may not appear to be very different in practice from Unix. There is no guarantee that Unix, which in a sense was developed within the old computer industry, will be the most appropriate system for all the new markets.

6. CONCLUSION

The rise of open systems shows how new technology can create the basic technical and economic conditions for open standards. The new technologies created new markets which naturally developed open standards. These not only have grown to threaten the traditional large systems markets but also have provided routes to establish open standards in the older areas. The exact form of the new standards depends on the strategies followed by the players and various outcomes are still possible. For example, had IBM responded earlier to the shift towards microprocessors then not only IBM itself but the computer industry as a whole might be taking a rather different path from the one which is now emerging.

A basic problem with open standards, of getting competitors to cooperate, has been resolved by a series of market generated coalitions. These confirmed that the standard would remain open, but probably still depended on there being a strong proprietary threat to unify the industry. Once the concept of open systems had been established, market forces have been the main determinants of the degree of openness.

It is hard to overstate the impact of this restructuring on the computer industry. Two major problems now facing the manufacturers are how to compete in an open standards world and how to stop the proprietary control from shifting from the broader computer market into the microprocessor or operating system markets. On the first, perhaps the best indication for continuation strategies is to look at the pattern in the personal computer market. This has effectively open standards, high competition (at least in hardware) and constant technological advance. The market has grown very quickly and made some very successful companies. Successful firms have found ways of differentiating their products without negating the open standard which makes the large market possible. This may be achieved via technical leadership, quality manufacturing or closer identification with user needs, but not by trying to reintroduce proprietary standards.

On the second, perhaps this too is approaching the problem from too traditional a viewpoint. For most of its history the semiconductor industry has not been characterized by strong proprietary standards, and for many reasons it has usually not been successful at integrating forward into computers. The current trends towards open standards and interoperable systems make it less likely that computer manufacturers are tied to a given component design. With open standards, component manufacturers (including computer manufacturers) also have to compete more on basic features such as speed, reliability and cost, and this must surely benefit the computer industry as a whole. The new focus of competition on chip performance, software features, service and even brand recognition, which seems to differentiate computer advertising today compared with the broad corporate images of a decade ago, may illustrate how far the shift to quality variables rather than lock-in has gone.

Appendix: Abbreviations

AIX	Advanced Interface Exchange
CAE	Common Applications Environment
CCITT	International Committee for Telephone and Telegraph
CISC	Complex instruction set computing
DCE	Distributed Computing Environment
IEEE	Institute of Electrical and Electronic Engineers (US)
ISO	International Standards Organization
LAN	Local area network
MULTIX	Multiple Interface Exchange
OSF	Open Software Foundation
OSI	Open Systems Interconnection
PC	Personal computer
POSIX	Portable Operating System Interface Exchange
RISC	Reduced instruction set computing
SAA	Systems Application Architecture
SNA	Systems Network Architecture
TCP/IP	Transmission Control Protocol/Internet Protocol
UI	Unix International
UNIX	Unified Interface Exchange
USL	Unix Systems Laboratories
XPG	X/Open Portability Guide

NOTES

1. Manufacturers with their main base in proprietary mainframe technologies include Digital Equipment Corporation (DEC), Unisys, Olivetti, Groupe Bull, and to a lesser extent Fujitsu and NEC. Computer manufacturers best known for supporting open systems include ICL (Fujitsu), Hewlett Packard, Sun, Compaq and Dell.
2. The early history of computers is given in Katz and Phillips (1982); a view on IBM's history is given in Watson and Petre (1990). Data from Watson and Petre (1990), 243.
3. There are several equivalent microprocessors, usually available to other workstation manufacturers, but there is also a high correlation between these and the manufacturer developing them (e.g. the Sparc chip is used by Sun, PA-Risc by Hewlett Packard, Alpha by DEC, Power by IBM, MIPS by Silicon Graphics). Of these Sparc is the most open. There are also chips from merchant semiconductor firms such as Intel and Motorola.
4. These use data for the 100 largest corporations only. Total world revenues are probably at least 30% higher, due mainly to the contribution of small firms in

the PC, peripherals and service markets. This also means that individual firm shares are overstated.

5. Charges for restructuring and accounting changes in 1992 were $11.6 bn.; a restructuring charge of $8.9 bn. was made in July 1993. The $8.1 bn. loss in 1993 is the biggest ever corporate loss, if the effects of accounting rule changes are excluded.

6. *The Economist*, 29 Jan. 1994.

7. In March 1993 John Akers was replaced as chairman by Lou Gerstner, from outside the computer industry.

8. The full extent of the PC market is understated here as figures exclude the small PC clone manufacturers, not covered in most surveys, which may add another 40% to sales, taking them to over 20% of the market.

9. *Datamation*, 15 June 1993.

10. This discussion draws on Manasian (1993).

11. Many of the firms competing for blocks of the IBM market, such as Fujitsu, Hitachi and National Advanced Systems (sold to Hitachi in the mid-1980s), were also in the compatible peripherals market. Thanks to Alan Robertson for noting this.

12. Windows is not strictly an operating system, but a graphical user interface (GUI) or 'environment' which runs on DOS operating system. Windows NT, introduced in 1993, is a true operating system.

13. All the microprocessors except Intel's Pentium are Reduced Instruction Set Computing (Risc) designs, which are designed to run faster by including only simple sets of instructions in the chip hardware. The Pentium and the rest of the ×86 series are Complex Instruction Set Computing (Cisc) designs, and contain about twice as many instructions built into the chip. Risc chips rely on the operating system software to provide a full set of instructions and so may be easier to interface with interoperable or 'platform independent' operating systems than Cisc.

14. Also included are 'specialized' environments for on-line transactions processing such as Tuxedo (from AT&T) and Encina (from Transarc), and distributed data base systems such as Oracle and Informix, designed to run on a combination of hardware systems.

15. The extent of structural change is indicated by the number of firms now in the industry. An estimate from IBM is that whereas there were about 2,500 firms involved in some part of the computer industry in 1965, there are now about 50,000 of significant size (Manasian, 1993).

16. Dataquest figures, in Manasian (1993).

17. Initially this was mainly for scientific and technical systems. A key step towards Unix acceptance was a DOD contract for minicomputers, worth $4.5bn., specifying Unix and won by AT&T in October 1988.

18. Estimates of the UK software industry are that only about 2,500–3,000 people were employed in independent firms in the UK in 1970, with revenues of £7.5–10 m., together with about 3000 development groups in-house, accounting for perhaps another 30,000 people (Foy, 1971). The total US market for software in 1970 was about $5 bn., of which in-house development amounted to $4.3 bn. and contract services to $650 m. (Fisher *et al.*, 1983).

19. Although production economies, affecting the core hardware, are important

they tend to be exhausted at smaller volumes than the demand side economies, affecting complementary software. For example, minimum efficient scale of production for microprocessors is likely to be (much) smaller than the total demand from the equipment market, whereas new software applications may continue to be developed as the installed base grows and makes new niche markets viable. Similarly, the fixed component of microprocessor production costs is likely to be lower than that for software production, where costs are more specifically for development. Also hardware costs are becoming a lower proportion of total systems costs than software. For general discussions of standards as they affect computers see Brock (1975a,b), Hemenway (1975), Gabel (1987a).

20. OSI model defines seven conceptual layers of compatibility for node-to-node communications paths between different systems. From the most basic to the most complex, these are (1) physical medium, (2) data link, (3) network, (4) transport, (5) session, (6) presentation, (7) application. It is the applications layer (7) which defines the specific services and protocols needed for interoperability as opposed to connectivity. Above it are the user application programs, which are not part of the OSI model. The OSI architecture is described in DTI (1988).

21. EITO (1993).

22. A related standard is the Portable Operating System Interface Exchange (POSIX) interface standard developed by the US Institute of Electrical and Electronic Engineers (IEEE). IEEE recommendations for LAN specifications are often converted into *de jure* standards and formally included in ISO recommendations, and hence become part of more comprehensive open standards.

23. Much of the OSI design was based on the SNA model, though there are differences.

24. As an example of common architecture, in the X/Open distributed transactions processing model there are two main interfaces: (*a*) the TX interface between the user application and the transaction manager, which standardizes the interfaces to different resource managers (e.g. file and database systems), and (*b*) the XA interface between transaction managers from different systems and specific resource managers. Together TX and XA provide a standardized application interface for accessing distributed resources in a network, rather than the many different specific resource manager (RM) interfaces needed otherwise (X/Open, 1993).

25. Some of the other methods ascribed to IBM in dominating the computer market are given in Delamarter (1986). Despite the controversy, it should be remembered that IBM has never been convicted of an antitrust violation. The US Department of Justice antitrust case, started in 1969, was finally dismissed as 'without merit' in 1982. By that time it had become a historical relic, in a vastly different market from what had existed when the case was filed (Fisher, McGowan, and Greenwood, 1983; Scherer and Ross, 1990: 459–462). Others have emphasized IBM's management skills as the source of its performance (Peters and Waterman, 1982).

26. For early history of X/Open see Gabel (1987b); for the technical description of CAE see X/Open (1988). History and technical description of SAA are in

Wheeler and Ganek (1988). IBM's difficulties in establishing SAA as a proprietary industry standard are foretold in Grindley (1990*b*).

27. Gabel (1987*b*).

28. Unix is an acronym for Unified Interface Exchange, though the name was coined directly as a derivative of the earlier system Multix, or Multiple Interface Exchange. Similarly AIX is Advanced Interface Exchange.

29. SAA incorporates IBM's SNA network standards, which were influential in the initial design of OSI standards, later to be incorporated in X/Open's CAE.

30. OS/2 may have a new lease of life as a system for PC networks, as a competitor for Windows NT and others.

31. *Datamation*, 1 Jan. 1991.

32. Dataquest, quoted in *Guardian*, 23 Dec. 1993.

33. See McKenna (1989), and press articles following IBM's announcement of restructuring in 1991 (*Financial Times*, 18 Dec. 1991).

34. In minicomputers, IBM shares the market with a number of manufacturers following similar proprietary strategies to IBM. These had managed to establish themselves in the new market in the early 1970s, before IBM entered.

35. In 1988 IBM announced software products to ease networking between its own SNA standard and OSI, and a number of open products (*Financial Times*, 21 Sept. 1988).

36. IBM restructured into smaller more autonomous divisions in 1990 to try to get closer to individual markets; this strategy was reversed in 1993 (*Financial Times*, 26 Oct. 1990; *Business Week*, 9 Aug. 1993; *Guardian*, 14 Apr. 1994).

37. *Guardian*, 28 Aug. 1988.

38. UI backed AT&T/Sun's System V, Release 4.0, promising the reintegration of AT&T V Release 3, Berkeley 4.2 and Microsoft's Xenix. System V, Release 4.0 emerged in late 1989.

39. In 1989 UI had 45 member firms and OSF had 56, with 13 common to both. For a game model of alliance membership decisions, see Axelrod *et al.* (1993).

40. The announcement was made by OSF members IBM, Hewlett Packard, Sun Microsystems, and Santa Cruz Operation, and by Unix Systems Laboratories and Novell (the successors to UI). This was motivated by 'pressure from customers and the threat of a new operating system called NT from Microsoft' (*Wall Street Journal*, 17 Mar. 1993: 10; 22 Mar. 1993: 1). USL had announced a broad coalition of manufacturers and software developers to develop a new version of Unix—Unixware—in 1992, signalling the end of the war between USL and OSF (*New York Times*, 15 June 1992).

41. Campbell and Kelly (1989), 356.

42. Campbell and Kelly (1989), 355.

43. Andy Grove, CEO of Intel Corporation, said in 1994: 'Unix is under threat today. It has gone from being an attacker to being a defender without ever having won in the process. . . . Unix must work fast to fulfil the promise of a single, consolidated Unix in the face of a threat from Windows NT . . . Windows has already won the battle for the desktop, the key niche is now applications servers' (*Electronic News*, 28 Apr. 1994).

44. Hewlett Packard announced an expected 15% stake in Taligent in January 1994; Taligent was formed in March 1992 (*Guardian*, 13 Jan. 1994).

45. Taking the PC market as an example, this implies that systems designers and applications software producers will no longer be limited to following the ×86 standard. Since the changes effectively will allow many more types of design to compete in the microprocessors market, this may signal the end of dominance by the ×86 standard. The new systems will provide emulators for the ×86, though it is not clear how efficiently they will run existing DOS software.
46. *Financial Times*, 20 Sept. 1993.

8

High-Definition Television:
The Failure of International Co-operation

SUMMARY   High-definition television (HDTV) is a prime example of the difficulties of achieving international agreement on standards—a combination of strategy and policy. It highlights a general problem of co-ordinating strong complementary interest groups, aligned nationally and focused by national standards authorities. Consensus is especially difficult for HDTV as there are three groups of complementary producers—equipment manufacturers, programme producers, and broadcasters—as well as the users. Also, as a replacement standard, HDTV must be significantly better than colour television to be adopted over the existing standard, creating additional resistance. Japanese developers followed what seemed a powerful strategy by establishing a domestic consensus between manufacturers and the state broadcaster, and introducing the global standard in stages—for programme production then transmission. However, international adoption was blocked by European and US manufacturers and broadcasters, acting through their national standards bodies. The Europeans chose a similar technology to the Japanese, but failed to hold the internal consensus, and this was dropped. However, the US used an unusual procedure for determining a standard, combining market and official processes, in which the authority acted as a referee for proposals invited from industry. Although structured to protect US local broadcasters, this policy led to an advanced digital system, which may now become the global standard. This is technically more acceptable than the earlier systems, and has possible links to computer and telecommunications applications. It also offers a more equal international distribution of benefits. Manufacturers are now cooperating privately. Although the Japanese strategy was effective in deciding on *a* standrad, this only applied in Japan and may have been made obsolete by the new developments. The case shows some strengths and limitations of official adoption, which focuses national interests but may generate an unacceptable standard. Other strategic issues include the dangers of premature standardization and the use of evolutionary versus radical introduction strategies.

1. INTRODUCTION

Few new consumer products have aroused as much interest, or been as thoroughly discussed before their launch, as high-definition television

(HDTV). Under development in Japan for over twenty five years, and in Europe and the USA for eight, this next-generation television system represents potentially one of the largest consumer electronics markets of all time. Interest has been intense since 1986, when a bid to have the Japanese system adopted as the world standard was stalled by European broadcasters and manufacturers, who proposed an alternative system. The USA later proposed a third and more advanced system. So far no HDTV products have appeared on the consumer market and although Japan has started a pilot service this is faltering. The outcome is finally becoming clearer, with the late-arriving US system now likely to be adopted around the world. This is not only technically more acceptable than the other systems, being fully digital and with links to computer and telecommunications developments, but also offers a more equal international distribution of benefits. The independent European effort has been dropped and even the Japanese may switch to the US standard.[1]

The reason for this unprecedented pre-launch activity is not just that HDTV is a new technology, but that it aims to become a global standard for television. It is a network product, which works effectively only if programme production, transmission, and reception all use the same standard. Coordinating adoption requires agreement between three groups of complementary producers. This is especially difficult at the international level, because there are separate groups in each country, acting through national standards authorities with the power to control local broadcasting rights. Consensus is hard to achieve, given the huge winner-take-all payoffs involved, and the fact that potential losers are able to block adoption via the standards bodies. Within countries, given the limited bandwidth available, any changes in technology may involve reallocation of property rights to use the broadcast spectrum, aggravating the co-ordination difficulties. Also, HDTV is a replacement standard, and must be significantly better than colour television to be adopted over the existing standard. These issues make HDTV introduction a much more complicated process than simply adopting a new technology. Yet the advantages of a unified global standard are great, allowing programmes and transmissions to be shared internationally without expensive, time-consuming, and quality-reducing conversion.

There are two main themes: the strategies of the manufacturers to try to establish global HDTV standards, and the contrast between government policies in the three regions for the role of the official standards authorities. Manufacturers have used a wide range of strategies to coordinate introduction, including the use of standards bodies. The Japanese strategies came near to success in introducing the 'Hi-Vision' standard, and probably would have succeeded had the technical and economic performance of the system been more favourable. Similar strategies may come into their own in establishing HDTV in future. Japanese developers first established a national

consensus for developing and introducing the standard between the manufacturers and the state broadcaster. To ease the introduction they separated
the effort into stages, first aiming at studio production and later extending
this to broadcasting and receiving. They also used a balance of evolutionary
and radical introduction techniques, and developed an array of supporting
equipment, such as video cassette recorders (VCR) and laser discs (LD), as
well as HDTV programming. Together these could have created a strong
demand for transmissions and forced official adoption. However, the failure
of the standard also shows the risks of premature standardization to which
a concentration on the mechanics of consensus, at the expense of allowing
market demand to express itself, may lead. The Japanese strategy was
effective in deciding on *a* standard, but was not fully in touch with demand,
and even in Japan the system has been regarded as outmoded and expensive. Also the consensus was too nationally oriented.

Policy approaches have been quite different in three regions, and the
centrally orchestrated policies in Japan and Europe may have been less
effective than the hybrid policy used in the USA, combining market and
official processes. The Japanese model of 'administered guidance' effectively ensured consensus but chose a conventional and apparently low-risk
technology, which proved unappealing to users. The politically motivated
European 'central direction' model chose an unlikely technology, partly
because of pressure to remain compatible with existing receivers, and failed
to hold the internal consensus. In the apparently more successful US approach the authority acted as an 'independent' referee—using supposedly
objective criteria—of proposals invited from industry. This offered some of
the benefits of variety and motivation from competitive standards, but
avoided the fragmentation possible with fully market determined standards. Although structured to protect US local broadcasters, this process
produced an advanced digital standard in a short time, which seems to have
a good chance of being accepted internationally. Manufacturers are now co-
operating privately. This may be a valuable model for standards setting in
other contexts.

The case gives some useful insights into the strengths and weaknesses of
using official adoption as part of standards strategy. In areas such as broadcasting some official involvement in standards is unavoidable, due to the
need to regulate the use of radio spectrum. However, relying solely on
official approval is risky. Even official standards ultimately depend on
market acceptance and may be bypassed if unattractive. Market strategies
have had a great deal of success. Although the Hi-Vision standard may be
defunct, many elements of the Japanese strategy are valid. They have
established *de facto* standards for studio equipment and will have a major
share of the consumer market whatever transmission standard is chosen.
They established the concept of HDTV and of using enhanced definition
television (EDTV) as an intermediate step. And it was the near success of

Hi-Vision which prompted other governments to act. Although official adoption was an important part of this strategy it was important to combine this with market forces. The more complete reliance on official adoption in Europe proved to be misplaced. However, the use of prospective market competition, before products appear, to generate the US standard has had a favourable outcome for US communications technologies. As for policy, the international bodies proved unable to resolve conflicts of national interests, and have come close to endorsing three regional standards, threatening to repeat the fragmentation of current colour television standards throughout the world

In the remainder of this chapter, Section 2 gives the background of HDTV development, and describes the history of the competing systems. Section 3 outlines standards theory applied to HDTV, including the advantages of a single standard, the contrast between evolutionary and radical strategies, and the need for official standards. Section 4 studies the different strategies used to try to establish HDTV, comparing the Japanese and European approaches. Section 5 studies the role of the institutions and how they may be integrated with market driven mechanisms, comparing Japan, Europe, and the USA. Section 6 draws some conclusions for strategy and policy. An appendix lists HDTV abbreviations.

2. HISTORY OF HDTV

2.1 Overview

HDTV is the next generation of television technology. It offers high quality pictures, almost as clear as cinema, and 'perfect' digital sound. Compared to the existing systems, HDTV has a wider screen with more lines. New transmission techniques, including satellite broadcasting and optical cable, though not restricted to HDTV, give pictures virtually free of interference.

It has been developed to supplement or replace existing colour television. There are currently three different colour television systems in use around the world. The US introduced the first colour services in the 1950s, using the US National Television System Committee (NTSC) system, which Japan also uses. Most of Europe uses the phase alternate line (PAL) system, developed about ten years after NTSC. The performance of NTSC had been compromised partly by the requirement that it was backwards compatible with the existing black and white system and could be received on existing sets. PAL required new sets, and together with technological advances made in the interim, was technically superior to NTSC. SECAM, a variant of PAL, is used in France and Russia. There are also minor differences between national standards. None of these systems are compatible with each other, and programmes must be converted from one to the other.

Television services are also organized differently in different countries, and this affects the response to HDTV proposals. In most European countries there is a state broadcaster and some independent broadcasters, with services presented, for the most part, on a nation-wide basis. There are usually only a few channels offered. Governments are closely involved in allocating broadcasting bandwidths and frequencies, and either operate services themselves or issue licences to operate. There are also cable and satellite services, though in Europe these are still not very extensive. Japanese television is also provided by state and independent broadcasters, similar to Europe. In the US, television services are provided by local independent stations, who either carry programmes from one of the major networks or provide their own programming. Some of the stations may be owned by a network. There are usually many stations in any local area. The government's main role is to regulate the use of radio spectrum and allocate bandwidths or broadcasting rights. There are extensive US cable services, but little satellite broadcasting at present.[2]

Development of systems for producing, transmitting and displaying HDTV programmes began in Japan over twenty five years ago, and trial broadcasts began in 1989. The Japanese standard, 'Hi-Vision', was developed by the Japanese state broadcaster (NHK) in collaboration with the major Japanese electronics manufacturers. Although Hi-Vision has an enormous lead in product development, it is not the only contender. A Japanese move to gain world-wide adoption of Hi-Vision at the meeting of the International Radio Consultative Committee (CCIR) in 1986 was stalled by opposition from European manufacturers, who began to develop an alternative system, multiplexed analog components (MAC), with government support. Having at first supported Hi-Vision, US manufacturers later proposed a third standard. Initial US proposals for Advanced Compatible Television (ACTV), similar to MAC, were soon superseded by fully digital Advanced Television (ATV) systems, made possible by the rapid improvement in digital technology in the intervening period. This has given potentially three regional standards. Hi-Vision, MAC and ATV, oddly similar to the divisions for existing colour television.

The contest between these alternative systems has taken place on three levels: technical, strategic, and political. Technically Hi-Vision and MAC are similar. They both use analog transmission, as in current television systems, though this may be combined with digital cameras and receivers. In contrast, ATV uses digital signals end-to-end.[3] It also has greater potential for future development, including links to computer and telecommunications applications. All three have generally equivalent picture quality. Development of studio production equipment, broadcast equipment, receivers and other consumer products are much further along in Hi-Vision than the other standards, though Japanese manufacturers claim that these products may be switched easily to any standard. Hi-Vision is well on the way to acceptance as a *de facto* production standard for studio equipment, which is switching to digital technology. However it is far from acceptance as a transmission standard for broadcasting.[4]

2.2 Technical description

The main features of the three HDTV standards, as well as the interim EDTV system, are given in Table 8.1. HDTV pictures are wider than current television and have finer detail. The screens have an aspect ratio (width to height) of 16:9, compared with 4:3 currently. Hi-Vision has 1125 lines per screen, compared with 625 or 525 lines now. Pictures are scanned with a frequency of 60 frames per second (f.p.s.) but, in common with current television systems, each pass only scans alternate lines, with the two partial images interlaced to give 30 full pictures a second (frame rate), saving transmission requirements and giving a brighter image (this is written as a 1125/60/2 system) The number of lines was chosen with enough resolution for the eye to see a 'perfect' picture at normal viewing distances, and to be most easily convertible to existing standards. With double the number of lines, and double the number of picture cells (pixels) per line, Hi-Vision has four times the resolution of colour television. It also needs about four times the bandwidth to broadcast the full standard, unless compression techniques are used. In comparison, MAC has 1250 lines and 50 f.p.s. The ACTV proposals had 1050 lines and 60 f.p.s. It is possible that digital ATV system will also have 1050 lines and 60 f.p.s., though this is not yet decided[5] Comparable data for existing colour television standards are given in Table 8.2.

A major difficulty for HDTV is its bandwidth requirements. Current television broadcasting requires 6 Mhz bandwidth per channel. Transmission of a full HDTV signal takes up more than four times this bandwidth, with Hi-Vision taking 27 Mhz and full HD-MAC taking 32 Mhz. This

Table 8.1. *Standards for different HDTV systems*

	Hi-Vision	MAC	ACTV	ATV	EDTV
Developer	Japan	Europe	USA	USA	Japan
Main patents	NHK	EBU	Zenith	GI/MIT	—
Prototype	1974	1987	1990	1991	1989
Lines	1125	1250	1050	1050/787.5*	525/1125
Frequency (Hz)	60	50	59.94	60/30	60
Interlace	2	2	2	2/1	2
Aspect ratio	16:9	16:9	16:9	16:9	4:3/16:9
Transmission	Analog	Analog	Analog	Digital	Analog
Back-compatible	—	√	√	—	√

* Later versions of ATV have proposed 960 and 720 lines.

Table 8.2. *Existing colour television standards*

	NTSC	SECAM	PAL
Introduced	1954	1967	1967
Patents	RCA	Thomson	Telefunken
Usage	USA/Canada	France, USSR	Europe (excl.
	Japan	Africa	France), ROW
Instal. base (m.)*	280	150	270
Lines	525	625	625
Frequency (Hz)	59.94	50	50
Interlace	2:1	2:1	2:1
Aspect ratio	4:3	4:3	4:3

* Installed base (m.): NTSC: USA (195), Canada (14), Japan (71)

PAL: UK (30), Germany (23), Italy (22), Spain (13)

SECAM: France (22), USSR (107), Eastern Europe (22)

Source: Unesco, 1988.

is far more than is available for terrestrial (land-based) broadcasting, where almost all the radio spectrum is fully allocated for existing broadcasting and telecommunications services. This means that full HDTV requires the use of direct broadcasting by satellite (DBS), where spectrum is available at the higher frequency satellite channels, or optical cable. However, compression techniques have been developed to allow HDTV to use less bandwidth (e.g. by only transmitting moving parts of the image). This has led to a number of transmission standards for each of the systems, mainly aimed at reducing the bandwidth requirements. Transmission requirements for the different standards are given in Table 8.3. Hi-Vision has developed the multiple sub-nyquist sampling encoding (MUSE) transmission system, which reduces the bandwidth requirements to 9 or 6 Mhz, though with some effect on picture quality. These would allow Hi-Vision to take up fewer satellite channels, use optical cable, or fit within two terrestrial channels. Similar MAC com-pression techniques have been developed, such as C-MAC and D-MAC. Compression methods work best for digital signals, but until recently it was thought that these would not be adequately developed for several years. New compression techniques using advanced digital signal processing (DSP) have been developed very recently to allow bandwidth to be reduced from 30 Mhz to the 6 Mhz needed to fit within one terrestrial channel. A problem with compression is that overall picture quality may be compro-mised. For example, for ATV the number of lines per screen and the scanning rate may have to be reduced, unless there are further advances in DSP techniques.

The standards under debate are for transmission and display, and the bulk of equipment such as cameras, editors, VCRs and monitors may be

Table 8.3. *HDTV transmission requirements*

Standard	Bandwidth (Mhz)	Medium
NTSC }		
PAL }	6	Terrestrial, DBS, cable
SECAM }		
HD-MAC	32	DBS
B-MAC	27	DBS
C-MAC	27	DBS, optical cable
D-MAC	10.5	DBS, optical cable
D2-MAC	7	DBS, cable
Hi-Vision	27	DBS
MUSE	8.1	DBS, optical cable
MUSE-6	6	Enhanced NTSC
MUSE-9	6 + 3	Terrestrial, cable
Narrow-MUSE	6	Terrestrial, cable
ACTV-I	6	Terrestrial, cable
ACTV-II	6 + 6	Terrestrial, cable
All-digital HDTV	30	DBS
ATV	6	Terrestrial, cable

manufactured in versions for any standard with only moderate redesign. It is also possible to design converters between standards to operate at the production, broadcast or reception point, though this adds to the cost and may reduce picture quality to some extent. The systems have many uses beyond television. Hi-Vision has been promoted, with some success, as a system for film production for computer graphics, printing, and other image applications. It has also been presented, with less success so far, as an alternative to 35 mm. movie.[6] Digital systems are more easily interfaced with computer applications, with huge potential markets in multimedia and telecommunications areas.

The greatest product problem is the display. Large screens are needed to justify the fine resolution of HDTV, which requires a massive picture tube. Flat screens and projectors are probably the key to consumer acceptability, but these are still a long way from being economically acceptable for major consumer markets. Great development efforts are underway for LCD and other displays, but bringing prices down to the 'cost effective' region could still be several years away.[7] The price of sets is one of the main reasons for expecting the introduction of HDTV to be quite gradual.

2.3 Development history

(a) Hi-Vision (Japan)

The main dates in the development of the Japanese standard are given in

Table 8.4. NHK began research into HDTV in 1968, soon after it had adopted the NTSC colour standard from the USA in 1960. Its original objectives were technical, to secure high quality pictures in poor reception conditions, with compatibility with existing systems secondary. The effort was coordinated by the Ministry of International Trade and Industry (MITI), which worked to ensure consensus between manufacturers, supported basic research and ensured that bank funding was available.[8] It recruited NHK to develop the standard and the basic circuitry, and manufacturers such as Sony to begin developing products. The basic NHK patents were made openly available, though the key patents are likely to be on the equipment developed by the manufacturers around the standard, and these are unlikely to be freely accessible. The system was demonstrated in Japan in 1980, and in the USA in 1981. As a measure of progress, live public demonstrations of satellite transmissions were made across Japan in 1988 of the Seoul Olympic games. This had probably been technically feasible for the Moscow Olympics in 1984 had the political climate allowed. NHK began daily test transmissions in June 1989 and a (rather uninteresting) eight hour daily public service in November 1991. Purchases of the large and expensive sets have been very low, even in Japan. Sets are costly.

Table 8.4. *Timetable for Japanese HDTV (Hi-Vision)*

Date	Event
1968	NHK starts research
1974	First HDTV demonstration
	First CCIR working group mention
1981	Prototype systems demonstrated—Sony
1983	Production equipment marketed—Sony
1984	MUSE compressed transmission standard announced
	TV sets available—Sony, Matsushita
1985	CCIR study group recommends Hi-Vision
1986	CCIR meeting (Dubrovnik) fails to adopt Hi-Vision
1987	HDTV promotion centre set up—MITI and 11 firms*
1988	6 Mhz transmission standard exhibited—CODEC
	NHK broadcasts Seoul Olympics live
1989	35 Japanese equipment manufacturers
	Korean manufacturers license Hi-Vision
	NHK demonstration broadcasts start—one hour daily
	Japanese EDTV sets appear—Clear-Vision
	Sony takes over Columbia Pictures
1990	CCIR meeting (Düsseldorf) fails to endorse any standard
1991	Regular MUSE broadcasts start—eight hours daily
1993	Only 10,000 receivers in use, price $6300—Sony

* Main firms: Sony, Hitachi, Toshiba, Matsushita, Sanyo, Mitsubishi, Sharp, NEC, JVC, Pioneer, Fujitsu.

In 1990 they cost about $43,000 but had been reduced to a little over $6,000 by late 1993.[9] Sets are also still very large: about the size and shape of a small desk. They are still custom built and not on general sale. So far only about 10,000 sets have been sold, mainly to public institutions or other electronics firms.[10]

Hi-Vision was making progress towards acceptance as the HDTV standard by 1986, when the attempt was made to have it adopted as a world-wide studio standard at the Internation Radio Consultative Committee (CCIR) plenary meeting in Dubrovnik in September, 1986. The Japanese had at this stage only sought to have Hi-Vision adopted as a production standard, presumably on the grounds that adoption as a transmission standard was too much for the national broadcasting authorities to accept in one step, but once the standard was established for production then broadcasters were likely to adopt it as a matter of course. It had already established a presence in the US studio equipment market, partly through Sony's association with CBS. Most important was that it was at first endorsed by the US standards body set up to consider HDTV, the Advanced Television Standards Committee (ATSC), which at that time was mainly influenced by the programme producers. There were as yet no other HDTV systems around. Despite already having been accepted by the CCIR study group, Hi-Vision was opposed by the Europeans. The decision on a world-wide standard was 'postponed' until 1990. Europeans began developing their own standard immediately. In the USA, different power groups became interested in HDTV. It became less attractive to the programme producers once the single world market for programmes had disappeared, and the US broadcasters and manufacturers became active as they realized what had nearly happened. The US began to consider a standard of its own. By May, 1990 the situation had not resolved itself and the long-awaited CCIR meeting in Düsseldorf again failed to adopt a standard. It was left to the individual national bodies.

Hi-Vision was designed as a radically new system, to avoid compromising the design by basing it on NTSC. The counter argument for receiver compatibility was made by MAC supporters, that an old set should be able to receive the new signals, though without improved pictures. Faced with a gap in their long range production plans, Japanese manufacturers eventually accepted this route and began to introduce an intermediate technology, EDTV or 'Clear-Vision', in 1989. By adding some additional transmitted signals and corrective circuitry in the set for digitally assisted pictures, EDTV gives clearer pictures than NTSC and negligible interference, together with digital sound. Sets sell for about $600, not much more than ordinary sets. This has helped fill Japanese production capacity, but is also an acknowledgement that an evolutionary approach to HDTV standards may be needed to educate the market and to phase in HDTV purchases. The next step, EDTV-2, is planned to have a wide screen with 1125 lines, more electronics and full digital sound, after which viewers should be ready to make the move to HDTV. Each stage is 'partially' compatible with the last, as initially EDTV sets will receive NTSC broadcasts, and vice versa, but as the systems diverge technologically converters between the two will be needed. Later EDTV-2 could be close to HDTV quality, possibly with built in converters to receive HDTV transmissions. A concern is that EDTV will be close enough that users will not want to pay the much higher price for HDTV, for quality which to the average viewer is not that different. Even so, this step-by-step approach may be the best chance to establish HDTV, which has to reach moderate price levels in any case to get accepted.[11]

The costs of Hi-Vision so far have included $150 m. spent on R&D for the basic technology by NHK over 25 years, as well as the very much larger amounts spent on equipment development by the Japanese manufacturers, an estimated $1.3 bn.[12] As many as 40 Japanese firms are now developing and offering Hi-Vision products, such as studio equipment, transmission equipment, cameras, recorders, monitors as well as receivers, VCRs, and LDs. However, most of these products may be produced in versions for other standards, so the equipment development costs are not exclusively tied to Hi-Vision and should give the Japanese a huge first mover advantage once a global standard emerges.

(b) MAC (Europe)

The timetable for MAC development is given in Table 8.5. The European broadcasters and manufactures had been considering standards for satellite broadcasting since the early 1980s. The shift in delivery systems gave the opportunity to unify the many different European standards (national variants of PAL and SECAM) with economies of scale in production and Europe-wide transmission. MAC was first developed by the Independent Broadcasting Authority (IBA) in the UK. Progress on agreement was slow until the threat of Hi-Vision concentrated the attention of those concerned. As with many such agreements, an external threat was needed to facilitate co-ordination.[13] By the time of the CCIR meeting in 1986 European Union (EU) member states had a co-ordinated response, with the original MAC repackaged as the first stage of HDTV. A project within the Eureka collaborative R&D programme (Eureka 95) was announced with initial funding of 200 m. ecu ($240 m.). Development is carried out by Thomson, Philips and, at one time, Nokia. The total budget for 1986–92 for Eureka 95 was 625 m. ecu ($750 m.), shared between government and industry, together with other state aid. In 1990 Thomson and Philips agreed to spend $3.2 bn. on a joint venture to develop MAC.[14]

MAC was intended to be introduced in two stages, with an interim standard, D-MAC, providing somewhat enhanced pictures and sound compared to PAL, but without a wide screen. D-MAC would be only partly

Table 8.5.   *Timetable for European HDTV (MAC)*

Date	Event
1983	EBU begins considering DBS standards
1985	IBA exhibits C-MAC standard
	EBU accepts basic MAC for DBS
1986	IBA and BBC oppose MUSE—UK
	French reject MUSE, propose HD-MAC
	Europeans reject NHK standard at CCIR
1987	EUREKA project (EU 95) to develop HD-MAC—ecu 200 m.*
	D2-MAC prototype demonstrated—France, Germany
	Thomson buys RCA brand from GE
1988	D-MAC prototype demonstrated—UK
	MAC adopted for national DBS services
1989	Sky and other DBS begin using PAL—UK, Germany
1990	ARD, ZDF confirm use of D2-MAC—Germany
	BSB begins D-MAC broadcasts—UK
	BSB merges with Sky and abandons MAC—UK
1991	Private broadcasters reject commitment to D2-MAC
1992	Public broadcasts of Olympics planned
	UK blocks further EU support for MAC
1993	MAC abandoned
	EBU indicates it will follow FCC choice

* MAC manufacturers: Thomson, Philips (Nokia).

compatible with PAL, as it could be received on PAL sets but would require adding a converter. This was to be followed by HD-MAC with full HDTV quality, including double the number of lines (1250 versus 625) and a wide screen. HD-MAC pictures were reported to be of slightly lower quality then Hi-Vision. Various versions of the MAC standard have been developed, almost threatening to fragment the standard. D2-MAC, with analog, non-stereo sound, was a 'simplified' version of the full standard, which may be transmitted by copper cable as well as DBS, and was adopted in Germany and France. The UK, with little cable, developed D-MAC, with digital sound. Full-bandwidth standards are B-MAC and C-MAC.

MAC development efforts are mainly concentrated on receiving sets and transmission, rather than studio products. Satellite receivers were on the market by about 1990 which allowed existing sets to receive D-MAC signals. Production D-MAC sets are not generally available. Large scale demonstrations of HD-MAC were planned for the 1992 Olympics, as Japan had done in 1988, but were postponed. MAC development was probably five to eight years behind Hi-Vision and no attempt was expected to be made to challenge the Japanese in the studio or professional display markets. Support for MAC throughout the EU was not uniform and began to unravel after about 1990. A major blow was that although supported by the public broadcasters, private DBS services have chosen PAL. In the UK, Sky Television began broadcasting in February 1989 using PAL rather than D-MAC, more than a year ahead of the officially sanctioned British Satellite Broadcasting (BSB), which was required to use D-MAC. For Sky, MAC offered little and MAC equipment was not ready in time. BSB, licensed in December 1986, only began broadcasting in April 1990, by which time Sky had 1.5 m. viewers. This lead in establishing an installed base ensured the failure of BSB, which was forced to merge with Sky in November 1990 to form British Sky Broadcasting (BSkyB). This removed the only UK MAC service.[15] In 1991 German public DBS stations (ARD, ZDF) only agreed to stay with MAC under pressure from France. PAL and PAL + (with digital sound) offered as much as D-MAC when transmitted by satellite or cable, and most broadcasters were not enthusiastic about investing in a new system which offered little to attract viewers.

A major part of the problem in maintaining consensus was the uneven distribution of benefits. The main beneficiaries of MAC were the French and Dutch manufacturers, Thomson and Philips. The last UK television manufacturer, the Ferguson division of Thorn-EMI, had been sold to Thomson in 1987, and the German manufacturers, Telefunken and Grundig, had been sold to Thomson and Philips respectively. For broadcasters the system looked expensive with little advantage. In particular the German broadcasters were involved in converting former East Germany from SECAM to PAL and PAL+, and did not want further costs. Eureka 95 ended in 1992, but a proposed five year action plan to succeed it, with a total budget of 850 m. ecu ($1.1 bn.), was vetoed by the UK in 1992. Several efforts to maintain EU support were made during this period, but doubts arose even amongst the manufacturers about the technical and economic viability of MAC compared with the new US digital systems. Philips withdrew plans for MAC in January 1993 and in February 1993 the EU declared that it would follow US standards. Both Thomson and Philips were already involved in US consortia for ATV. EU manufacturers, broadcasters and government bodies formed the European Launching Group for Digital Video (ELGDV) to co-ordinate the development and introduction of digital systems.[16]

(c) All-digital ATV (USA)

The US timetable is given in Table 8.6. The US Society of Motion Picture and Television Engineers (SMPTE) set up a task group to study HDTV in 1977, responding to initiatives from Japan, but did not set up the ATSC committee to consider standards until 1981, two years after NHK had demonstrated Hi-Vision in the USA at the SMPTE annual conference. At the 1986 CCIR meeting the USA at first supported Hi-Vision. The main interested parties influencing the ATSC at that time were the US television

Table 8.6.   *Timetable for US HDTV (ATV)*

Date	Event
1977	SMPTE study group on HDTV
1979	NHK demonstration at SMPTE conference
1981	ATSC set up to advise on HDTV
1984	CBS developing studio equipment—Hi-Vision
1985	ATSC supports Hi-Vision
1986	CCIR fails to adopt Hi-Vision
1987	ATSC study group on HDTV
1988	FCC general guidelines—unfavourable to MUSE
1989	US firms (AEA) seek government support—$1.35 bn.*
	DARPA supports $30 m. graphics development
	US Government rejects support
1990	NBC, Thomson, Philips link announced
	FCC requests terrestrial HDTV proposals
	First all-digital signal technology announced—General Instrument
1991	FCC testing of 4 digital and 2 analog systems begins
1993	FCC decision recommends 'grand alliance'
1994	Single ATV prototype expected
1995	HDTV broadcasts possible

* AEA firms: IBM, DEC, Apple, 12 others.

Table 8.7.   *US-produced programmes broadcast in Europe per day, 1985*

Country	Broadcasts (%)
France	16
Germany	25
Italy	31
UK	24
TOTAL	25

Source: ATSC 1985.

and movie producers, who would benefit from a single world standard, and US subsidiaries of Japanese companies. These ensured the US support for the Japanese standard. Programming was especially of interest for the main export market in Europe, which already devotes 25 per cent of its air time to US programmes, as in Table 8.7. The broadcasters and manufacturers so far had shown little interest in HDTV. Most US television manufacturers are foreign owned; the only US-headquartered firm is Zenith, which mainly manufactures in Mexico.[17]

After the attempt to establish Hi-Vision standards failed, the programme producers' interest declined and opposition started to grow from US local broadcasters. The concern of the 1350 or so local stations has not only been that HDTV would be expensive to install, and that costs would be hard for local stations to recover through increased viewing rates. They have been more concerned that HDTV mainly benefits cable and DBS services, who are increasingly strong competitors for the television market.[18] Full HDTV requires satellite or optical cable, which could exclude local stations. In addition, DBS and cable can charge viewers premium rates for the new services while the local stations must rely on effectively fixed advertising revenues. Whereas the need for satellite transmission may initially have limited the threat from HDTV (there are few US DBS services), the in-roads which cable services have made since the early 1980s, and the potential increase in DBS and optical cable services, have left the local stations vulnerable. The introduction of HDTV could be a decisive blow unless the local stations could participate fully.

At the same time US electronics and computer manufacturers became worried that the enormous market for integrated circuits for Japanese HDTV would fund the destruction of the US semiconductor industry. They began major lobbying efforts for HDTV research, seeking huge aid from the Department of Defense. HDTV, with its high demand for integrated circuits and potential spillovers into computing and graphic displays, was portrayed as the last blow to the US electronics industry. Although this generated much excitement these arguments were eventually rejected by the government in November 1989. The Defense Advanced Research Projects Agency (DARPA) agreed in December 1989 to provide $30m. for HDTV graphics research, which has been seen as important symbolic support.[19]

These moves focused opposition to Hi-Vision, and the US Federal Communications Commission (FCC) began to seek a US standard after 1987, largely at the urging of the local broadcasters concerned that cable and DBS services could leave them behind by setting up their own HDTV system.[20] Compared with the speed of the EU response, the FCC has moved slowly in setting standards and the situation only started to become clear by about 1992. The FCC has been keen to protect existing NTSC owners and broadcasters and initially indicated that it would require any HDTV system to be compatible with NTSC. It modified this in 1988 to require that for an interim period programmes broadcast in HDTV must also be made available to NTSC receivers, which allowed non-compatibility provided there were simulcasts.[21] It also made a significant policy shift by deciding, after reviewing the allocation of (scarce) spectrum, that most stations could be allocated one additional 6Mhz channel, but HDTV had to fit within this. Based on these requirements the FCC invited proposals from industry groups for HDTV systems, to be tested beginning in April 1991. The requirement to fit a simulcast signal in only 6 Mhz was a key constraint. It ruled out MUSE in its original form, which required 8.1 Mhz, and MUSE-9, which required one additional channel of 6 Mhz plus an augmentation channel of 3 Mhz.

In a further attempt to let the market generate the standard, testing was not carried out by the FCC directly, which wished to stay clear of charges of 'picking winners'. Instead it was allocated to a private committee of broadcasters, electronics firms and programme makers, the Advanced Television Testing Committee (ATTC), with additional testing by CableLabs and the Advanced Television Evaluation Laboratory (ATEL). The cost of testing has been low, the ATTC's budget being only $15 m., entirely funded by the industry. Testing has been designed to use mainly technical criteria rather than make economic analyses, although system cost was a consideration. The standards were required to be made available to all manufacturers at reasonable royalties. An announcement of the winner was planned for mid-1993, with broadcasts potentially to begin in 1995.

A large part of the FCC's motivation has been to respect the needs of the local broadcasters, who have a good deal of political influence. Although other potential providers of HDTV services, such as DBS and cable services as well as non-broadcast VCR and LD, are not bound by FCC regulations, it would be difficult to establish a standard which was incompatible with an FCC standard, as this would confuse the market and possibly fragment the standard. These other groups, including the Japanese manufacturers, have waited to see what standard would be decided. The local stations' interests seem to have been twofold: to delay HDTV for all services, and, once HDTV was seen as inevitable, to ensure that the stations could compete on an equal footing with the other providers. Had the broadcasters wished to speed up the introduction of HDTV they could well have acted earlier than 1987, and ensured that ATTC would complete testing in less than the year or more planned (proposals were tested consecutively rather than concurrently).[22]

In many ways the stations may have preferred that no one adopts HDTV. It does not benefit the stations as a group, but once one has adopted all are likely to be forced by inter-station competition to adopt in suit—a situation similar to the prisoners' dilemma game, described in chapter two. However, the need to transmit HDTV in the narrow bandwidth may have limited the capability of the standard, so that HDTV as a whole may be less attractive (see below).

The response of the electronics industry, given only about two years to generate standards and prototypes, has been impressive. The first contenders were for ACTV systems, similar in concept to MAC. The main one was developed by RCA Sarnoff Laboratories (an independent organization) and promoted by Thomson. ACTV was derived from NTSC in a similar way that MAC is derived from PAL. It came in two stages, ACTV-I and

ACTV-II. The quality of ACTV was limited by NTSC, which has notoriously poor colour quality due to transmission problems. It would have been broadcast terrestrially. North American Philips and Zenith considered similar systems. NHK considered variants of MUSE which would be compatible with NTSC.[23]

However, by 1991 technology had moved on quickly and four of the six proposals finally submitted to ATTC were all-digital systems. The six contenders are given in Table 8.8. Although it was known that digital signals are highly suitable for compression, little work had been done on this for video and it was thought that the technology was years away from development. In fact DSP techniques originally developed for military and aerospace uses were soon adapted to the task. Digital systems were rendered feasible by the continual advances in semiconductor and microprocessor technology generally. The reductions in cost and increases in performance which had taken place since the analog systems had first been proposed, made digital solutions cost effective which could probably not have been considered in 1986. General Instruments (GI), in association with the Massachusetts Institute of Technology (MIT), announced a digital compression system in 1991 which changed the course of HDTV decisively. The four digital proposals were two systems from GI/MIT, called Digicipher (interlaced and progressive versions), one from Philips/Thomson/Sarnoff/NBC, called Advanced Digital Television (ADTV), and one from Zenith/AT&T, called 'Spectrum Compatible' SC-HDTV. The two analog systems were a compressed version of Hi-Vision, called Narrow-MUSE, and an EDTV system from the Philips/Thomson/Sarnoff/NBC consortium. NHK continued to argue that fully digital systems were unnecessarily advanced for a consumer product.

The outcome was announced in February 1993. ATTC found value in each of the digital systems and recommended that the three groups co-operate in a 'grand alliance' for ATV to develop a single standard.[24] The analog systems, including MUSE, were eliminated. The final test was planned for September 1993, with prototypes expected by mid-1994. There

Table 8.8. *US HDTV system proposals to FCC*

System	Proposer	Method	Lines	Scan (f.p.s.)
Digicipher	General Instrument/MIT	Digital	1050	30
Digicipher	General Instrument/MIT	Digital	787.5	60
SC-HDTV	Zenith/AT&T	Digital	787.5	60
ADTV	Philips/Thomson/Sarnoff/NBC	Digital	1050	30
ACTV	Philips/Thomson/Sarnoff/NBC	Analog	1125	30
Narrow-Muse	NHK	Analog	1125	30

have been some differences over standard specifications, including whether the system should be interlaced or progressive and whether there should be different versions for different applications, but the schedule seems to be on course.[25] ATV promises to combine technologies from around the world. Transmission elements will depend heavily on DSP techniques led by the USA, and EU manufacturers should participate through their membership of the grand alliance. The basic ATV standards are openly available and Japanese manufacturers should be able to adapt the many products developed for Hi-Vision to the new standard. How great the gains are to each group is not clear, but the fact that all regions should be participating to some extent should help the international acceptance of the ATV standard.

The costs to a television station of converting to HDTV have been estimated as about $10–12 m. for the first stations, falling to half that in a few years, and perhaps only $1 m. to pass through a network signal. These costs are not very different from those of re-equipping a station using existing technology, so that if the introduction of HDTV can be phased in as equipment needs replacing—and the period during which simulcasting is needed is not too long—the incremental cost to the stations need not be very high.[26]

There remains a question of how closely ATV may be interfaced with computer applications. The US computer industry had originally been opposed to Hi-Vision on the grounds that whoever developed HDTV would become a serious threat in computer graphics markets. Current concerns are that HDTV may be hardr to adapt to computer uses than once thought. To accommodate the resolution and flexibility needed for computer graphics, some observers have advocated Open Systems transmission standards capable of even higher resolution screens with 1600 or 2000 lines, and progressive scanning rather than interlacing. Analog system such as Hi-Vision were designed around the transmission problems of television and are not suited to computer interfacing. ATV is easier to interface with graphics, computer data, text and still images; nevertheless the digital proposals use only 1050 or 787.5 lines, partly dictated by the bandwidth restrictions.

2.4 Market prospects

TV and video products account for about 40 per cent of the world consumer electronics market, which had $76 bn. annual sales in 1986. Predictions for the HDTV market vary. In the late 1980s, Nomura estimated the market for HDTV at $25 bn. annually for receivers and $16 bn. for VCR by the year 2010. MITI projected in 1987 that by the year 2000 the HDTV market would be $40 bn. The AEA also estimated that the total market would be $40 bn., with $11 bn. in the USA. The EU has estimated the European market for television, including HDTV, at $70 bn. Most of these estimates must be seen as optimistic projections of the total television market and the rate at which it would switch to HDTV, based on previous experience with successful consumer products.

Forecasts of both the size of the market and the rate of growth have been scaled back considerably since then, following the delays in introducing HDTV and greater realism about the rate at which consumers may adopt the new system, especially given its cost and performance compared with existing systems—such as current television delivered by cable or DBS, and EDTV. Large-scale adoption by viewers is now not expected before the end of the century, and the system could still flop. However, although the early figures may be unrealistic, they set the scale for future markets, and the size if not the timing may still be valid. There are currently around 680 m. television sets installed world-wide, of which Japan has 71 m., USA 195 m., Europe 134 m. (Unesco, 1988).

Most consumer responses to HDTV demonstrations have been very positive as to the picture, but unimpressed by the size and cost. Sony predicts that HDTV sets (Hi-Vision or ATV) will eventually be priced less than twice as much as current colour television, at around $1,000. With prices now around $6,000, down from about $40,000 a few years ago, this target seems achievable with large volume production. However, a price of $1,000 may not compare well with EDTV, which may also be around $500 and offer many of the features of HDTV. The first HDTV sets on the US market are expected to cost about $4,000. In some professional uses, Hi-Vision sets are now fairly common for graphic displays.

2.5 Comparison with the introduction of colour television

There are several parallels between HDTV and the introduction of colour television in the 1960s. The NTSC colour television standard for the USA was set by the FCC in 1954, following a contest between systems from CBS and RCA. Although the CBS system arrived first and had initially been adopted by the FCC, in 1950, it was later dropped in favour of the RCA system. The RCA system was technically more advanced (the CBS system used mechanical rather than electrical picture scanning) and, critically, was compatible with the old black and white standard. Reputedly, compatibility was insisted on at the time partly for emergency broadcast reasons. This experience probably influenced the FCC in requiring that HDTV broadcasts should be receivable in some way be existing television sets. Though technically unimpressive, the NTSC standard was also adopted by Japan in 1960. European systems were developed ten years later (PAL in UK and Germany, SECAM in France) which were technically superior to NTSC. It was hoped that a world-wide colour standard similar to PAL could be adopted at a CCIR meeting in 1966. As at the HDTV meeting 20 years later, national interests prevailed and no agreement could be reached. Although PAL was technically preferable, France was committed to SECAM and the USA and Japan had already installed NTSC. National standards have additional minor differences, so that even PAL standards within Europe are not quite equivalent.[27]

For colour television there was a lag of ten years after setting the standard until large scale purchase of colour sets began in the USA in the mid-1960s, and it was 1975 before 50 per cent of US homes owned a colour set. Although most television stations had adopted colour capacity almost immediately, it took many years before large amounts of colour programming were available.

3. INFLUENCE OF PRODUCT STANDARDS

3.1 Value of a global standard

Compatibility standards define the interface requirements between complementary products. For television, three groups of products and services are needed for the system to work: programme production, broadcasting and television sets. Interface standards are needed between programme production and broadcasting and between broadcasting and receiving. Although it is possible to have different standards for production and transmission—indeed, programmes produced under one studio standard may often be broadcast abroad in a different standard—there are limits to how much conversion may conveniently take place (e.g. converting between different frame rates or line counts) and generally a single standard is necessary throughout the whole system. Conversion is also expensive and time-consuming.

Standards add value to a product by network effects, working through the demand for broadcast services. Any standard is more valuable the larger the network of core and complementary goods. On the broadcasting side, the more receivers the greater the audience and so the greater the number and variety of broadcast services and programming which may be offered. Similarly, the more programmes there are available the more viewers buy receivers and watch television. This makes programmes and transmission less expensive per head and increases the advertising revenue available for programming, in turn making owning a set more valuable. On the production side, the more studios using a production standard the easier the distribution of programmed output, as well as the greater the availability of equipment and trained personnel. Between the two, having the same standard in production and transmission saves the cost and quality reduction involved in conversion.

With a single standard there may also be economies of scale in manufacturing and development for studio equipment, transmission equipment and receivers, designed around a single set of specifications. This increases the supply and lowers prices. Provided there is open access to the standard, this also increases competition, further reducing prices.

The value of a single world-wide standard is that these demand and supply side economies are taken on a global scale. Savings are in programme production and distribution, without conversion costs or loss of picture quality, and in world-wide broadcasting, again without conversion problems. Broadcasting and production, for good or ill, are becoming more and more global industries. Programmes are produced for international markets, often as joint ventures between corporations from different countries. US programming accounts for 25 per cent of broadcasts in Europe, possibly more in Japan. Global media corporations, such as News Corporation and CNN, have appeared and are likely to be permanent features of the world economy. Broadcasting is crossing national boundaries, especially aided by satellite broadcasting and cable. A news network such as CNN now supplies the same programmes live world-wide. The advantages of a single standard are particularly strong for live events, such as news and sports, as instantaneous standards conversion is difficult. The high cost and often reduced picture quality of Eurovision links, broadcast between European countries nominally using similar standards, are witness to this.

On the manufacturing side, a regional market such as Europe may not be large enough to achieve full scale economies in equipment production. Although the scale may be enough to ensure that direct manufacturing costs can be brought in line with world levels, as was one of the original motives for a pan-European MAC standard, this does not account for the duplication of development costs, especially for the range of equipment needed. Development of technology and products for Hi-Vision have already cost $1.3 bn. and MAC was expected to be equally expensive (with plans for a total of $1.8 bn. in EU programmes plus the $3.2 bn. Philips/Thomson joint venture to exploit MAC). Digital ATV may be just as costly. These costs must ultimately be borne by the viewer or the taxpayer. Development and manufacturing economies may be most significant for studio and transmission products, with smaller unit sales. The effect on equipment prices due to the adoption of MAC was inevitably upward. Significantly, Thomson put most of its effort for MAC into developing receivers and broadcast equipment, as the studio production market was already covered by Hi-Vision.

A major advantage of a new system is also that it gives an opportunity to correct the current fragmentation of colour television standards, between three major systems and further national differences within these. The demand for a single world standard to support global media, and the escalating costs of developing new television equipment, may be decisive motivations for establishing HDTV. It may be the best chance for uniting global standards and offer enough to each of the interested groups (manufacturers, programme producers, broadcasters and viewers) for it to be worthwhile making the joint investments. The fact that two of these groups, the producers and broadcasters, are becoming increasingly concentrated makes it more likely that the joint investments will be made, as the coordination problems of negotiating simultaneous investments are simplified.[28] These potential network advantages work in addition to the product attractiveness of HDTV, i.e. HDTV may be adopted not only because of high quality pictures, but because it reduces the duplication costs of the existing three-way system. In a sense, HDTV may provide a vehicle for setting global standards, and if successful will greatly influence the structure of the world-wide broadcasting industry. Also, other prospective markets in computers, telecommunications, graphics and printing will not be organized nationally, making the case stronger for a single standard.

3.2 Strategies for setting standards

The aim of standards strategy is to build up the installed base of support for the standard and establish its credibility with potential adopters. For television the base consists of the combination of programme producers, broadcasters, viewers and manufacturers. The main aim in a contest is to be first to build the installed base to a 'self-sustaining' level. In HDTV many of the usual market oriented strategies for doing this are in evidence, but the main difference between this and purely market determined standards is the central role of the standards authority. The standards authority in this case has a very different status than the consensual industry bodies in, say, the computer industry. Broadcasting standards within each country are controlled to a greater or lesser extent by national regulatory authorities. These authorities have the legal responsibility for the assignment, and reassignment, of rights to use the broadcast spectrum. Thus they not only represent the common interests of the industry, but have independent interests. This introduces a further player into the standardization process. Part of strategy is involved in influencing adoption by the various groups via market forces, and an equally important part is in ensuring the adoption of the standard by the standards bodies, national and international.

For most broadcasting standards these two elements of strategy interact, so that evidence of broad market support for a standard will influence the authority in its favour, while official adoption may be a prerequisite for establishing the standard. The standards authorities often have the power to veto a standard and unless endorsed by the authority a market standard is unlikely to have much credibility. However, official adoption is not sufficient to ensure success for a standard on its own. There may also be ways to bypass or pre-empt official adoption, by creating strong demand for a standard which the authority may have to acknowledge. We may separate strategy into these two aspects, to establish support by market forces and to ensure adoption by the standards authority.

(a) Market strategies

As with any new product, introduction of HDTV is partly a question of product development, marketing, distribution, and market education. As a new standard there are also special considerations not covered by conventional strategy. Some of the strategies with particular relevance to HDTV are as follows:

Commitment: The key to standards adoption is the installed base. Establishing a base requires large up front investments to develop the standard, and may also involve subsidizing adoption by users and producers of complementary goods. Methods include promotion and low initial pricing to attract early users, encouraging complementary production and alliances with other manufacturers to ensure adequate supply of products. The sponsor must be fully committed to the standard to make these investments and to ensure the standard's credibility, as below.

Credibility: Early adopters make decisions based on their expectations of which standard will win, making the credibility of the standard very important. This may lead to enormous pre-announcement activity and a reluctance by manufacturers to launch products ahead of standards approval for fear of confusing consumers. It helps explain how a standard may lose momentum once the initial enthusiasm is diffused and why a gradualist approach to standards may be ineffective. Maintaining credibility adds to the need for commitment and indicates that openly following hedging strategies may be difficult. Hedging may be necessary to reduce risk but it also helps the credibility of competing systems. When Japanese manufacturers stated that they were able to produce to any standard, this reduced the potential payoffs for the EU and US manufacturers from pursuing their own standards and so may have weakened their resolve, but it also raised the credibility of these other standards and lowered that of Hi-Vision.

Timing: The dynamics of standards are that once a standard has sufficient installed base, new buyers gravitate to it, making it cumulatively even more attractive and creating a 'bandwagon'. The critical period for a new standard is the 'window of opportunity' from the time the standard has reached a basic level of user acceptability until it or another standard has enough bandwagon momentum to win. Being first to the market is not enough, since the product may be not yet acceptable and the standard premature, leaving its supporters locked into an obsolete system. Hi-Vision should in theory have had timing advantages, being years ahead with products which were believed to be ready for the market. Some of its problems may be due to trying to set a standard prematurely, even after years of development.

Co-ordination: The main strategic problem faced by new standards is to build up the installed base in several inter-dependent areas at the same time. No one wants to adopt until the standard is proven, which acts as an introduction barrier. The problem is that instead of the usual two producer groups to co-ordinate (e.g. hardware and software producers in computers) before offering an acceptable package to the users, for HDTV there are three complementary producers—programme producers, broadcasters, and manufacturers. One way to simplify this is to separate the problem into two stages of studio production and transmission, with only two producer groups each, as the Japanese manufacturers have attempted to do.

Replacement standards: Replacement of an existing standard with a strong installed base is often much more difficult than establishing a new standard in a new market. The new standard has to offer sufficient improvement over the existing one to justify not only the new investment by users and producers, but also to overcome the network externalities of the established standard. This 'excess inertia' makes standards very difficult to change when there are large sunk investments in complementary goods. For viewers the incremental advantage of HDTV over colour television has to justify the full expense of a new set. This is partly offset if the user can delay adoption until an old set needs replacing, but usually adopting the new system will mean making the old one obsolete. Also, some of the network benefits of the existing system in the stock of television programmes in the old format are balanced by the ability to present the stock of movies and live programming in high definition.

Avenues of entry: It may be easier to introduce a new standard in steps, first in a small segment of the market and then expand from this installed base, rather than try to co-ordinate investments in the main market right away. On a large scale this is the logic of the separation into two stages, production and transmission. It is also the logic of trying to establish an installed base via standalone VCR/HDTV combinations, to create a base of sets to attract broadcasters (see below). For a replacement standard it may be possible to use the existing standard as the base, introducing minor modifications then using this as the installed base for further modifications, as in EDTV. This is the argument for an evolutionary rather than radical approach, discussed below. HDTV standards should also be easier to establish if they can be linked to developments in computers and communications which already have huge installed bases, though as yet it is not clear how similar the requirements in these different areas will be.

(b) Official standards

The complication for radio and television, as for other regulated networks such as telecommunications, is that standards are not a pure market issue but depend on being approved by the industry standards authority. Broadcasting standards are central to HDTV. Although it is possible to split the adoption into production and transmission standards the standard loses much of its value and credibility if different standards are used. The risk of relying on official adoption is that this does not guarantee the system will be successful, especially as the authority is removed from the market and may be poorly placed to judge the business prospects. Official bodies necessarily tend to concentrate on technical criteria, which can be evaluated objectively and appear impartial, rather than economic potential, which can usually only be resolved by market competition and which firms are less keen to reveal to competitors ahead of time. Approval takes time and effort, with a lot of political lobbying, and may still need to be backed up by market pressures. Even in Japan official sponsorship of Hi-Vision did not ensure its success.

Part of the issue is that there are limits to the powers of the national standards authorities and there are several routes by which they may be bypassed by more attractive standards generated by the market. An important gap is that national standards bodies do not regulate all media or even all the radio spectrum, especially for uses such as satellite broadcasting which are essentially international in character. Thus, D2-MAC standards were bypassed in the UK by Sky Television broadcasting PAL on satellite channels not covered by standards regulations. Also it was only the threat of cable, DBS and VCR preempting HDTV standards which induced the US local broadcasters to seek regulated standards before it was too late.

The further risk of focusing too closely on official adoption is that standards body approval becomes the focus of the game, the object being to influence the regulatory authorities rather than ensuring that the standard is acceptable in the market place. This can easily become non-productive. The means are political as much as economic, a mix of building market pressures, as above, and lobbying at the national and international levels. There are many questions about the effectiveness of the official approval process, and of whether policy interests can and should outweigh market forces, discussed below.[29]

3.3 Evolutionary and radical standards

One of the key distinctions for HDTV is that it is a replacement standard. Introduction is especially difficult as the new standard has to compete against an existing network, and has to offer significant improvement to overcome the incumbent's network externalities. In such a case it may be easier to introduce the system in steps as an evolutionary standard, each stage compatible with the old. The evolutionary approach was widely promoted by MAC supporters. At each step, old sets may receive the new signals (backwards compatibility) and new sets may receive the old broadcasts (forwards compatible), though without improved quality. In a true evolutionary approach the old standard is included as a subset of the new and compatibility does not need old sets to be fitted with a converter or 'gateway' technology. For HDTV 'evolutionary' is something of a misnomer, as some form of converter at the set is needed for all standards, including MAC.

Evolutionary standards are about timing decisions for producers, broadcasters, and viewers. For each group they reduce the investment hurdle as the standard can tap the existing installed base. Each player has more freedom to choose when, and if, they should switch to HDTV, reducing the initial investment and risk. Broadcasters do not have to set up a new service without any viewers but can operate a service which reaches both old and new. They can choose when to upgrade without losing audiences. Features can be added in stages and the investment may be spread out in smaller lumps as old equipment wears out. Firms may also monitor the progress of HDTV to reduce risk. With a radical standard broadcasters must make large up-front investments in equipment, initially without an audience. If they adopt HDTV, they must either abandon their old audience or, if bandwidth is available, broadcast simultaneously in two standards.[30]

Viewers have similar concerns, though the investment and risks are lower. Evolutionary introduction may be smoother, allow users to be educated to the new product in steps, and get introduction underway more quickly. If HDTV programmes can be received on current sets viewers can upgrade when they wish, as HDTV services expand and as old sets wear out. They may be 'educated' into the charms and expense of HDTV gradually. Programme producers also may prefer their upgrades in stages, though they are somewhat insulated from the problem as they may switch to HDTV when they wish, ahead of the market if needed, and convert to any standard at output.

Problems with the evolutionary strategy are that although the first step is quicker the whole process of introduction takes longer and the total costs may be greater. Paradoxically it may also further entrench the old system. Each step has a cost and has to be a sufficient improvement over the last to justify the new expenditure. By breaking down the overall performance improvement into small increments, the introduction could stall. This happened with D-MAC, which could not prove that it was significantly better than PAL, whereas full MAC, had it been available, might have justified the switch. Perhaps most important in the long term is that evolutionary standards restrict the technology, making it less attractive. It must be tailored to fit the old standard, which may be obsolete but held in place by inertia. A radical system provides a clean break. It may be more advanced and have more development potential. New technology also gives an opportunity to change the market structure.

A radical strategy, setting up a parallel network, is indicated where the attractions of the new standard are strong, compatibility restricts technology too much, and converters are expensive. An evolutionary strategy, building on the old standard in steps, may be more effective where the new system does not have a clear advantage and the network externalities of the existing standard are strong. Until the arrival of ATV, the latter seemed to be the case for HDTV. Both Hi-Vision and MAC offered an evolutionary route with compatibility between stages using converters. Hi-Vision had tried a radical approach but was forced to reconsider. It relies more on converters than MAC, which is technically closer to PAL than Hi-Vision is to any of the three standards it is designed to replace. For ATV the requirement not to impose new costs on existing set owners ruled out converters, and once analog ACTV was rejected in favour of digital systems, a radical approach using simulcast was unavoidable. Even so, EDTV may still be part of ATV introduction, as part of educating the market and filling manufacturing capacity until HDTV comes into its own.

4. MARKET STRATEGIES

Although most attention has been focused on the national and international standards bodies, in the long run what has been happening in the market may be most important. Until recently almost all of the significant activity was by the Japanese manufacturers. They have used some instructive strategies to build the installed base, if with mixed success. An aim has been to establish global markets for Hi-Vision products and hope that market pressures would convince international standards bodies to adopt this as the standard. These strategies have been put on hold by opposition from national standards bodies, since on political grounds the Japanese could not be seen to impose a standard on the rest of the world. Once international standards are agreed these strategies should come into force to establish HDTV, and we concentrate here on understanding these market routes.

The problems for HDTV have been in two areas: to develop a product which is acceptable to the market, and to coordinate adoption by the various players. HDTV is still being developed, and there remain doubts about its consumer acceptability. The initial attempts to establish HDTV standards may have taken place before an acceptable design exists. The technology has developed rapidly and has threatened to overtake each standard as it appeared. Efforts are underway to improve HDTV, in particular to develop low cost flat displays and reduce prices to make the product acceptable to the users, and digital transmission technology should make the system more attractive to users and complementary producers. Thus the window of opportunity may only now be opening.

The co-ordination issue is that there are no fewer than four interested parties to co-ordinate: the manufacturers, programme producers, broadcasters and viewers, each unwilling to adopt independently. These exist afresh in each country. With Hi-Vision, by separating programme production from broadcasting, the Japanese simplified the co-ordination problem by in effect partitioning the installed base, treating the different groups as far as possible in isolation. Whatever standards are now adopted these strategies are likely to continue with a three-pronged attack: concentrating on studio production standards ahead of transmission standards, building an independent base of receivers and other equipment in niches such as video or cable, and allowing broadcasters and viewers flexibility using evolutionary standards. The fact that the basic standards for Hi-Vision and ATV are open should also be seen as part of strategy.

(a) Studio standards

Sony has said that the key to HDTV is programming.[31] This may be set up independently of the rest of the broadcast chain. If studio standards are high enough they may be converted to any of the transmission standards without appreciable loss of quality. Establishing the production standards first gives an initial base from which to attack the transmission standard. The system is also being developed for use in film production and other areas, giving HDTV bases in niches outside television.

This part of the Hi-Vision strategy appears to have been successful. NHK claim with justification that 'more Hi-Vision hardware is on the market each year, putting it well on the way to becoming the *de facto* standard for studio and the other areas.'[32] This range includes cameras, recorders, editors, film readers and printers, and special effects. The same is not true for film production, which remains unconvinced that HDTV is an adequate substitute for 35 mm.[33] It is possible that this situation could change as the use of animation and digital editing in film making increases. It should also play a role in the expected growth in multi-media. Hi-Vision is also entering the market for high quality display systems such as in graphic design, printing, computer graphics, medical imaging, and reference libraries. Future uses are in information technology, telecommunications, and defence applications.[34]

Since this equipment uses digital technology it should be more than capable of accommodating digital transmission standards, either on output or by modifying the equipment. There is little risk for production studios in choosing Hi-Vision today, even though ATV may be chosen for broadcasting. Manufacturers have stated that they have versions of equipment ready whatever format is chosen. Output may also be converted down to the existing television standards.[35]

(b) 'Stand-alone' receivers

'Stand-alone' HDTV using VCRs and laser discs with pre-recorded movies gives a route to establish an audience for HDTV programming which under

some circumstances could pre-empt broadcasting standards. If the base of
sets becomes large enough this would create demand for HDTV broadcasts. This might be hard for the authorities to refuse, depending on how far
broadcasting has progressed by that time. DBS or optical cable also provide
a route for HDTV entry independent of the standards authorities. Standards for these media are not regulated in either the USA or Europe in the
same way as terrestrial broadcasting. As noted previously, it was this threat
of VCR and private DBS that finally motivated the US broadcasters to
press for compatible HDTV standards, allowing them to participate centrally in HDTV and control its introduction.[36]

The manufacturers have not pressed this route. Although VCRs are
ready they have been reluctant to sell them outside Japan until broadcast
standards are decided, to avoid confusing the consumer and of splitting the
standard, with different systems for VCR and broadcasting. The cable and
DBS operators have held back from new services for similar reasons. There
are also the usual problems of coordinating core and complementary goods
in a new market. The main target for Hi-Vision currently is not the consumer but the industrial market, for uses ranging from promotion to computer monitors.[37]

(c) Evolutionary strategy

HDTV has provided an interesting contrast between the radical approach
of Hi-Vision and the evolutionary approach of MAC. Faced with tepid
consumer interest the Japanese also switched to an evolutionary strategy.
They have accepted that this may be the only way to establish the standard
at the moment. It is the quickest way to make a start, and appeals to their
manufacturers at a time when they need new consumer products to take
over from declining colour television and VCR sales.

Hi-Vision is being pursued in Japan in three hierarchical stages. Clear-
Vision (EDTV) sets and VCRs are on sale in Japan and broadcasts started
in 1989. This removes much of the interference in conventional television,
and adds digital sound. The next stage will use a wide screen and simulate
Hi-Vision picture quality. The third stage is full Hi-Vision. Existing sets can
receive Clear-Vision signals but ignore the extra data. Converters are reportedly under development which would allow NTSC and Clear-Vision
sets to receive Hi-Vision signals. For later EDTV sets these converters
could be built into the set, so that the broadcaster may switch to Hi-Vision
without losing an audience, and viewers have Hi-Vision broadcasts ready
when they wish to trade up. Stations and viewers may postpone investment
in HDTV until it looks more certain to pay off. However, the actual cost of
converting broadcasting and studio equipment is not greatly different for
EDTV and HDTV.[38]

The European plan, which started the interest in evolutionary systems,
was very similar. D-MAC and D2-MAC broadcasts started in 1990 but were

mainly only received on PAL and SECAM sets. Of the 2.8m. European households receiving satellite television in 1991 only 170,000 (6 per cent) used D2-MAC. Broadcasts of MAC stopped in the UK with the demise of BSB in late 1990 and in the rest of Europe in 1993.

(d) Open standards

The basic standards for Hi-Vision and ATV are open. NHK's policy for Hi-Vision has been to make its patents available to any manufacturer, Japanese or foreign, at minimum cost. ATV standards are required by the FCC to be made available under similar conditions. This does not cover other features of products developed around the standards, but it does rule out proprietary control of the core standard. This encouraged a large number of Japanese manufacturers to adopt Hi-Vision, which helps build the installed base more quickly and establishes credibility. There is more competition, the standard is likely to be around a long time, and access will not be restricted at some future date.

In contrast the main objectives in developing MAC were to keep the technology proprietary, with great attention given to the security of the basic MAC patents. This restricted support and made MAC products more expensive and risky. Manufacturers showed little enthusiasm for MAC, other than the direct beneficiaries, Thomson and Philips. In the USA the intention seems to be try to gain some substantial part of the market for ATV systems, particularly transmission, but to accept that much of the equipment will be foreign made. Attempts to insist on progressive rather than interlaced scanning, which would benefit US computer makers, were rejected by the US and grand alliance manufacturers as this would harm ATV's chances of success.

5. ROLE OF STANDARDS INSTITUTIONS

5.1 Policy aims

Some questions for government standards policy are how the approval process takes place, how it compares with market determined standards and whether it can be improved. There are a number of issues concerning the interaction between market forces and policy. Some government involvement in television standards is unavoidable because of the need to allocate broadcast channels. However, other interests inevitably become part of the process. Standards may be used to further other policy aims, particularly to protect national industries. These may distort the standards and make them less attractive. However, intervention may also avoid some of the problems of market standards, such as fragmentation and stranding.

At one level HDTV shows the risks in a strategy relying too heavily on official approval unless also backed by market forces. Official standards often concentrate on technical measures, which may bear little relation to potential commercial success. Agreement is hard to achieve and even when achieved the consensus may not hold. International agreement for HDTV has still not been reached and if a global standard emerges now it is likely to be the result of market-mediated competition and co-operation between national standards rather than negotiation. The pan-European consensus broke down once competition from other standards became intense. At another level, the experience with ATV standards in the USA may provide a useful model for involving markets in developing standards. Though strongly influenced by a particular interest group the process developed an advanced standard in a short time, with good prospects for being accepted globally.

5.2 Technical focus

The focal point for international opposition to Hi-Vision was the CCIR conference in 1986. Although Japanese manufacturers had prepared their position by ensuring that working parties had recommended the standard and had the support of the US standards body, the standard was rejected by the Europeans. At first sight this failure may appear surprising. The advantages of a single global standard were apparent in an age of world-wide communications. Hi-Vision was considered technically adequate and each of the objections raised by the Europeans were answerable. Concerns were that as a studio standard it would not convert adequately to HD-MAC, that it was not a replacement for film, and that the images could not be manipulated digitally were answered within Hi-Vision.[39] Other arguments, that as a radically new standard it would place an unfair cost on broadcasters and viewers, were countered by the promise of converters, and eventually the Hi-Vision strategy was modified to include an evolutionary path with EDTV. The objections did not in themselves justify an entirely new standard with its own set of problems.

Committee standards are often negotiated at a technical level using apparently objective criteria such as technical merit, availability, applicability and cost, but behind these may be more powerful commercial and political issues. Technologists are often surprised that the technically most advanced standard is not adopted, but this ignores vital commercial interests which may be too important to the firms involved to be negotiated away in a committee. Resolution may require market competition, as has been shown by the experience with MAC and indeed with Hi-Vision, in the market.

5.3 Negotiating conflicts

Agreement is needed between four different interest groups: the programme producers, broadcasters, manufacturers and viewers. We may add a fifth, the standards bodies themselves. Each group has further divisions, such as film and television producers; cable, DBS and local broadcasters; studio, transmission, television receiver and VCR equipment manufacturers; national authorities, policy makers and international bodies. There are also groups who are not yet directly represented, in markets to be opened up by the new technology, such as in computing and other electronics. It is not feasible to cover the interests of all these groups in committee negotiations, where agreement is voluntary and each group effectively has veto power.

Progress towards international standards approval may be seen as the rise and fall in the influence of different groups. In Japan the interests of the producers, broadcaster, and manufacturers coincided. The main groups threatened by HDTV in Europe are the few remaining television manufacturers and in the USA are the local television broadcasters and electronics firms. They have successfully blocked the Japanese standard. At first programme producers supported Hi-Vision but later the other groups became more active and blocked the standard.

In Europe the television manufacturers are influential as they still supply the majority of sets. The market has been protected partly by the PAL patents, which expired in the mid-1980s. Firms feared that Hi-Vision could be the end of television manufacture in Europe, while MAC would continue the patent protection. However, after the merger activity in the 1980s only two firms were left, Thomson and Philips. Other European countries saw less value in supporting MAC, private DBS services rejected it and MAC was dropped.

In the USA, the television manufacturers are less influential, as most leading brands are now foreign owned, though there is still an active studio equipment industry. The broadcast networks and local stations were initially poorly organized, and this allowed early decisions to be determined by the programme producers, who wanted Hi-Vision. Later the broadcasters became involved and endorsement of Hi-Vision was dropped. These were joined by component manufacturers and computer firms. The result is that the FCC has sought a standard favourable to the local broadcasters, but fairly neutral to US manufacturing interests. Until the all-digital proposals the manufacturers most likely to benefit from a separate US standard were French and Dutch multinationals. The all-digital proposals have breathed more life into the issue with US transmission technology likely to be of central importance.

Given the conflicting interests represented in the national and international standards bodies, it may be missing the point to call the lack of agreement so far a failure of institutions. The standards bodies can only represent the interests of their members, and these are at variance. National standards bodies may have powers to co-ordinate domestic efforts; at the international level agreements are voluntary and can only operate by consensus. The committee may express differences which must be resolved elsewhere. With many interested parties with something to lose, market competition and co-operation may be the only recourse.

Given all this, it seems clear that the Japanese innovators could have handled their strategy better. With hindsight it may have been naive to expect automatic adoption, especially given the history of colour television. While divisions may have been unavoidable, more effort to share the benefits and enrol support from national manufacturers and broadcasters would have helped. Perhaps this was not appreciated in 1980. The reputation of the Japanese for keeping manufacturing and components supply at home certainly fuelled protectionist arguments. More sharing of the manufacturing technology, not just for programming, would have helped allay suspicions.[40] A more even sharing of benefits may occur with ATV, which should have the US and European support which eluded Hi-Vision.

5.4 Combining official and market standards

The eternal problem for standards policy is balancing the roles of market forces and standards body approval. Agreeing on standards ahead of product development may avoid duplication of effort, take confusion out of the market, avert costly standards wars and avoid fragmented standards. Unfortunately such a situation rarely arises. Yet standards body leadership remains the philosopher's stone of product innovation. It is difficult to define a standard before development, which usually means competing proposals for standards from the beginning. The standards bodies are not well placed to decide what the market wants. They may seek elegant technical solutions, although commercially successful standards are often not technically the most advanced. They also take a long time to come to agreement, whereas standards success depends on timing. Finally, they are open to vested interests, in a contest which would be carried out very differently in the market-place.

The US process for combining market and official standards processes in an R&D contest may be a useful example for avoiding the difficulties of centralized standards while still deciding a single standard before services are started. Competition (between market participants if not between market products) is used to generate proposals, but centralized testing is used to select the winner. The regulator set goals for standards but put few constraints on the means used to achieve those goals. The industry responded by developing a system which was advanced enough to appeal to the range of interests above. Most important, the process should avoid the fragmentation of the standard which could occur if the standard had been left entirely to the market.

However the US process has not avoided the problem of allowing an external policy agenda to restrict the standard and possibly reduce its attractiveness. The requirement for transmission within a single additional terrestrial channel has led to a simplified version of HDTV which may not provide such high quality pictures possible with broader satellite channels. Protecting the interests of the US local broadcasters may yet cost HDTV dearly. Part of the problem with the US position is the contradiction of regulating standards in one medium for a system which is transmitted better by other (DBS and cable). National authorities in the USA and elsewhere are closely involved in regulating terrestrial broadcasting channels in the lower frequency ranges (below 1 Ghz or 1,000 Mhz) used by current television, where the radio spectrum is most congested. Their role for the higher frequency channels used in satellite broadcasting (3 Ghz to 30 Ghz), where there is much more spectrum available, is more limited, and has mainly consisted of allocating spectrum, with the format of the channels left to the operators.

One way to avoid this conflict may be to treat all media equally and leave standards completely to the market, with broadcasters able to trade spectrum to establish a winner. But there may be valid reasons for trying to set standards centrally, *ex ante*, for terrestrial broadcasting, which do not apply in the less congested higher frequencies.[41] There is less need for regulation in the high frequencies where ample unused spectrum allows services more scope for competition. Terrestrial channels are a scarce resource, with only 1 Ghz of bandwidth for television, radio, mobile radio, cellular telephone and other uses. This would be wasted if it were fragmented between incompatible standards, as can easily happen with market determined standards. Market processes for correcting fragmentation, such as by allowing services to sell spectrum, may not be effective for terrestrial broadcasting, since sales of the limited resource affect consumer interests, but are made by firms. For example, networks may be established for a local standard using the only available channels, and an entrant wanting to introduce a more widely supported standard would have to replace the whole local network of broadcasters and users. Fully market derived standards may leave significant pockets of stranded services and users, which can only be replaced in blocks, probably over a long period.[42]

An alternative is to limit HDTV to the satellite channels and cable services with enough spectrum for its needs, as Japan and Europe have already done, rather than try to tailor it to an unsuitable terrestrial medium. This would free scarce terrestrial channels for other uses such as cellular telephone and other telecommunications, with pressing needs for more spectrum.[43] The dilemma is that this also deprives broadcasters and consumers of choices.

6. CONCLUSION

The case has illustrated some of the complexities of trying to establish international standards in the presence of strong national interests. These interests take effect via negotiations between national standards bodies in international committees. HDTV does not speak strongly for the international standards institutions as co-ordinating mechanisms. Although there seems to be a net advantage in a single world standard we may still see incompatible systems. Part of the difficulty is that the standards authority in each country has the power, and responsibility, to set standards centrally, so that players become grouped in national blocks, each representing an array of interests. Also the history of existing standards and the institutions for controlling standards differ between countries, and these lead to genuine differences in national interests. Yet at the international level, agreement must be by consensus, and this is hard to achieve.

Perhaps surprisingly, the more cohesive policies in Japan and Europe have been less successful in generating standards which the rest of the world can support than the more flexible approach taken in the USA. Central direction has shown that it can be effective in coordinating national players and establishing *some* national standard, but not necessarily a standard which consumers want to buy. The more market-oriented US approach has been more successful in generating an attractive technology and encouraging private co-operation between firms, including international links. It offers more to the various players in different countries and appears to have a good chance of international acceptance.

HDTV also shows a number of specific market strategies for establishing standards, which are likely to come into their own once official adoption questions are resolved. One is to minimize the co-ordination hurdles by taking them separately, setting up a base first in studio production and using this to supply programming with which to attract broadcasters and viewers. Similarly stand-alone systems using VCR may provide a useful route to building the installed base independently of broadcasting. Another is to use an evolutionary approach, to move to the new standard in two or more steps. Originally the Japanese may have misread the demand for HDTV, seeing it as a radically new product rather than a replacement, but they later switched to an evolutionary strategy. This has been needed while the attractiveness of HDTV has been in doubt, but once displays and other technologies are developed, a radical approach may be justified.

The case also illustrates some policy problems of using official standards bodies to achieve industrial objectives. Direct manipulation of standards does not guarantee commercial success, and may even be overturned by market forces. It may divert effort and in the long run fail to protect the national industry. The European standard has been particularly ineffective.

Policy and strategy may need to rely more on market forces. Even the US policy has not escaped this problem, and the aim of protecting local broadcasters may still limit the potential for HDTV. The standard could be bypassed by less restricted DBS and cable delivery standards once the official standards position is clarified.

After decades of effort the prospects for HDTV are finally becoming clear. The technology issues are being resolved and the standards now being defined should open the way for product introductions. Developments in global broadcasting, especially DBS, have increased the demand for a single world-wide standard. At this point the most important question may be whether it will be one of the existing standards, such as PAL or EDTV, rather than HDTV. As for the applicability of any lessons to other standards contests, many of the issues are similar to those found in other communications and telecommunications areas, with national regulations and global scope.

Appendix: *HDTV Abbreviations*

Products:	CD	Compact disc
	CTV	Cable television
	DAT	Digital audio tape
	EDTV	Enhanced-definition television
	DBS	Direct broadcasting by satellite
	DSP	Digital signal processing
	HDTV	High-definition television
	IDTV	Improved-definition television
	LCD	Liquid crystal display
	LD	Laser disc
	VCR	Video cassette recorder
Standards:	ACTV	Advanced Compatible Television—US
	ATV	Advanced Television—US
	MAC	Multiplexed analog components—EU
	MUSE	Multiple sub-nyquist sampling encoding—Japan
	NTSC	National Television System Committee—US
	PAL	Phase alternate line
	SECAM	Sequentiale couleur à mémoire—FR
Institutions:	AEA	American Electronics Association—US
	ATEL	Advanced Television Evaluation Laboratory—Canada
	ATSC	Advanced Television Standards Committee—US
	ATTC	Advanced Television Testing Committee—US
	BBC	British Broadcasting Corporation—UK
	BSB	British Satellite Broadcasting—UK
	BTA	Broadcast Technology Association—Japan
	CCIR	International Radio Consultative Committee
	DARPA	Defense Advanced Research Projects Agency—US
	EBU	European Broadcasting Union
	ELGDV	European Launching Group for Digital Video
	EU	European Union
	EUREKA	European R&D Programme
	FCC	Federal Communications Commission—US
	IBA	Independent Broadcasting Authority—UK
	ISO	International Standards Organization
	ITU	International Telecommunication Union
	MITI	Ministry of International Trade and Industry—Japan
	MPEG	Motion Picture Experts Group—US
	NHK	Japanese Broadcasting Corporation (Nippon Hoso Kyokai)

OTA   Office of Technology Assessment—US
SMPTE   Society of Motion Picture and Television
             Engineers

NOTES

1. This chapter discusses the situation current in late 1994. It concentrates on the attempts over the previous decade to establish the Japanese Hi-Vision system as the international standard, and the ensuing contest between three regional standards. The outcome of this process, including the future of the US digital system, is still unresolved.
2. For the history of colour television standards, see Pelkmans and Beuter (1987), and later in this chapter.
3. The three stages of programming, transmission, and reception for television broadcasting are analogous to the analog or digital steps in recording, mastering, and reproducing music on compact discs (e.g. AAD, ADD, DDD). In HDTV, Hi-Vision would be a DAA or DAD system, while ATV would be DDD.
4. Articles summarizing HDTV history and technology are Iredale (1987); Cripps (1988); Donahue (1989); Kupfer (1991); Farrell and Shapiro (1992); Depma (1992); Bruce and Buck (1993); *New Scientist*, 3 Feb. 1990; *The Economist*, 27 May 1989; 27 Feb. 1993.
5. It is not clear whether the ATV system will use progressive (non-interlaced) scan, as in computer systems, or continue to be interlaced. The original digital proposals were with 1050 or 787.5 lines, and 30 or 60 f.p.s., non-interlaced (1050/30/1 and 787.5/60/1). Probably both progressive and interlaced scans will be allowed. Using progressive scan would mean developing new television receivers and cameras, and would hold up the introduction of ATV, even though it would make interfacing with computer applications easier (*Electronic News*, 31 May 1993; 5 July 1993).
6. Graphics applications should benefit greatly from the wider availability of equipment, but often require much higher resolution than even HDTV: for graphic arts 200 to 1000 lines *per inch* is routine (Schreiber, 1988). Full HDTV does not have high enough resolution for printed graphics, being adequate for prints only up to about 3–6 inches wide (Quantel, 1990*a*).
7. The most likely technology is liquid crystal display (LCD). Screens up to 14 inches have been developed, but currently cost around $75,000. Other contenders include plasma technology, electro-luminescence, vacuum microelectronics (microtips) and deformable mirrors (*The Economist*, 13 Apr. 1991; 31 Aug. 1991; *Business Week*, 26 Feb. 1991).
8. For the typical mode of MITI operation see Ouchi and Bolton (1988).
9. The current lowest price is $6,250 for a Sony 28 in. screen; a JVC set with 32 in. screen costs $8,175 (*Electronic News*, 13 Sept. 1993).
10. *The Economist*, 27 Feb. 1993.
11. *New Scientist*, 3 Feb. 1990.

12. OTA (1990).
13. Standards collaboration on joint systems facing a strong proprietary threat is a feature of the PC, Open Systems, and VCR cases above.
14. Bruce and Buck (1993).
15. *The Economist*, 10 Nov. 1990. By 1991 in Europe 2.8 m. households received DBS: all used PAL except for 170,000 using D2-MAC (*The Economist*, 16 Mar. 1991). The reasons behind BSB's failure are foretold in Grindley (1990*a*) and discussed in Chapter 1 of this book.
16. *The Economist*, 23 Feb. 1991, 16 Mar. 1991; *Financial Times*, 9 Feb. 1993.
17. Only Zenith remains as a US supplier with 13 per cent of the market, mainly manufactured in Mexico. RCA, with 30 per cent of the market, is owned by Thomson, which acquired it from GE in 1987 (GE acquired RCA consumer electronics in 1986); Magnavox and Silvania, with another 10 per cent, are owned by Philips. The main US studio supplier is Ampex. For an analysis of the politics of the attempt by US program producers to secure Hi-Vision approval in 1986 see Neil (1988).
18. Cable penetration in the USA is over 60 per cent of homes, with only 66 per cent of viewing time to the three major networks, ABC, NBC, CBS (*International Broadcasting*, Dec. 1988; *The Economist*, 31 Mar. 1990).
19. The campaign was carried out under the auspices of the American Electronics Association (AEA), with IBM, DEC, Apple, and many others. A Congressional study concluded that the prospects for HDTV had been exaggerated and the semiconductor industry itself later questioned some of the linkages between mass produced HDTV memory chips and other IC development (*Financial Times*, 31 July 1989; 11 Oct. 1989). Arguments for policy intervention in HDTV for the USA are summarized in Hart (1989), for Europe in Carpentier (1989). DARPA was renamed ARPA in 1993.
20. This and the following sections draw on Farrell and Shapiro (1992).
21. FCC (1988). At the time this was widely misreported as requiring compatibility with NTSC. The FCC made this clear in a later ruling in favour of non-compatible simulcast systems, in March 1990. I am grateful to William Schreiber for noting this.
22. Farrell and Shapiro (1992). The FCC chairman reportedly 'warned broadcasters urging delays in HDTV deployment that UHF spectrum for HDTV cannot be held indefinitely,' (*Broadcasting*, 28 Oct. 1991). Stations are offered the additional channel for HDTV provided they begin broadcasting within six years of a standard being adopted.
23. Other proposals included Super-NTSC, from Yves Faroudja—an inexpensive EDTV system which corrected many of NTSC's problems and mimicked HDTV pictures by doubling the number of lines (Donahue, 1989).
24. This was counter to some expectations that as the only fully US based bid, the Zenith/AT&T system would be selected (*The Economist*, 13 Apr. 1991).
25. *Electronic News*, 5 July 1993.
26. Cost estimates in *TV Digest*, 13 May 1991. These compare with initial estimates as high as $38m. made initially by ATSC, to be compared with the $25 m. average price of a local station in the 1980s. Other recent estimates have been much lower, with the costs of new equipment and upgrading put at $1–2 m. per station (Kupfer, 1991).

27. For further details of the background of colour TV standards see Pelkmans and Beuter (1986); Besen and Johnson (1986); Farrell and Saloner (1992); *The Economist*, 27 Feb. 1993.

28. The success of News Corporation in establishing the Sky Television DBS service in the UK is an example of the co-ordinated investment strategy in product development, programming, satellite transmission, and subsidized receivers, which may be needed to establish HDTV.

29. Many of the issues surrounding the use of official approval as part of standards strategy and the combination of market forces and official adoption are similar to those in the Telepoint case, in Chapter 9.

30. Whether it costs more to simulcast or broadcast a single 'compatible' signal, however, is not clear, as new equipment is need in both cases.

31. This is a lesson learned from VCR and compact disc (CD), where software availability was crucial, and digital audio tape (DAT), where the lack of pre-recorded music blocked its introduction as a consumer product.

32. *International Broadcasting*, Jan. 1989.

33. Total movie production costs are claimed to be 30 per cent lower by reducing production and editing time. This is an optimistic figure, given movie production methods. Final prints are either transferred to film for distribution or displayed electronically. Hi-Vision is of equivalent quality to moving 35 mm., but not to 35 mm. slides (Quantel, 1990*a*, *b*).

34. Garner (1989).

35. Conversion is most difficult when there is a frame rate change from 60 Hz to 50 Hz for PAL and HD-MAC, with some picture deterioration.

36. Interview with William Schreiber of MIT in Donahue (1989).

37. *New Statesman*, 5 May 1990; *The Economist*, 4 Aug. 1990; *Business Week*, 1 Apr. 1991.

38. Conversion requirements and comparisons of different systems are discussed in Schreiber (1991, 1989).

39. Michel Carpentier, director-general of DG XIII, EC (Carpentier, 1989).

40. That a more subtle approach was not taken may not be surprising, given the market oriented approach taken in other standards contests by the main manufacturer, Sony.

41. These different levels of intervention in standards setting may also be partly historical, as the higher frequencies have only become useable with developments in communications technology, including satellites.

42. Examples where broadcasting standards have been left completely to the market, such as AM stereo in the USA, have left significant stranded networks. However they have also been characterized by rapidly determined standards and fast adoption of the leading standard in new areas once the winner has been established (Berg, 1987). UK proposals to sell rights to radio spectrum are discussed in Radiocommunications Agency (1994).

43. This would strengthen the trend towards cable and DBS as the main media for television which is evidently taking place anyway. For further discussion see Farrell and Shapiro (1992).

9

Telepoint Cordless Phone:
Regulation, Markets, and Policy

SUMMARY   A central problem in setting standards is finding a balance between the use of government standards bodies and market forces. Telepoint, a UK public cordless telephone system, provides a valuable example of an attempt to use market forces within a regulated framework. The exercise has had an unhappy history. The initial services were withdrawn within two years and a subsequent service was also withdrawn. Basic strategic problems were that the operators did not make the full-scale commitment essential to establish new standards. They introduced trial services with few base stations and high prices, and rather than focusing on a single standard they tried to differentiate the services, fragmenting the installed base and reducing credibility. Yet many of these problems may be traced to contradictions in government policy. Despite intentions the regulator effectively defined the system. The initial configuration did not appeal to users and redefining it took too long. The high level of competition between licensees meant that the operators lacked commitment. As a result neither commercial nor policy aims have been achieved. Not only have the services miscarried but hopes that the system could become a *de facto* European standard have been set back. If hybrid policies are to work the framework may need to be more market responsive, and the private agenda of the regulator less evident, than here.

1. INTRODUCTION

One of the most poignant examples in recent years in the UK of the victory of hope over experience has been the number of 'Telepoint—Coming Here Soon' signs which appeared at street corners, train stations, shops, and other public spots. These announced the imminent arrival of a radio base station from which to use the latest portable phone system, telepoint. Poignant because many of the advertised bases have not yet arrived, and those which were installed were hardly used. The service which had promised millions of subscribers attracted only a handful. Launched in 1989, telepoint was expected to be a major step in bringing mobile telecommunications to mass markets with a low cost digital service, using pocket-sized handsets for access to the public phone network. It also involved an innovative approach to licensing and standards, which brought market forces into the standardization process. Services were licensed to four competing

groups, and instead of setting standards in advance they were to be determined by market competition as the technology was developed. Yet
telepoint appeared to be failing just two years later, when the initial three
licensed operators withdrew services. The fourth service was launched sub-
sequently and hoped to avoid the earlier problems, but this too was withdrawn after a year. Although there is still the possibility of issuing new
licences, the window of opportunity for telepoint in the UK may have
passed.[1]

The main problem has been that telepoint is a systems product which
needs standards, but never established sufficient installed base to survive.
Users did not favour the system as it only allowed outgoing calls. It was
launched with three incompatible services so that users were never sure
whether their handset could be used or not. And the service operators made
insufficient effort to publicize the system. At one level, this disappointing
outcome highlights the dangers of overlooking basic standards strategies
for network services. Service poviders did not make the full scale commitment essential to establish new standards. They introduced trial services
with few base stations and high prices, and made inadequate attempts to
promote the services. Rather than co-operating on a single standard they
tried to differentiate their services with pricing and other strategies. The net
results were tiny installed bases and low system credibility. Potential users
were confused and they ignored the system.

Yet although the operators made errors, many of the reasons for the
failure lay elsewhere. Telepoint was a victim of a perennial problem in
setting standards, of finding a balance between government direction and
market forces. It was an experiment which broke new ground by allowing
standards to be determined by market competition after licences were
issued, within a framework set by the regulator. This was intended to give
a standard which would be responsive to market needs and agreed quickly.
The outcome was different: the regulator effectively defined the system and
the standards remained incompatible to the end.

The role of institutions in standards setting is a topic of great concern.[2] It
has been shown that under certain conditions committees may outperform
the market as co-ordinating mechanisms, and hybrid systems may be better
still (Farrell and Saloner, 1988). Committee negotiations may help avoid
duplicate investments and this is enhanced if the parties can back up their
commitments in the marketplace. The problem is that pure co-ordination
towards a voluntary standard is rare, except in fully market driven standards. The committee itself often introduces its own agenda, especially in
regulated industries. Other policy aims interfere with the standardization
process and may not allow market forces to work, so that the theoretical
benefits of the hybrid system are not realized.

In supporting telepoint the authority was pressing its own industrial
policy objectives for managing competition in mobile telecommunications

and developing UK technology. This involved too many constraints to give the standard a fair chance. The initial configuration did not appeal to users and redefining it took too long. The high level of competition between licensees meant that the providers lacked commitment. Most critically the authority was also sponsoring other mobile systems which threatened the telepoint market and damaged its credibility. The result was that neither policy nor commercial aims were achieved. Not only have the services miscarried but their potential as a show-case for UK manufacturers, aiming at a *de facto* standard for European cordless telephone, has been set back. The one element of success has been the rapid definition of a common standard. However, the poor history of telepoint services in the UK has damaged its credibility and the interest shown by many European telecommunications services has waned.

The aim here is not to question the intentions of the key players in this technology; rather to show that if the standards policy is wrong then their efforts may be largely in vain. There are key strategies which the operators need to follow but the policy framework may make these difficult. The case implies that for a hybrid policy to work, market forces need to be given greater freedom than here. Mechanisms for responding to the market need to be quicker and more direct. In general the external agenda of the regulator should be kept separate from the standardization process, which is often too sensitive to disruption to be used as a policy tool. Only then, if a neutral committee is possible, may the policy help standards making.

In this chapter, Section 2 describes telepoint history and the licensing conditions. Section 3 outlines the role of standards for telecommunications networks and evaluates the operators' strategies to establish telepoint. Section 4 presents typical problems of market driven standards and Section 5 evaluates telepoint policy. Section 6 discusses the impact on European standards and future prospects for telepoint, and Section 7 draws some conclusions. A list of abbreviations is given at the end of the chapter.

2. HISTORY OF TELEPOINT

2.1 Product description

Telepoint is a public cordless telephone system using pocket-sized handsets for access to the public phone network via short-range radio base stations. It was originally intended as a mass market, low cost, mobile telecommunications service, made possible by new digital technology. The phones are about the size and appearance of a large hand calculator, similar to miniaturized cellular telephone handsets. Each base station, typically a small box on the side of a building, has a range of about 200 meters and can accept up to 40 users at the same time. There would be many thousands of these stations over the country, an estimated 40,000 being needed to cover the

UK. The cost of handsets and the service could be relatively low, certainly compared with cellular telephone. It has been called the 'poor man's mobile phone' or 'phonebox in your pocket'.

The technology is a development of the existing portable telephone. The main technical feature is that it uses digital transmission, called CT2 (cordless telephone, second generation). Its initial configuration only allowed outgoing calls—it could not receive calls. It is portable but not truly mobile, as the user has to stay close to the base station and there is no 'handover' from cell to cell on the move, as needed for car phones. The concept is thus somewhere between public payphone and cellular phone. It is used by first dialling a personal identification number (PIN) to validate the user. The telephone number is then dialled as usual. Charges are made to the user's account with the particular telepoint service with which the user is registered. Apart from telepoint, CT2 technology may be applied to cordless phones for business and domestic use, such as Cordless PABX and private portable phones, each potentially large markets. In the UK it was decided that the first application would be as a public service. Eventually the same handset could be used for all three areas, public, home and business.

The potential market for telepoint depends on the choice of product features and price. Its initial configuration in the UK placed it at the lower end of the mobile market. The limitation to only outgoing calls put it in close competiton with payphone. This may still have been more convenient than payphone, though it meant carrying a handset and there was no booth to cut down noise. However, with enhancements such as adding a pager telepoint may be as much as the average user needs in a portable system, provided it is priced competitively. Other possible system enhancements are mentioned below. Even with these, telepoint would not perhaps compete at the high end of the market with fully mobile two-way cellular systems or others being developed. There is a question whether there is too much overlap between telepoint and the other systems to leave a substantial market.[3] The available gap gets smaller the longer telepoint is delayed, as more advanced systems appear, payphones are improved and card payment is extended. It is difficult to estimate the intrinsic demand for telepoint as an established system. Original market forecasts believed that it would reach millions of users, though it is difficult to know how much reliability to place on these.

2.2 Licensing conditions

Licences to provide telepoint services in the UK were awarded to four operators by the DTI in January 1989. These were to Phonepoint (main shareholders British Telecom and STC), Zonephone (Ferranti), Callpoint (Mercury, Shaye) and BYPS (Barclays, Philips, Shell). Three services were launched at the end of 1989, with BYPS delaying introduction. The consortia membership for telepoint and for other UK mobile phone systems are given in Table 9.1.[4]

The broad product specification and the industry structure were determined by the regulator rather than by the technology. This was part of an unusual approach to standards by the licensing authority, here the Department of Trade and Industry (DTI). It outlined the basic requirements for the system, but did not specify detailed transmission standards ahead of awarding the licences. The intention was to speed up both introduction and standards setting by allowing the market to determine the standard. Most of

Table 9.1. *UK mobile phone consortia membership, 1991*

System	Licensed	Service	Membership	%
1 Cellular	1985	Vodaphone	Racal Telecom	100
		Cellnet	BT	60
			Securicor	40
2 Telepoint	1989	Phonepoint	BT	49
			STC	25
			Nynex	10
			France Telecom	10
			Bundespost	6
		Callpoint	Mercury	49
			Motorola	25
			Shaye (Nokia)	25
		Zonephone	Ferranti	55
			Cable & Wireless	5
			Venture capital	40
		BYPS	Barclays	33
			Shell	33
			Philips	33
3 PCN	1990	Mercury PCN	Cable & Wireless	60
			Motorola	20
			Telefonica	20
		Unitel	STC	30
			US West	30
			Thorn-EMI	25
			Bundespost	15
		Microtel	BAe	35
			PacTel	20
			Millicom	14
			Matra	10
			Sony	4
			IBA, Litel	17

the technical details were left for the services to define for themselves. The aim was a simple system which could be developed quickly and would not compete directly with more sophisticated mobile systems being planned. Many of the reasons for promoting a public rather than private service, for the product configuration, for using market standards to speed up standardization and encouraging bids from multinational consortia stemmed from DTI aims to use telepoint as a base for European standards. The hope was that a working public service would give UK manufacturers a lead in setting European CT2 standards and allow them to participate strongly in the private markets.

(a) Product definition

The main product restrictions imposed in the licences were that telepoint could not receive incoming calls, it was to use low powered base stations with limited range, and there was no provision for 'handover'. Several potential enhancements to the system were suggested after the launch, listed in Table 9.2. Most of these changes have been authorized but the process has been very slow. The main product weakness was one-way calling. The first response was to add a pager to the handset, initially billed and operated as a separate service. This was approved by the DTI in 1990. More substantially, a means of providing two-way calling was developed whereby the user may 'log in' on the nearest base station to a call routing system, called 'telepoint plus'. The handset can then receive calls. This has been approved in principle. Finally, the development of full two-way calling, called 'neighbourhood telepoint', was allowed in March 1991.[5] A further problem was the lack of mobility. The technical feasibility of limited 'handover' was demonstrated (by Northern Telecom), which allowed the user to move from one base station to another by automatic re-connection. However, although these enhancements increased the convenience of the system, they also increased its cost. All were eventually accepted in principle but came too late to affect the initial services. None of them were implemented by the original services, though some were included in the subsequent launch of the fourth service.

(b) Choice of standard

Each of four services was allowed to choose its own technology independently of the others. They were incompatible in that handsets could only be used on one service, though initially there were only two technical designs. The equipment manufacturers and investment for the four systems are shown in Table 9.3. Phonepoint and Callpoint used a Shaye design, Zonephone used a Ferranti design. BYPS, with no experience in telecommunications, decided to wait until a common standard was developed before selecting a technology. The licences specified that the operators must accept a common standard, Common Air Interface (CAI), within about a

Table 9.2. *Potential enhancements to telepoint*

Feature	Status
1. Proprietary handsets and base stations	Current
2. Handsets with built-in pagers	Approved 1990
3. Common air interface (CAI)	Defined 1990
4. Inter-system roaming	Defined 1991
5. Telepoint plus	Accepted 1991
6. Two-way telepoint	Accepted 1991
7. Limited handover	Feasible 1991

Table 9.3. *Telepoint equipment suppliers and operator investment*

Service	Leader	Bases	Handsets	Invest (£m.)
Phonepoint	BT	STC/Shaye	Shaye	25
Callpoint	Mercury	STC/Shaye	Shaye	20
Zonephone	Ferranti	Ferranti/AB	AB	20
BYPS	BYPS	Philips/GPT	GPT/Orbitel	25

Source: Company press releases; Fintech.

year, by the end of 1990, and convert their systems to this within a further year. Handsets from one system would then be fully usable on the others, with arrangements for billing between services—intersystem roaming (ISR)—by mid-1991. A common standard greatly increases the number of base stations available to any user, and hence the value of the system as a whole. The rationale given for the two stage approach was to exploit proprietary equipment immediately, as the authority 'does not want to restrict the services if they want to use their own equipment' (DTI, 1989). It was expected to take a year to develop all the technology for the standard interfaces.

The means by which this common standard was to be defined were not clearly specified. It was to be decided by the DTI but only after further consultation and taking into account how the existing systems had performed. It was widely expected that it would be a modification of one of the original designs, and it was on this basis that the early entrants began their services. In fact when the DTI chose the CAI standard in 1990 it was neither of the Shaye or Ferranti designs but a third design, not yet in use, developed by GEC-Plessey Telecommunications (GPT) and Orbitel. Market forces did not appear to have been considered after all; the standard had been chosen on *a priori* technical grounds. Its main feature was that it conformed to Integrated Services Digital Network (ISDN) standards, which the others did not. This was preferred by the DTI to make it compatible with data networks for the business market, also an advantage for becoming a European standard.[6] Since the ISDN interface was put in the handset rather than the base station and the only available chip had high power consumption this had the unfortunate side effect of greatly increasing the size of the handset. The initial CAI handsets were no smaller than cellular and four times the weight of the Shaye handset, negating telepoint's main selling point.[7] The sophistication of ISDN is probably more than the average telepoint user would need, especially with wide adoption of ISDN still years away (David and Steinmueller, 1990). In fact the operators delayed their phase-in of the new standard, as noted below.

(c) Other new systems

Part of the intention in restricting telepoint features was to avoid conflicts with the DTI's plans for two other new mobile systems and, probably misguidedly as it turned out, to avoid confusing the market. The first of these was digital cellular. European standards had already been set for this, called GSM (Groupe Speciale Mobile). Cellular telephone services using analog technology had operated in the UK since 1985, and digital systems with greater capacity were planned for 1991, now being introduced. The second was personal communications network (PCN). This is a mobile system similar to cellular, but with smaller cell sizes (1–5 km. radius) and lower power, which should make the handsets smaller, lighter and cheaper but require more frequent 'handover' on the move. It is similar to GSM but uses a slightly different standard, DCS1800, and operates in higher frequency bands where there is more spare capacity (1.8 Ghz compared with 900 Mhz). It was planned as a high capacity, low price system. A policy aim was that it should be able to rival the fixed link telecommunications services and was seen as a main plank in extending competition in the UK industry.

PCN was already being discussed in the late 1980s before telepoint licences were issued. Licences were awarded to three operators in 1990, less than a year after the telepoint launch. The two existing cellular telephone operators, Vodafone and Cellnet, were also allowed to offer PCN services. The first services were planned for late 1992. As with telepoint the design and pricing of PCN were not decided before issuing licences and were left to the operators. PCN competes closely with telepoint as a small cell mobile telephone but with the advantage of two-way access and mobility. On one reading of policy telepoint was intended as a temporary system until PCN was developed. On another it was intended to fill a low price niche between payphone and cellular/PCN mobile telephone.[8] The PCN services and the launch schedules have evolved slightly differently than planned. Facing the huge investment in infrastructure of around £1 bn. per service for PCN some of the consortia members dropped out. By 1992 two of the original three licensed operators, Mercury PCN and Unitel, had merged in a joint venture, Mercury Personal Communications (MPC), and Hutchison had bought Microtel.[9] The first service, called 'one2one', was launched in September 1993 by MPC. It is a low-priced system, comparing closely with fixed link charges. Hutchison Microtel launched its PCN service, called 'Orange', in 1994.[10]

(d) Competitive conditions and consortia

Policy considerations also aimed to ensure a high level of competition in the telepoint market. The number of operators was set at four, a large number in telecommunications. British Telecom (BT) and Mercury were allowed to bid for licences but were required to take minority stakes and set up their interests at arms length, to avoid possible cross subsidy or preferential treatment. The concern was that telepoint should operate independently of the fixed link services and should neither affect nor be affected by market positions in the fixed networks. Although Racal (a cellular operator) entered the bidding it was not licensed. The DTI favoured bids from groups of firms, especially including foreign firms, to equalize market power and to broaden the support for the eventual standards. Several US and European telephone services and equipment manufacturers took small stakes in the consortia, presumably to gain experience in the new services and gain access to the technology. Bidding costs were low as the technology had been developed already by Shaye and Ferranti, though there was an implicit commitment by successful licensees actively to pursue the service.

2.3 System history

The basic telepoint technology was developed well before services were set up. Ferranti and others had proposed a similar system in the mid-1980s, at about the same time as cellular telephone was being introduced. These suggestions were not acted on by the DTI until the awarding of licences in 1989, by which time cellular was safely established.

Telepoint services were begun in late 1989 by three of the groups, Phonepoint, Callpoint, and Zonephone, less than a year after licensing. BYPS, waiting for the common standard, announced its launch for summer 1990, a launch which did not take place until much later and under new ownership. Although the services got off to an early start this was on a small scale. The initial number of base stations at the end of 1989 and subsequent history are shown in Table 9.4, compared with the very large projections being made for the future network. The services were introduced at trial levels, to test the market for the new product. Largely for this reason much of the public were unaware that the services existed, according to private surveys. There was little advertising or distribution effort. There were several press articles when the licences were issued and services launched, but little more until the PCN announcements.

Table 9.4. *Installation of telepoint base stations*

Service	Launch date	Initial bases	Actual 1990	Plan 1990	Plan 1995	Close date	Final bases	Final users
Phonepoint	Aug. 89	100	1,050	5,000	25,000	Oct. 91	3,500	800
Callpoint	Dec. 89	150	1,000	2,000	25,000	July 91	1,000	<1,000
Zonephone	Oct. 89	150	1,000	7,500	25,000	July 91	1,000	<1,000
Rabbit*	May 92	500	—	7,000	20,000	Nov. 93	10,000	9,000

*BYPS interest sold to Hutchison Feb. 1991; launched as Rabbit May 1992.

Source: Company press releases; Fintech, May 1990, Oct. 1991, and March 1993.

The situation in 1990, a year after the launch, had not changed much. The introduction rate was far below the rapid build up envisaged in earlier plans. The installation rate of base stations was slow and by May 1990 the three services had only just topped 1,000 stations each.[11] This may be compared with the original projections for market growth in Table 9.5. Interest in the system by the public was disappointing: in 1990 the three services had together about 3,500 base stations, and admitted having 'less than 4,000' subscribers.[12] Possibly fewer people were aware of the system than at its launch. While original projections were that by 1990 there would be many thousands of stations and hundreds of thousands of users, the reality was only hundreds of each.

Market forecasts were reduced to about a third of the original estimates, but still projected a large market for telepoint. A forecast for the UK and other European countries is shown in Table 9.6. A late hope of the operators was that the business and domestic cordless market would provide the base of CT2 users which will then create demand for public telepoint. Some hopes were pinned on BYPS, which stated that it would invest heavily in base stations, and only launch its service, called 'Rabbit', once it had 500 stations in place. An added complication was the licensing of PCN at this critical time, in 1990. This was seen as a direct competitor and a number of press articles questioned the need for telepoint when it would be obsolete in a few years.[13]

Seeing the low user acceptance the operators successfully lobbied to modify the licence restrictions during 1990–1. The CAI standard was specified in May 1990, as planned. As this was significantly different from either of the existing designs and was not seen as commercially attractive the operators were reluctant to convert to it and lobbied for the

Table 9.5. *Telepoint income forecast, 1989*

Year	Users (m.)	Connection (£m.)	Subscription (£m.)	Sales (£m.)	Total* (£m.)
1989	0.2	7.0	16.8	30.0	53.8
1990	0.5	10.5	42.0	40.0	92.9
1991	1.0	17.5	84.0	50.0	151.5
1992	2.0	35.0	168.0	50.0	253.0
1993	3.0	35.0	252.0	50.0	337.0
1994	4.0	35.0	336.0	50.0	421.0
1995	5.0	35.0	420.0	50.0	505.0
2000	15.0	70.0	1,260.0	100.0	1,445.0

*Connection fee £35; subscription £7 per month; handsets £150 (1989) falling to £50 (1992 onwards).

Source: Retail business.

relaxation of the compatibility requirement. As a result in 1991 the operators were allowed to keep their own standards until they felt able to
convert.

All this came too late. The services seemed to be marking time until an
opportune moment to withdraw from operations. There was a last attempt
in mid-1991 to revive demand by dramatically reducing handset prices to
£99 (from £180) and call charges by 50 per cent. This went largely unno-
ticed. BYPS sold its interest in telepoint to Hutchison Telecom in February
1991, without launching a service. Callpoint and Zonephone both withdrew
services in July 1991 and finally Phonepoint announced its withdrawal
in September 1991. It finally became clear how few users there were.
The largest, Phonepoint, had installed 3,300 base stations but had just
800 subscribers. Each service had invested around £25 m. The DTI stated
that licences would be available for new operators, on the same terms as
before, though no new commercial interest has been evident. The promised
business and domestic products had not yet appeared on the market.

The fourth licensee, now owned by Hutchison, finally launched its Rabbit
service in May 1992, at first as a local operation in the city of Manchester.
It also followed an incremental approach, though with more commitment
than previous operators. It was careful not to promise services before it had
the infrastructure in place.[14] It extended coverage to other areas including
parts of London in 1993, though by late 1993 it had yet to launch the
planned national service. It took a more positive approach to installing base
stations (with 10,000 by March 1993), offered a combined handset and
pager and made a significant attempt to advertise the system (including a
£4 m. campaign in 1992). It also offered a home base station. Even
so, Rabbit reported only 8,000 subscribers in mid-1993 (against an initial
forecast of 50,000 by the end of 1992), despite offers cutting equipment
prices by half.[15] The service was withdrawn in November 1993. It had 9,000
subscribers and had cost £120 m. Hutchison stated that there was insuf-

Table 9.6. *European telepoint and mobile market forecast, 1990*

Country	Telepoint		Total mobile			
	Users 1995	Value 1995	Users (m.)		Value (£m.)	
			1989	1995	1989	1995
UK	1.66	496	1.48	5.15	986	2,500
France	1.38	368	0.41	3.81	408	2,646
Germany	1.10	144	0.37	3.81	476	3,675
Other	2.83	576	1.84	9.63	1,530	6,027

Source: MZA.

ficient demand for a restricted service, indicating that the window of opportunity for telepoint had passed.[16]

3. STRATEGIES FOR TELEPOINT

3.1 Standards and networks

Telepoint standards define the technical protocols used to transmit messages, such as the message formats, length of data packages, and other specifications, as well as the accounting codes to verify and bill customers. For handsets from one service to use the base stations from another, called 'roaming', the standards must be compatible. This may be achieved either by redesigning the handsets (or base stations) to use the same technical format, or by arranging for them to use both formats and select the right one in operation. There must also be accounting systems which can bill between services. There were originally two standards, from Shaye and the Ferranti, using slightly different transmission techniques. Each service agreed to convert to a common CAI standard, by replacement or modification of equipment. When it was finally defined, the CAI standard was neither of the existing standards but a third more elaborate one. Converting to compatibility was expensive and hard to justify for a simple portable phone system.

These are examples of compatibility standards, which allow different pieces of equipment to be interconnected in a system. They are important in areas such as telecommunications where the value of the service increases the greater the size of the network. These *network externalities* work primarily via the demand side. A larger telepoint network is more valuable directly by having more users to call and more support facilities, making it more convenient to use.[17] There may also be economies of scale in production of complementary equipment, such as handsets and base stations, and greater opportunity to share and resell equipment.[18] The general mechanism is that the larger the *installed base* of equipment on a given standard the cheaper and more various are the complementary goods and services provided. This in turn makes belonging to the standard more valuable. It usually makes a common standard more attractive than a system fragmented into several incompatible standards.[19]

The dynamics of standards setting are that as the installed base gets larger a standard gets cumulatively more attractive and 'bandwagon' effects take place. This makes the *credibility* of a standard in the early stages very important, when users are making purchasing decisions based on expectations of which standard will ultimately succeed. In a standards contest an early lead is often decisive, once the product has reached a basic level of user acceptability, giving a narrow 'window of opportunity' from the time an acceptable design appears until a bandwagon for some standard is established. After this a trailing standard has little chance of being accepted. This also means that standards are very sensitive to small events in the early stages, when apparently minor influences and errors in strategy may permanently ruin the standard's chances of adoption.

3.2 Operator strategies for establishing standards

The key requirements for setting standards are:
- building the installed base quickly
- establishing the standard's credibility in the early stages.

These need heavy investment and promotion, implying that strong commitment is needed to establish a new standard; a trial approach may be fatal. There are also a number of supporting strategies, echoing those used in many of the other market contests for standards:

- ensuring the product is developed to an adequate level of user acceptability before launch

- pricing for market penetration rather than skimming high margins
- co-ordinating efforts with competitors to agree a common standard
- timing in the window of opportunity
- linkage to an existing installed base

The strategies used to establish telepoint standards underemphasized these elements, as discussed below.

(a) Building the installed base

For telepoint the installed base is measured by the number of base stations, users, and handsets. The main determinant of telepoint usefulness is the number of base stations. Users must be sure of a base station nearby when they want to make a call. This means that the services have little choice but to build up a large network before they can attract subscribers, implying a large initial investment. Without this, other means of building the user base will not have much effect. This is a familiar problem that standards involved relatively large initial risks which do not allow the services to be introduced gradually. The risks may be reduced, such as by co-operating on a common standard, but can not be avoided altogether.

The cost of investment needed in base stations is not excessive. Base stations cost £700–1,500 each, so that the full 40,000 for the UK represents, say, £60m. with installation. The three services each expended about £25 m., but little of this seems to have been on base stations. For example, the cost of Phonepoint's 3,300 base stations may have amounted to about £5 m. Although these figures are significant, they are tiny compared with the £1 bn. or so estimated for PCN systems with fully self-contained communications links.

Instead of this, the initial three services followed a cautious schedule, installing services on a trial basis with limited coverage. There were operational problems in installing access points to the public phone system quickly enough, which contributed to the slow build up. An unfortunate response to this was to erect 'Coming Soon' signs, most of which turned out to be empty promises. This did little for the system's credibility. Base station numbers never really got beyond test levels. The subsequent entry by the fourth service, Rabbit, was accompanied by the installation of a larger number of base stations, but this was still essentially a gradualist approach.

This investment should be taken in parallel with other means of building the user base. These include initially subsidizing handsets and call charges, and strong distribution. As we discuss later, handsets remained expensive, indeed often more expensive than cellular, and call charges were kept high until too late. Users wishing to buy handsets had difficulty finding a retailer who stocked them. These all helped to hold back subscribers.

(b) Credibility

The lack of clarity and commitment also reduced the credibility of the system with potential users. Early users make their decisions based on expectations of whether the service is going to succeed. These are determined partly by the proven installed base but also by subjective evaluations of the value of the system and the commitment of the operators.

The definition of telepoint has never been completely clear. The system started out as an unfinished product, with private base stations and PABX applications to be added later. The terms of the licence were left vague and the system had difficulty finding its position in the market. Users were not sure where it fitted in with their needs or with future developments in telecommunications. Users were further confused by the many changes in telepoint. Specifications have changed twice, to add pagers and then allow incoming calls. To this were added concerns about the number of incompatible systems and how these would be resolved. The common CAI standard expected to clear up these doubts only added to them, as one more complication. It was different from the preceding standards, seemed over elaborate and left the suspicion that it too would soon be changed.

The dedication of the initial operators to the future of telepoint was also not obvious from their trial approach and less than 'full-scale' promotion of the service. They made limited efforts to publicize the system or educate the public. Surveys indicated that few people were aware of telepoint's existence. If people had noticed the signs at base stations or seen a handset they were often mystified as to what they could all mean. The operators' limited commitment may have been inevitable given the licensing terms. The requirements for four operators and a simple service ensured that margins would be low. This was compounded by the fact that the operators were consortia of large firms, each with parallel interests in other services. It was difficult for telepoint to be a primary interest under such conditions.

The biggest blow in this respect was the announcement of PCN licences only a few months after the launch, in January 1990, with services initially planned for late 1992. Though PCN was not fully defined, this could potentially do all that telepoint could do plus two-way communication and mobility, and it was also intended as a low cost service. This severely damaged what was left of telepoint's credibility.[20] Had telepoint already become established within its first year, before the PCN announcement, this would have been less of a problem. Telepoint would have had an installed base and may have found a place alongside PCN. Even though it became apparent that PCN services would not be introduced as quickly as planned, and were delayed by about a year, the threat they posed to Telepoint was the last straw. Although the effect on telepoint by PCN was largely a consequence of policy decisions, the operators also did not make strong efforts to reduce the potential conflicts between the systems.

(c) Product acceptability

A standard has to have reached a basic level of user acceptability before it is launched on the market. Because of credibility problems it is particularly hard with a network product to make major modifications once it is launched, as might be quite usual for other products. Similarly, once a basic level of acceptability is achieved, further technical improvement may be less effective in building the installed base than more direct methods, so that adding product sophistication is usually not a very useful strategy for setting standards. The important step is to get the product 'acceptable' first time.

As became apparent very soon after launch, telepoint entered the market below a basic level of acceptability. The initial definition of telepoint was set primarily by the authority and did not have an obvious market niche. The main problem was the limitation to outgoing calls. This did not make it clearly more attractive than payphone, especially as the price was significantly higher. To make the product acceptable it needed some form of two-way access or at least a built-in pager. Even though the operators successfully lobbied the DTI to allow pagers and telepoint plus to allow limited two-way access, it never recovered from this initial loss of interest. The time taken to make these changes was crucial. It was nearly a year after launch before pagers were allowed and telepoint plus was still being discussed when the initial services were withdrawn.

The implication is that not enough market research had been done prior to setting up the licensing conditions and launching the services, while the operators with their trial approach believed they had adequate time to make changes later. This was not the case and once the initial interest had been dissipated it did not recover.

(d) *Pricing policy*

The most valid niche for telepoint seems to be at the lower end of the mobile market, where it competes most closely with payphone. Market positioning depends on the bundle of features offered and the price. 'Mapping' consumer tastes onto product attributes is hard for new untried products. The relevant characteristics for mobile phones may be placed in five groups:

1. Access:	One-way or two-way calling
2. Mobility:	(i) Calls made anywhere or only when close to a base station
	(ii) Used on the move with 'handover' from cell to cell
3. Usability:	Lightweight handset, easy to handle and use
4. Coverage:	National or local
5. Service:	Data transmission, interference, security, other quality features

No one of the existing systems is superior on all counts. Basic telepoint has only one-way access, localized base stations, and no handover but has a lightweight handset and national coverage via the public phone network, provided there are enough base stations. It compares poorly with cellular other than on usability. It is closer to payphone, being more mobile but less useable. For the service to survive it has to appeal to groups of users with specialized and limited needs (e.g. who do not need full mobility) and be priced competitively enough to outweigh the limited characteristics. This calls for a price well below cellular and not far above payphone. It also needs wide coverage of base stations.[21]

This implies that telepoint should be positioned as a low price, large scale system. This coincides with one of the main recommendations from the standards analysis to use low penetration pricing to establish the installed base quickly. In fact the initial services were predominantly high price, small scale, trial introductions. Call charges were closer to cellular prices than payphone. Some representative call charges are given in Table 9.7. For some time bands some telepoint services were actually priced above cellular. In addition there was a connection fee of £20–30 and a monthly subscription charge of £8–10. Handsets cost £170–200. These compared badly even with cellular, which subsidized handsets to attract users and sometimes even gave them away to new subscribers.

Pricing was essentially based on the fixed link charges plus the cost of telepoint access, with price structures which were various hybrids of payphone and cellular. The service operators claimed that they were limited in their pricing strategy as they must charge for their service on top of those for using the public network. Little attempt seems to have been made

Table 9.7.   *Representative telepoint call charges**

	Peak**		Standard		Cheap	
	Local	Long†	Local	Long	Local	Long
Home telephone	13	44	9	31	4	22
Public payphone	26	87	17	61	10	44
Cellular phone:						
Cellnet (in M25)††	99	99	99	99	30	30
Cellnet (out M25)	75	75	75	75	30	30
Telepoint:						
Phonepoint	39	90	39	90	30	75
Callpoint	60	60	48	48	30	30
Zonephone (in M25)	38	125	25	88	13	63
Zonephone (out M25)	30	100	20	70	10	50

* Charges in pence for 3 mins. (incl. VAT), 1989.
** Peak 8 a.m.–1 p.m.; standard 1 p.m.–6 p.m.; cheap 6 p.m.–8 a.m.
† Long: over 35 miles (56 km.).
†† In M25: Within London area.
Source: Operator price lists.

to negotiate lower block rates. The prices were too far above payphone to be attractive. The original claims were that telepoint would cost little more than payphone.

The reasons for a high price policy may either have been because the operators at first misread the market as a premium product, or because they were following a price skimming policy as part of their trial approach, intending to reach first the 'high value' users then gradually to bring down prices to expand the market. It was clear early on that positioning as a premium service in the initial configuration was not appropriate. The premium service was cellular telephone, which continued to attract more users while telepoint stalled.

A response to the slow take-up of the services could have been to abandon the skimming policy and reduce prices substantially to develop the market and the installed base quickly in a penetration strategy. The services did not do this. Continuing the trial approach they moved in the opposite direction, taking the product up market to make it look more like the cellular systems its prices resembled, rather than bringing prices down to what the product may have justified. Adding new features, other than a basic way to alleviate one-way calling (i.e. built-in pager or telepoint plus), was probably the wrong focus for strategy. Instead of technical improvements, standards analysis shows that the services needed to concentrate on radically expanding demand and the installed base, to start the bandwagon effects. First this meant getting the pricing low. While some of the enhancements, such as pagers, were cheap and effective, the others required new development which added substantial delays and costs. Also there needed to be broader publicity and distribution. It was not easy to find any handsets to buy for the initial three services, and then they were often sold as luxury items. What had been billed as the 'poor man's mobile phone' was only retailed in London by two luxury department stores, Harrods and Selfridges. Making an initial misreading of the market is understandable, but the response once the error was clear was unfocused. The firms seemed to realize the pricing error only towards the end, in mid-1991, when they halved the price of handsets and call charges. This was too late to have any effect.[22]

(e) Collaboration vs. differentiation

A major problem with the installed base was that it was fragmented between three, and possibly four, services. To get around this the initial services could either have collaborated to establish a single standard, or one could have made a determined effort to establish itself as the *de facto* standard by building up a dominant position. Either would have increased the available installed base of each of the services and raised the credibility of the system, at a stroke. Yet the three initial services did neither. Instead of converging they tried to differentiate their services from one another. This is a strategy which might be expected with normal products but which is often counter-productive where network externalities are involved. By emphasizing the differences between the standards the effect was to convince users that each standard was separate and could only count on its own small installed base.

An example of the effect of differentiation was that the services followed intricately different pricing policies for call charges, subscription charges, and handset costs. Some of these complexities are indicated in the charge schedules, which involved a different blend of fixed and variable charges for each service, shown in Table 9.8. There were different time bands for peak, standard, and cheap rates, shown in Table 9.9. The different call rates are shown in Table 9.10. Phonepoint used only two time bands and two distance categories. Callpoint had three time bands but only one distance category. Zonephone had three time bands with four distance categories plus different rates for calls initiated within the London area. It was virtually impossible for potential customers to compare prices between services. These intricacies further confused users who now had to make fine decisions on the features of the individual systems. The pricing structures also made it harder to devise a common standard with an accounting procedure for 'roaming'.

Under the terms of the licences the operators were required to adopt a common standard after a year. The uncertainty about how this would be decided, whether by authority or by market forces, and the short time

Table 9.8. *Telepoint charge structures*

	Conn.	Subs.	Call	Dist.	Zone*	Peak	Duration
Phonepoint	√	√	√	√	—	√	√
Callpoint	√	√	√	—	—	√	√
Zonephone	√	√	√	√	√	√	√
Payphone	—	—	√	√	√	√	√
Cellular	√	√	√	—	√	√	√
Pagers	√	√	—	—	—	—	—
PMR**	√	√	—	—	—	—	—
PCN†	√	√	√	√	—	√	√

√ Charge levied.
* Zone: Within London area.
** Personal Mobile Radio.
† Mercury one2one (1994).
Source: Operator price lists.

Table 9.9. *Time charge bands (24 hrs.)*

Service	Operator	Peak	Standard	Cheap
Telepoint	Phonepoint	8–20	—	20.00–8.00
	Callpoint	7.30–13	13.00–18.00	18.00–7.30
	Zonephone	9–13	8.00–9.00, 13.00–18.00	18.00–8.00
Payphone	BT	9–13	8.00–9.00, 13.00–18.00	18.00–8.00
Cellular	Cellnet	8–22	—	22.00–8.00
	Vodaphone	7.30–21.30	—	21.30–7.30
PCN	Mercury	7–19.00	—	19.00–7.00

Source: Operator price lists.

allowed may have left the services little incentive to attempt to establish a market standard. With the services making little effort to define a common standard the responsibility returned to the authority. The one devised, though intended to be set in consultation with the services, was neither of the existing standards and probably not one they would have chosen based on market acceptance.

The differentiation strategy shows the dangers of mistaking the competitive objective when standards are involved. Firms may be overly competitive for market share at the expense of market size. Collaboration on standards increases the size of the total market. Although this helps competitors as well as oneself, so that investment in common base stations helps

Table 9.10. *Comparative call charge schedules**

Service	Distance	Peak		Standard		Cheap	
Phonepoint	Local	39		—		30	
	National	90		—		75	
Callpoint	Local	60		48		30	
	National	60		48		30	
Zonephone	Local	37.5	(30)	25	(20)	12.5	(10)
	≤35 mile	87.5	(70)	62.5	(50)	25	(10)
	<35 mile (low)	100	(80)	75	(60)	37.5	(30)
	<35 mile	125	(100)	87.5	(70)	62.5	(50)
Home tel.	Local	13.2		8.8		4.4	
	≤35 mile	30.8		22		8.8	
	<35 mile (low)	35.2		26.4		13.2	
	<35 mile	44		30.8		22	
Payphone	Local	26.1		17.4		10	
	≤35 mile	60.9		43.5		17.4	
	<35 mile (low)	69.6		52.2		26.1	
	<35 mile	78		60.9		43.5	
Cellular	Local	99	(75)	—		30	(30)
	National	99	(75)	—		30	(30)
PCN**	Local	75		—		0	
	National	75		—		30	

*Charges in pence for 3 mins, 1989 (excl. VAT); charges outside London M25 in parenthesis.
** Mercury one2one introduction prices (1994), plus £12.50 per month charge.
Source: Operator price lists.

all services equally, this may be the only way to ensure any market exists. Competition may then take place using other variables.

(f) Timing

As with most standards there was a narrow time window during which to establish telepoint, from the time the product was technically possible until competing systems or standards became serious threats. There was also a need to maintain the momentum of the new standard to keep its credibility. Once the standard was seen as a failure it was very hard to regain credibility. As the initial services were launched the time window for public telepoint was closing rapidly. Both the size of the market and the time available before telepoint became obsolete were shrinking. The market niche at the low end of the mobile market, between cellular/PCN and pagers/payphone, became smaller as telepoint took longer to establish itself. At the high end, newer more advanced technologies were on the near horizon, while at the low end of the market, payphones were becoming more numerous and reliable in the UK. The services did not respond adequately to this double threat. The time window had already been narrowed by the issue of licences some years after the system was technically feasible, and the planned arrival of PCN gave a limit of about three years to establish telepoint. The trial approach and high price entry route suggest that the operators did not fully appreciate that timing had to be well focused.

(g) Linkage

An area which was not stressed by the initial services, though was made more central by Rabbit, was the advantage of using the same handset at home, at the office and in the street. This would enable telepoint to have access to an existing installed base of home portable phones. It may also be one of the few advantages telepoint has over PCN, which, for the initial services, requires that users subscribe to a separate service operating in parallel with the fixed link, and may not be as convenient to use at home. Part of the reason that this was not pursued was that home digital base stations were not initially available, the consequence of introducing the public system first (see below). The timing was difficult, as it meant that users had to invest in a new digital PABX at home or office at the same time as taking up telepoint. If CT2 had already been in use for private portables then the public service would follow naturally.

4. STANDARDS POLICY

4.1 Problems with market standards

Markets are usually effective in converging quickly to a single, proven standard. However, this is not always the case, and from a public policy viewpoint there may be other problems which justify government policy intervention. Problems to be considered include the following:

(a) Fragmentation

Multiple standards with small groups of users occur if several standards establish self-sustaining installed bases before one becomes dominant. Subscribers to a minority standard are stranded with a poorly supported system but cannot justify the switching costs needed to change to the leading standard. They have fewer complementary goods and services, and the equipment costs are high if the standard has not reached minimum efficient scale. All users suffer by being locked into standards with smaller installed bases. This holds back total market growth. Whether this is a major danger for technologies which are widely realized to have network externalities is an open question. Even so, though markets may converge quickly to a single standard, they are harsh on failed standards and their supporters.[23]

(b) Duplication of effort

Market competition for standards duplicates development and promotion costs, and has high risks. Setting a standard requires large scale investment and strong commitment just to compete, with no guarantee of winning. At worst the risks may mean that no individual firm is prepared to make an attempt and the product stalls, as was the case with telepoint. As far as this is 'wasteful' competition, resources could be saved if producers use the same standard from the beginning and risks are reduced. Against this, even if standards can be set ahead of development, it is not clear that this is different from other aspects of competition, which is generally approved of. Also commercial risks may not be reduced by trying to set standards before the technology is proven in the market place.

(c) Technical inferiority

A standard established by the market may be inferior to others available, technically or otherwise. The market process depends on establishing the installed base and complementary support as much as on the product itself. Once a standard is established users may be locked into an obsolete standard. The problem with focusing on technical superiority is that there is more to creating a successful product than this. The criteria used to decide what is technically 'best' may not be what the market wants, whereas a standard established by the market has at least passed this important test. A basic level of user acceptability from which to build a support base may be more important than fine technical distinctions.

(d) Market power

The above are essentially co-ordination problems. A further set of problems concern the potential market power given by proprietary rather than open standards. The problem is that this is part of much broader industrial and trade policy issues with implications beyond those of setting standards. Standards certainly may bestow market power. However, standards setting is sensitive to small disturbances in the crucial early stages so that results are unpredictable. Standards strategy may be more likely to be influenced by market power than have the strength to influence it.

Whether such problems seriously offset the advantages of market standards depends on the particular case. Whatever the balance, the fact remains that there is some level of problems with markets. Firms may become locked into standards they would like to change, often say that they would prefer a standard to be set before development to avoid wasted investment, and tend to adopt standards set by the firm with the largest resources rather than necessarily the best design. In theory such problems could be avoided by an official standard set by negotiation before substantial development takes place, possibly backed by regulatory power. Alternatively an official body may try to modify the market process to avoid the problems. The question is whether such action can be effective.

4.2 Government vs. market standards

Basic questions for standards policy are whether official standards bodies are more or less effective than market forces in reaching a workable standard (*de jure* vs. *de facto*) and whether it is possible to combine the two in a superior hybrid policy. Farrell and Saloner (1988) have shown that in theory committees may outperform the market as coordinating mechanisms, and hybrid systems may be better still. Their reasoning is that a committee is more likely to arrive at a common standard than an industry which only communicates by (investment) actions. Negotiations take place before irreversible investments are made and there is less chance of choosing fragmented standards by mistake. In their analysis, committee standards may be set later than pure market standards since firms delay agreement until the last moment, but the cost of delay is more than offset by the greater likelihood of agreement. Without negotiations firms try to pre-empt each other: 'pure market' standards are set earlier but with greater chance of fragmentation. The most unexpected result from Farrell and Saloner is that in the hybrid system the ability to make pre-emptive investments strengthens the ability of the firms to make commitments in the negotiation process and so this may be best of all.

The problem with this result is that the analysis by Farrell and Saloner is really about co-ordination in setting *market* standards rather than policy intervention in a directive sense. It shows that market standards may be set more efficiently if firms are permitted to negotiate with each other. The committee itself has a purely co-ordinating role giving the firms' repeated opportunities to state their preferences verbally rather than revealing them via sunk investments. The value of committees as talking shops is not controversial. The trouble is that in practice committees are rarely neutral over which standard is preferred. There are a number of reasons why involving an official standards body in the standardization process is not costless. These may override theoretical advantages of committees or hybrid systems over market standards, as follows.[24] ·

(a) External policy agenda

The basic problem is that the approach introduces an extra player into the standardization process, in the form of the standards body itself. Standards bodies have agendas of their own beyond facilitating co-ordination, which, although consensus may appear to be reached, may influence the standard in ways which make it unacceptable in the market. Private agendas are especially likely in regulated industries, which are just the areas where official standards committees are likely to have power and to try to use this to further exterior policy aims. This applies to bodies such as the US Federal Communications Commission (FCC), the DTI, or, for that matter, the International Consultative Committee for Telephone and Telegraph (CCITT), as sponsors of influential committees. It certainly applied with telepoint. Attempts to use standards for industrial policy aims may seem costless but are likely to interfere seriously with standards co-ordination. Decisions are made not on the basis of setting an efficient standard but on other grounds. The success of a standard is very sensitive to its credibility in the early stages, and any interference can easily destroy this. The existence of the separate body may also divert the firms' efforts away from establishing the standard towards lobbying the authority. The focus changes from an economic to a political process. These are particular problems in regulated industries, where standards authorities are strongest.

(b) Remoteness from the market

Because of its distance from the market the standards body may not have sufficient information or indeed motivation to choose the most attractive standard. This is unlikely to be an issue if the committee merely represents a consensus of its members (as Farrell and Saloner assume). If, as is more likely, it has independent influence on the standard it may be too far removed from the business to be adequately informed about user needs or technological and commercial realities. A consequence is that official standards are decided outside the market forum and tend to concentrate more on technical performance than market criteria.

(c) Slow procedure

The committee process is usually slow and may operate on a much longer time scale than the market needs. Fact finding and negotiations, especially for voluntary agreements, inevitably move slowly. Decision mechanisms are cumbersome, so that changes may not be feasible once the process is far advanced. It is also often unclear what criteria are being used in the process. Delay is occasionally an advantage if it avoids premature standardization.[25] More often it is a problem, especially in technically an advanced industries where the technology and industry structure change very quickly. Committees can have difficulty keeping abreast of market developments and may only confirm what has already happened.

(d) Unreliable consensus

Committee agreement is elusive and even when achieved it may be reneged on unless backed up by market forces. The standards issue may be too important to the future of the firms to be settled by committee negotiations. Where members are under pressure to generate agreement, consensus may ostensibly be achieved but with the players not truly committed. Such standards are often worded ambiguously for this reason, and effective standards may still have to be determined *de facto* by market competition. This is especially so if the process is slow and the conditions which led to the original agreement change over time.

5. EVALUATING TELEPOINT POLICY

5.1 Policy performance

Telepoint involved a hybrid policy which it was hoped would combine the best features of government and market approaches. The regulator defined the broad technical specifications of the system, set the number of operators and other licensing terms, and acted as standards co-ordinator. This was combined with market forces in three ways: (*a*) technical details of the systems were to be developed by the services, (*b*) a single common standard was to be agreed after the experience in the market, and (*c*) any changes to the regulations were to be agreed with close consultation between the service operators and the authority. The intention was to involve the market in defining those aspects of the product which could not be known in advance.

In practice the policy has not worked so clearly in this way. Rather than combining the best of both worlds, the hybrid policy still showed many of the problems of using official standards while the use of market forces only added problems. The introduction of market elements did little to reduce the potential problems of government directed standards, other than increasing the speed with which services were started:

(*a*) Standards definition

The basic product configuration was defined by the authority with insufficient consultation with the industry. It proved to be different from what the users wanted, particularly the one-way access. The situation was arguably made worse by leaving many of the details vague, for the services to develop as they wished. The combination restricted the product in a critical way while the remaining ambiguity confused users and operators alike. It was not clear what the product was meant to do, or whether there was genuine demand. This was a case of technology looking for an outlet. Though there is often a case for technology push to introduce breakthrough innovations before a market exists, this still requires close understanding of the business and the flexibility to change the product. These were not evident here.

(*b*) Responsiveness to market signals

The mechanism for authorizing product changes, such as telepoint plus, was slow and unwieldy. Although the approach was quick to define the basic product, necessary changes in the configuration which became clear very early on took many months to get through the permission process. Changes are needed on a faster clock once the product is launched to maintain the credibility of the standard. This happened even though modifications had been expected and were implicit in the policy. Meanwhile the services 'marked time' with their trial approach. A powerful example of this problem was the mechanism for deciding the common standard. CAI was due within a year but it was not clear which standard this would be or how it would be chosen. The two stage process turned out to be a serious problem for user confidence. Users did not know whether the handset and service they had subscribed to would still be valid with the new standard, whether they would have to pay the costs of changeover themselves or even whether their service would still be in existence. Operators did not know whether they should try for market dominance or try to avoid it. Everyone had to make a leap of faith.

(c) Failure of consensus

Though the operators had agreed in the licence terms to the basic product definition and the rules for setting a common standard, consensus proved hard to maintain when faced with the experience in the market. The product configuration and CAI were not fully supported by the operators, who lobbied for changes. Agreeing the common standard in the first place was also difficult and was eventually decreed by the authority. Having a pre-announced date for common standards rather than an open ended contest may have aggravated the agreement problem. The date was inflexible and gave insufficient time to build up pressure for a market standard. With a common standard coming no firm wanted to make investments which would probably soon be obsolete or at best benefit its three competitors as much as itself. Each waited for the other to move. The problem became more acute as the firms developed stronger vested interests. Increasingly the decision needed either an official decision or full market competition; consultation alone could not work.

The effectiveness of a hybrid policy depends on the balance between the authority and the market. For telepoint, this rested mainly on the side of the authority, perhaps by default as much as intent, which may explain the weak market effect. Yet there were few advantages of *de jure* standards. Intervention tended to add to the confusion and did not discourage fragmented standards, avoid duplicated investments or lead to an acknowledgedly superior standard.

5.2 Conflicts in policy design

The policy had been conceived according to a broad industrial policy agenda which tended to override what was needed to establish standards.

The result was a series of conflicts which ensured that neither commercial nor policy aims were achieved. In a sense, policy tried to do too much with telepoint. The various objectives interfered with the product so that it became difficult to market in its own right. The effect was to reduce the commitment of the operators, who then failed to make the necessary investment in the installed base, as outlined above. The main aspects of this disconnect are the following.

(a) Restricted product niche

Telepoint was restricted to the low end of the mobile market and delayed to keep it from challenging what were seen as more important services in digital cellular and PCN. One-way calling put telepoint down market where it did not always compare well with payphone. Telepoint was defined too negatively, so as not to interfere with other systems, rather than by trying to find an optimal market. The responsibility for making the product marketable was given to the services, who by then were boxed in. Operators had wanted a service in the mid-1980s, but the licensing of telepoint had been held back until 1989 to allow cellular to be established. The approval of two-way telepoint was delayed, critically, until 1991 because 'the duopoly policy [for fixed link services] . . . precluded the licensing of neighbourhood telepoint before the conclusion of the duopoly review'.[26] PCN was seen as particularly important as it was presented as a new technology which could introduce more competition in UK telecommunications services (DTI, 1991). This role is now less apparent. Following the duopoly review, greater competition in telecommunications is being introduced with a range of policies.

(b) Conflicts between systems

Not only was telepoint restricted by these other systems but one of them, PCN, directly threatened to make telepoint obsolete within a few years. This was known as telepoint services were being launched, and some commentators at the time warned that telepoint was 'set for disaster', 'already outmoded' and possibly 'redundant' from the start.[27] This had an obvious effect on the system's credibility. The policy started too many systems at once without fully acknowledging the difficulties of promoting more than one standard at a time, and the damage this would do to telepoint.[28] The result has been that neither PCN nor telepoint have worked out quite as planned.[29]

(c) High level of competition

Having four service operators was a high level of competition in a market which was already defined as a low margin, high volume product, especially when the market potential was uncertain. This discouraged investment. It was clear that policy efforts would be made to keep the competition balanced, so that there was little point in trying to dominate the market. This fragmented the installed base and made it hard to establish critical mass, especially in the crucial early stages before common standards. The three active services initially made closely matching investments and kept their services at trial levels.[30]

(d) Selection of common standard

The common CAI standard was not chosen solely on the basis of market acceptability, which would probably have favoured the miniature Shaye handset, but was swayed by the desire for ISDN compatibility, possibly to make it acceptable as a European standard. This feature made the handsets as heavy and power hungry as cellular phones. Also it came from a third manufacturer, again apparently to balance competition and ensure that no service achieved a dominant position. Whether there would have been insufficient competition in handsets without this is not clear. Motorola was committed to produce CAI handsets and was expected to dominate the market. Japanese manufacturers refused to produce handsets even for CAI, explaining that they thought the market would be too small.

(e) Use of consortia

The consortia structure exacerbated the decision making and commitment problems. Consortia were favoured by the DTI to broaden the exposure of the system, especially to foreign firms. Members had various motivations and individual interests were diffused. For example, in BYPS two of the three members had no previous experience in telecommunications. The DTI had encouraged licensees to get overseas connections to help in the standards battles and some overseas firms had been added to the bids at the last minute. The consortia also inevitably involved some conflicts of interest. Membership covered the industry, including the leading firms with parallel interests in mobile phones. Fear of undermining investments in public payphone, cellular, and PCN may have been a consideration for firms such as BT, Hutchison, Mercury, STC, and Bundespost. Motorola, Philips, and Shaye all provided services and at the same time supplied equipment to competitors. These potential conflicts strengthened the need to differentiate telepoint from other mobile systems.

5.3 Positive results

Although the policy has been disappointing overall, there have been some positive aspects. The main one is that the technology and the standards, including CAI, were developed very quickly. Systems were developed and services running within a year, a consequence of allowing the services to use their own designs. A common standard was set a year later. This compares well with timetables for committee standards which may normally take five to ten years, as with recent European Union (EU) standards for mobile telephones, though this is not a strict comparison as for telepoint the basic CT2 technology already existed. The speed of introduction as an operating service was important as this could have given telepoint a strong selling point for EU cordless standards as a tried and tested system. CAI standards were endorsed as an interim EC standard and seven European countries agreed to trial services, as discussed below. Had the other aspects of the policy worked as well as the basic idea then telepoint could have been in a strong position.[31]

6. EUROPEAN STANDARDS

6.1 European standards approach

The market oriented process used for telepoint in the UK contrasts with the more traditional committee approach being used for mobile telephone standards in the European Union. This aims to replace the existing fragmentation in the European telecommunications market with a set of common standards. This was set out in the Green Paper on telecommunications in 1987. The European Telecommunications Standards Institute (ETSI), which includes non-community members, has been set up to do this. It is working to establish Pan-European standards in three areas: digital cellular, digital cordless and paging. The intention is to avoid the situation for analog cellular phone services, for which there are at least five standards across Europe.

The standards for the different mobile phone services are shown in Table 9.11. ETSI has adopted a digital cellular standard, GSM, and a paging standard, ERMES. Cellular services using GSM were introduced in summer 1991, in Scandinavia, and ERMES were introduced in 1993. ETSI was working on a standard for digital cordless telephone, Digital European Cordless Telephone (DECT) in 1994. The main technology being studied is the system being developed by Ericsson, Philips, and Siemens, now called CT3 to distinguish it from telepoint. DECT is intended as a standard for both private and public systems in the same markets as telepoint. Recently the DCS1800 standard, similar to GSM, has been chosen for PCN applications; its compatibility with DECT is under consideration. DECT has not been finalized, and it is here that attempts have been made to introduce CAI. CAI was adopted as an interim DECT standard for five years in 1990, and has recently been accepted as a potential final standard.

6.2 Telepoint and European standards

A main aim behind the telepoint policy was to help UK manufacturers develop cordless technology for business and domestic markets, and be-

Table 9.11. *European mobile phone standards*

System	UK standard	Other European
Cellular phone	TACS	RC-2000 (F); Netz B (D); RTMS (I); NMT-450 (Rest)
Digital cellular	GSM	GSM
Telepoint	CAI	CAI/DECT
PCN	GSM/DECT	GSM/DECT

come the *de facto* European standard. Experience with a proven technology is an important selling point, and European companies and Public Telecommunications Operators (PTOs) have been encouraged to take an interest in telepoint.

Adoption by European interests seemed a strong possibility in 1990 at the introduction of telepoint. The opinion of a GPT spokesman at the time was: 'European acceptance of telepoint, we couldn't stop it now even if we wanted to.'[32] A significant move in its favour was the Memorandum of Understanding (MoU) signed in March 1990 between seven major European telephone operators and the four UK telepoint services, committing each operator to set up trial services by the end of 1990.[33] This included a framework for roaming to allow the same handset to be used in different countries. Trials with CAI equipment were soon underway in several countries, including Germany, France, Netherlands, and Finland, also in New Zealand. The Deutsche Bundespost, for example, ordered 2,000 CAI handsets and base stations in 1990 from Siemens-GPT for field trials. The fact that CAI was already available and incorporated in a range of products could have allowed it to bypass the committee process with an established standard already in use.

With the difficulties of telepoint in the UK this possibility seems more remote. European cordless standards are more likely than ever to be set by the traditional committee process. The UK standard is not well placed in this with the stigma of having been rejected by the market. After the period of optimism in early 1990, the introduction of telepoint services in Europe was cautious. Commercial services have been started after 1992 in Germany, Netherlands, Finland, and Belgium. The main European effort has been in France, which launched its Pointel service, nicknamed 'Bi-Bop', in May 1993. Trial services in Strasburg, begun in 1992, were extended to Paris and La Défense, the business and financial centre, in 1993. There are plans to include a log-in capability for receiving incoming calls similar to telepoint plus, but the initial services are one-way only. Take up of the service has been modest, with 20,000 subscribers by late 1993. This is possibly because users are waiting for the two-way service but also because Bi-Bop has initially been marketed as a high price, 'fashion accessory' system.

The only real successes with telepoint have been in Hong Kong and Singapore, whose dense urban areas are well suited to the service. Hong Kong services were started in March 1992. There are now three operators, Hutchison, Chevalier and Pacific Telelink. By late 1992 there were 30,000 subscribers, with 7,000 newcomers a month. It is similar to the UK system, but Hutchison began trials on two-way telepoint in 1993. The Singapore service, Callzone operated by Singapore Telecom, was started in January 1992, and now has 24,000 subscribers.

6.3 Future prospects

It is an open question whether telepoint can recover in its current form. This seems a pity. Objectively there seems to be a market for a simple, low cost portable phone system, to complement sophisticated, high cost cellular services. Telepoint, with two-way calling or a pager, could potentially supply this market segment quite adequately. Telepoint is more attractive in the absence of PCN, though this depends partly on how PCN is defined and priced. PCN may still be a premium product or could merge into digital cellular, leaving the low cost segment open for some time. Telepoint also seems to have advantages as an 'integrating' system, using the same handset at home, office, and outside.

One possibility is still that new operators take over the licences. There is a clear idea now of what telepoint could look like and can offer the user. It seems that only a redefinition of the market and a change away from a gradualist approach could make telepoint a success. At the time of writing, there is little evidence of such a change. Just before their closure the initial operators were still talking of waiting 'two or three years' before services would take off and for demand to build up. The introduction of the Rabbit service was pursued with more attention to building an adequate installed base before each local launch, but the overall process proceeded gradually and eventually also failed.

The remaining route for telepoint would be for an installed base to be built up first in the business and domestic portable phone markets and then create a demand for a public service. This was a late hope voiced by the initial operators and part of Rabbit's plan. This is a reversal of the approach originally taken, in which telepoint was launched as an 'unfinished' system for public services and followed by domestic and business applications as they were developed. This could revive the system, though it is not clear that the private markets could be large enough to create an adequate base of users. Also some aspects of these systems are likely to be technically different from current telepoint, and developing fully compatible equipment will require additional investment. A problem with this approach, and part of the reason the public service route was followed in the original policy, is that this is a slow way to build the installed base and inevitably puts telepoint further back. Before demand could build up in this way, telepoint could be obsolete.

Looking more widely, the UK manufacturers may still participate in some way in European markets if they can disassociate the technical development of telepoint from its commercial problems. The technology and standards were developed quickly and UK firms have some lead. The failure of UK services provides a poor example for customers, and negates any benefit from being first. Also the expertise may turn out to be with the wrong standard.

7. CONCLUSION

Telepoint involves two major standards issues: strategies for establishing a winning standard, and the role of official standards bodies. Both have been causal factors in telepoint's problems. The strategic problems in introducing telepoint were in both building the installed base and establishing credibility. There may have been less than whole-hearted commitment to the service by the initial operators, which contributed to insufficient investment in the access network and promotion of the system. The specifications of the system needed modification to make it fully attractive to users, and these changes were slow coming. This places significant responsibility for the problems on the operators. The result is doubly unsatisfactory as UK manufacturers' hopes for defining a European standard have been set back.

Many of these strategic problems had roots in government policy. The intention was to allow the market to determine the standard, but for one reason or another the market was not allowed to work. The system was defined by the licensing authority and the degree of competition imposed may have been too great for the operators to justify major investment. The standardization rules themselves added to the confusion. Other problems were in resolving internal concerns for firms with parallel interests in other mobile services for which telepoint could become an added complication.

The underlying question is where to strike a balance between markets and regulation. Had telepoint been left more completely to the market the product and industry structure would probably have looked quite different. In this sense the mix of market and official direction has not worked. The main problem was that the regulator brought in a strong external agenda when the market could well have been allowed more freedom. Despite intentions the temptation to use standards for general policy aims was too strong. A hybrid policy need not automatically combine the best of market and regulated standards; it may increase confusion.

The policy lessons may be two-fold. The first is that if hybrid policies are to work then it may be better for the authority to take a more neutral role as facilitator and coordinator rather than try to manipulate decisions directly *as the standards are being set*. Markets can be very effective at setting standards but they need freedom to work—especially in the early stages where the process is sensitive to small disturbances. The decision making, flexibility and fast reactions needed do not allow for much official intervention. This means letting firms make most of the decisions themselves, though faster mechanisms for market feedback may help. The role of standards bodies may lie before and after the standards 'contest' takes place, in a support role leaving selection to market competition.

The second is that however standards are set, they do not mix well with other industrial policy aims, which may be better dealt with separately. Standards may look like an inexpensive way to pursue industrial policy. This is misleading. The cost is that it is easy to harm the new standard in the process. New standards are not robust enough for general policy use and the other aims, such as industrial development and balancing international market power, may be pursued more directly.

Appendix: Abbreviations

BAe	British Aerospace
BT	British Telecom
CAI	Common Air Interface
CCITT	International Consultative Committee for Telephone and Telegraph
CEPT	European Conference on Posts and Telecommunications Administrations
CT2	Cordless telephone, second generation
DECT	Digital European Cordless Telephone
DTI	Department of Trade and Industry
ERMES	European Paging Standard
ETSI	European Telecommunications Standards Institute
EU	European Union
FCC	Federal Communications Commission—US
GPT	GEC-Plessey Telecommunications
GSM	Groupe Speciale Mobile
ISDN	Integrated Services Digital Network
MoU	Memorandum of Understanding
MPC	Mercury Personal Communications
PCN	Personal Communications Network
PIN	Personal Identification Number
PSTN	Public Service Telecommunications Network
PTO	Public Telecommunications Operator
TACS	Total Access Communications System—cellular

NOTES

1. This chapter considers the situation current in early 1994. It focuses primarily on the experience of telepoint up until the withdrawal of the three initial services (Phonepoint, Zonephone, Callpoint) in late 1991, with only brief discussion of the implications of the introduction of the fourth service (Rabbit) in mid-1992 until its withdrawal in late 1993. It draws on Grindley and Toker (1993, 1994).
2. For a review of standards policy issues, including problems with market standards and justification for policy intervention, see Rosenberg (1976); Dybvig and Spatt (1983); David (1986, 1987); David and Greenstein (1990); Farrell and Saloner (1986, 1988); and Chapter 3 of this book.
3. The size of this gap varies by country. It may be larger in the rest of Europe, where cellular telephone is not yet as well established as in the UK, and narrower in the USA and Japan, where payphones are more easily available. Thanks to Edward Steinmueller for noting this.
4. The table shows the consortia membership at the beginning of 1991, as they were when the licences were issued. The BYPS service was sold in February

1991 to Hutchison Telecom. There have also been substantial subsequent changes of ownership of the PCN interests, noted below.

5. DTI (1991). Hutchison Telecom began trials on two-way telepoint with its telepoint operation in Hong Kong in 1993 (Fintech [Financial Times Business Information], March 1993).

6. This coincided with expectations that CT2 would eventually be used in the office for connecting various types of data processing equipment (e.g. fax machines, computers, and printers) as well as voice communication to telecommunications networks via private base stations.

7. The CAI handsets used by Rabbit in 1992 were about the same size as the Shaye handset.

8. The current approach for policy has been to invite industry responses to a discussion document before deciding policy. For example, a discussion document for Personal Communications systems emphasized that the DTI had 'no unique insight into the future' and invited 'informed discussion' about what 'appear to be the main trends . . . towards digital technology', (DTI, 1989). Recently a green paper on the fixed link duopoly review outlined the policy issues (DTI, 1990), followed by a white paper that stated policy (DTI, 1991).

9. In 1991 Motorola and Telefonica withdrew from Mercury PCN, and Bundespost withdrew from Unitel. Mercury PCN and Unitel merged in March 1992 to form Mercury Personal Communications (MPC), a 50/50 joint venture between Cable and Wireless (Mercury) and US West. Meanwhile PacTel, Matra and Millicom withdrew from Microtel in early 1991, leaving it controlled by British Aerospace (BAe). Other original members of Microtel (Sony, IBA, and Litel) had already withdrawn. It was sold to Hutchison (30 per cent owned by BAe) in July 1991.

10. One2one met its target of installing 6,000 base stations within six months, by March 1994. It is not clear how many subscribers PCN has attracted and the new services may be suffering similar problems to telepoint. They face strong competition from the cellular service providers, Vodafone and Cellnet. Vodafone introduced a digital cellular service, using the GSM standard, in 1993 and a lower priced system, MetroDigital, in October 1993, in direct competition with PCN (though still more costly than PCN). MetroDigital is run on the back of the GSM service but will involve building 3,000 new micro-cells to provide extra capacity. However, users will also be able have access to Pan-European GSM services, at premium rates. Cellnet plans to introduce digital cellular in 1994. Vodafone currently has 1m. analog cellular subscribers, Cellnet has 0.8m. US trials of personal communications system (PCS) began in April 1993, with FCC licences of PCS services expected to be auctioned off in mid-1994 (*Financial Times*, 8 Sept. 1992; 18 Oct. 1993; *The Economist*, 23 Oct. 1993).

11. *Fintech*, 24 May 1990.

12. Ibid.

13. For example, *Guardian*, 10 Nov. 1989; *New Scientist*, 4 Nov. 1989.

14. *Financial Times*, 8 Sept. 1992.

15. In early 1993 Rabbit made offers cutting equipment prices by half for business users (reducing a GPT handset from £128 down to £69; a Rabbit Recall with pager from £177 to £99; a GPT private base station from £85 to £69); prices for residential users were unchanged but they already were given free connection and some other incentives (*Fintech Mobile Communications*, 11 Mar. 1993).

16. *Financial Times*, 6 Nov. 1993.

17. The direct benefits of having more telepoint users are spread over all users of the public fixed link network, not just telepoint users. With two-way access, all phone users have more people to call. Even if telepoint has only one-way access, all phone users benefit by receiving more calls and potentially relaying telepoint messages. Benefits are externalities because new users benefit existing users as well as themselves.

18. On the production side, incompatibility and fragmented standards may raise costs because: (*a*) the smaller market for each standard's hardware reduces economies of scale and experience effects and there are fewer units to cover R&D costs, (*b*) there is less competition between fewer producers, and (*c*) there is less opportunity for small specialized producers. These effects may be less important if hardware production has reached minimum efficient scale (Gabel and Millington, 1986).

19. The advantage of a single standard may be lower where variety is important (Matutes and Regibeau, 1987).

20. Press comments warned that telepoint was 'set for disaster' (*Guardian*, 10 Nov. 1989) and 'already outmoded' (*New Scientist*, 4 Nov. 1989). Even though it was not clear how much PCN and digital cellular would overlap with telepoint at the low end of the market, the uncertainty was damaging. The PCN services being introduced may in fact be no more expensive than telepoint.

21. For a comparison of prospective UK mobile services and their pricing policies see Toker (1992).

22. As noted above, Rabbit's strategy has put more stress on market penetration than the initial services. It has made handsets more broadly available, including distribution through electronics retail stores. It also halved some equipment prices and service charges in early 1993, in a move some observers saw this as a last attempt to expand the market, reminiscent of moves by the initial services two years previously.

23. This is seen in standards contests such as for PC, VCR, CD vs. DAT, audio cassette vs. 8-track, and 33 r.p.m. vs. 45 r.p.m. LP records. Many fragmented standards exist either where the technology was in wide use before network effects became an issue (railways, screw threads, fire-hose connectors) or at an international level where national standards bodies have tended to be concerned about the effect of adopting external standards on domestic industry (telecommunications, colour TV, HDTV).

24. The many aims and activities of standards bodies other than negotiating conflict are described in Sanders (1972) and Verman (1973). Enabling activities such as facilitating discussion, information sharing, user education, technical evaluation, standards drafting and compliance testing are seen as valuable in their own right and are not considered here.

25. This may be the case with HDTV in the USA, where delays in approving standards have given superior digital systems time to be developed (Farrell and Shapiro, 1991).

26. Brian Carsberg, Director of Oftel (CBS, 1991: 147).

27. *Guardian*, 10 Nov. 1989; *New Scientist*, 4 Nov. 1989; *Communicate*, Sept. 1989.

28. It was believed that 'telepoint would have at least three years to . . . consolidate its market before it would be feasible for PCN to become operational', (DTI, Jan. 1989).

29. For a comparison of prospective UK mobile services see Toker (1992).
30. It should be remembered, however, that the investment requirement was relatively low, possibly a twentieth of the £1 bn. estimated for a cellular or PCN operator.
31. A useful comparison of the use of markets to set standards is the US development of AM stereo in the 1980s (Berg 1987). Standards converged towards a single standard (Motorola C-QUAM) within a three-year period, but left a sizeable minority stranded with the first acceptable entrant (Kahn). The FCC was criticized for being excessively slow by first taking twenty years, from 1961 to 1982, evaluating proposals without action before a policy change to allow users and manufacturers to decide. Services were then introduced within a few months. Comparisons may be made with the use of national and international standards bodies in regulated industries to set international television standards. These have usually resulted in fragmented standards along national boundaries (see Crane, 1979, Besen and Johnson, 1986, Pelkmans and Beuter, 1987, and Grindley, 1991).
32. *Electronics Weekly*, 11 Apr. 1990.
33. *Financial Times*, 15 Mar. 1990.

REFERENCES

ANSOFF, H. (1965), *Corporate Strategy*, Harmondsworth: Penguin.

ARROW, K. (1962), 'The Economic Implications of Learning by Doing', *Review of Economic Studies*, 20: 155–73.

ARTHUR, B. (1988), 'Self-Reinforcing Mechanisms in Economics', in P. Anderson and K. Arrow, *The Economy as an Evolving Complex*, Redwood City, Calif.: Addison-Wesley: 9–31.

—— (1989), 'Competing Technologies, Increasing Returns and Lock-in by Historical Events', *Economic Journal*, 99: 116–31.

AXELROD, R., MITCHELL, W., THOMAS, R., BENNETT, S., and BRUDERER, E. (1993), 'Coalition Formation in Standard-Setting Alliances', mimeo, University of Michigan.

BAJARIN, T. (1993), 'Apple's Cloudy Future', *Bay Area Computer Currents*, 20 July 1993: 49–51.

BERG, S. (1987), 'Public Policy and Corporate Strategies in the AM Stereo Market', in Gabel (1987*a*).

BESEN, S. (1992), 'AM vs. FM: The Battle of the Bands', *Industrial and Corporate Change*, 1: 375–96.

—— and FARRELL, J. (1994), 'Choosing How to Compete: Strategies and Tactics in Standardization', *Journal of Economic Perspectives*, 8: 117–31.

—— and JOHNSON, L. (1986), *Compatibility Standards, Competition, and Innovation in the Broadcasting Industry*, Santa Monica, Calif.: RAND Corporation.

—— and SALONER, G. (1989), 'The Economics of Telecommunications Standards', in R. Crandall and K. Framm (eds.), *Changing the Rules: Technological Change, International Competition and Regulation in Telecommunications*, Washington, DC: Brookings Institution: 177–220.

BROCK, G. (1975*a*), *The US Computer Industry*, Cambridge, Mass.: Ballinger.

—— (1975*b*), 'Competition, Standards and Self-Regulation in the Computer Industry', in R. Caves and M. Roberts (eds.), *Regulating the Product: Quality and Variety*, Cambridge, Mass.: Ballinger.

BRUCE, A., and BUCK, T. (1993), 'The State Promotion of High Definition Television (HDTV)', Discussion Paper 1993. VII, University of Nottingham.

BUTCHER, L. (1988), *Accidental Millionaire*, New York: PMB.

CAMPBELL, A., and KELLY, T. (1989), *ICL: A Business and Technological History*, Oxford: Clarendon Press.

CARPENTIER, M. (1989), 'An Action Plan for HDTV in Europe', *Telecommunications*, Sept.: 23–5.

CARROLL, P. (1993), *Big Blues: The Unmaking of IBM*, New York: Crown.

Centre for Business Strategy (CBS), (1991), *Lectures on Regulation 1991*, Centre for Business Strategy Report, London Business School, 106 pp.

CHPOSKY, J. (1989), *Blue Magic: the People, Power and Politics Behind the PC*, London: Grafton Books.

CLARK, K. (1985), 'The Interaction of Design Hierarchies and Market Concepts in Technological Evolution', *Research Policy*, 14: 235–51.

Consumers' Association (1990), *The Price of CDs*, Consumers' Association Report: 59.

COTTRELL, T. (1994), 'Fragmented Standards and the Development of the Japanese Microcomputer Software Industry', *Research Policy*, 23: 143–74.

CRANE, R. (1979), *The Politics of International Standards*, Norwood: Ablex.

CRIPPS, D. (1988), 'Understanding the MAC Objective', *International Broadcasting*, Dec.: 36–45.

CUSUMANO, M., MYLONADIS, Y., and ROSENBLOOM, R. (1990), 'Strategic Manoeuvering in Home-Video Standardization', CCC Working Paper No. 90-5, Center for Research in Management, University of California, Berkeley.

DAVID, P. (1985), 'CLIO and the Economics of QWERTY', *American Economic Review*, 75: 332–7.

—— (1986), 'Narrow Windows, Blind Giants and Angry Orphans: The Dynamics of System Rivalries and Dilemmas of Technology Policy', in F. Arcangel *et al.* (eds.), *Innovation Diffusion*, iii, New York: Oxford University Press (forthcoming).

—— (1987), 'Some New Standards for the Economics of Standardization in the Information Age', in P. Dasgupta and P. Stoneman (eds.), *Economic Policy and Technological Performance*, Cambridge: Cambridge University Press.

—— (1991), 'Narrow Windows, Blind Giants and Angry Orphans: The Dynamics of System Rivalries and Dilemmas of Technology Policy', in F. Arcangel *et al.* (eds.), *Innovation Diffusion*, iii, New York: Oxford University Press.

—— (1992), 'Heroes, Herds and Hysteresis in Technology and History: Thomas Edison and the "The Battle of the Systems" Reconsidered', *Industrial and Corporate Change*, 1: 129–80.

—— and GREENSTEIN, S. (1990), 'The Economics of Compatibility Standards: An Introduction to Recent Research', *Economics of Innovation and New Technology*, 1: 3–42.

—— and STEINMUELLER, E. (1990), 'The ISDN Bandwagon is Coming, but Who Will Be there to Climb Aboard', *Economics of Innovation and New Technology*, 1: 43–62.

DAY, G. (1990), *Market Driven Strategy*, New York: Free Press.

DELAMARTER, R. (1986), *Big Blue: IBM's Use and Abuse of Power*, New York: Macmillan.

Department of Trade and Industry (1991), *Competition and Choice: Telecommunications Policy for the 1990s*, House of Commons, Cm. 1461, London: HMSO.

—— (1989), *Phones on the Move: Personal Communications in the 1990s (discussion document)*, London: DTI.

—— (1990), *Competition and Choice: Telecommunications Policy for the 1990s (discussion document)*, House of Commons, Cm. 1303, London: HMSO.

Depma (1992), *Japan Electronics Almanac 1992*, Tokyo: Depma Publications.

DONAHUE, H. (1989), 'Choosing the TV of the Future', *Technology Review*, Apr.: 31–40.

DYBVIG, P., and SPATT, C. (1983), 'Adoption Externalities as Public Goods', *Journal of Public Economics*, 20: 231–52.

EITO (1993), *European Information Technology Observatory 93*, Frankfurt: EITO.

Electronics Industries Association (EIA), (1992), *Electronic Markets Data Book, 1992*, New York: EIA.

FARRELL, J. (1990), 'The Economics of Standardization: A Guide for Non-Economists', in J. Berg and H. Schumny (eds.), *An Analysis of the Information Technology Standardization Process*, Amsterdam: Elsevier.

—— and SALONER, G. (1985), 'Standardization, Compatibility and Innovation', *Rand Journal of Economics*, 16: 70–83.

—— —— (1986a), 'Economic Issues in Standardization', in J. Miller (ed.), *Telecommunications and Equity*, New York: North-Holland.

—— —— (1986b), 'Standardisation and Variety', *Economic Letters*, 20: 71–4.

—— —— (1986c), 'Installed Base and Compatibility: Innovation, Product Preannouncements and Predation', *American Economic Review*, 76: 940–55.

—— —— (1988), 'Coordination Through Committees and Markets', *Rand Journal of Economics*, 19: 235–52.

—— —— (1992), 'Converters, Compatability and the Control of Interfaces', *Journal of Industrial Economics*, 40: 9–36.

—— and SHAPIRO, C. (1992), 'Standard Setting in High Definition Television', *Brookings Papers on Economic Activity: Microeconomics*.

Federal Communications Commission (FCC), (1988), 'Tentative Decision and Further Notice of Inquiry', *Federal Communications Commission Record*: 6520–53.

—— (1991), 'Fourth Interim Report of the Advisory Committee on Advanced Television Service'.

FERGUSON, J., and MORRIS, C. (1993), *Computer Wars*, New York: Times Books.

FISHER, F., McGOWAN, J., and GREENWOOD, J. (1983), *Folded, Spindled and Mutilated: Economic Analysis and US vs. IBM*, Cambridge, Mass.: MIT Press.

—— McKIE, J., and MANCKE, R. (1983), *IBM and the US Data Processing Industry*, New York: Praeger.

FOSTER, R. (1986), *Innovation: The Attacker's Advantage*, London: Pan.

FOY, N. (1971), 'Government Strategy for Computer Software and Services', in E. Moonan (ed.), *British Computers and Industrial Innovation*, Oxford: Oxford University Press.

GABEL, L. (ed.) (1987a), *Product Standardisation as a Tool of Competitive Strategy: INSEAD Symposium*, Paris: North-Holland.

—— (1987b), 'Open Standards and the European Computer Industry: The Case of X/Open', in Gabel (1987a).

—— (1991), *Competitive Strategies and Product Standards*, London: McGraw-Hill.

—— and MILLINGTON, R. (1986), 'The Role of Technical Standards in the European Cellular Radio Industry', mimeo, INSEAD.

GARNER, R. (1989), 'The Japanese Gain a Clear View of TV's Future', *Financial Times*, 8 May 1989.

GRAHAM, M. (1986), *RCA and the Videodisc*, Cambridge: Cambridge University Press.

GRANSTRAND, O. (1984), 'The Evolution of the Video Tape Recorder Industry and the Mainframe Computer Industry in Japan', Working Paper, Chambers University of Technology, Gothenburg, Sweden.

GRANT, R. (1987), 'The Effect of Product Standardization on Competition: The Case of Octane Grading of Petrol in the UK', in Gabel (1987a).

GRINDLEY, P. (1990a), 'Winning Standards Contests: Using Product Standards in Business Strategy', *Business Strategy Review*, 1: 71–84.

—— (1990b), 'Standards and the Open Systems Revolution in the Computer Industry', in J. Berg and H. Schumny (eds.), *An Analysis of the Information Technology Standardization Process*, Amsterdam: Elsevier: 99–110.

GRINDLEY, P., and TOKER, S. (1993), 'Regulators, Markets and Standards Coordination: Policy Lessons from Telepoint', *Economics of Innovation and New Technology*, 2: 319–42.

—— —— (1994), 'Establishing Standards for Telepoint: Problems of Fragmentation and Commitment', in G. Pogorel (ed.), *Global Telecommunications Strategies and Technological Changes*, Paris: Elsevier: 201–25.

GUPTA, A., and TOONG, H. (1988), *Insights into Personal Computers*, New York: IEEE Press.

HART, J., and TYSON, L. (1989), 'Responding to the Challenge of HDTV', *California Management Review*, Summer: 132–45.

HEMENWAY, D. (1975), *Industrywide Voluntary Product Standards*, Cambridge, Mass.: Balinger.

HENDERSON, B. (1979), *Henderson on Corporate Strategy*, Cambridge, Mass.: ABT Books.

HERGERT, M. (1987), 'Technical Standards and Competition in the Microcomputer Industry', in Gabel (1987*a*).

IREDALE, R. (1987), 'Proposal for a New HD-NTSC Broadcast Protocol', *IEEE Transactions on Consumer Electronics*, CE-33 1: 14–27.

JONES, J. (1986), *What's in a Name? Advertising and the Concept of Brands*, Lexington, Mass.: Lexington Books.

KATZ, B., and PHILLIPS, A. (1982), 'The Computer Industry', in R. Nelson (ed.), *Government and Technical Change: A Cross-Industry Analysis*, New York: Pergamon.

—— and SHAPIRO, C. (1985), 'Network Externalities, Competition and Compatibility', *American Economic Review*, 75: 424–40.

—— —— (1986), 'Technological Adoption in the Presence of Network Externalities', *Journal of Political Economy*, 94: 833–41.

—— —— (1992), 'Product Introduction with Network Externalities', *Journal of Industrial Economics*, 40: 55–83.

KAY, J. (1993), *Foundations of Corporate Success*, Oxford: Oxford University Press.

KHAZAM, J., and MOWERY, D. (1993), 'The Commercialization of RISC: Strategies for the Creation of Dominant Designs', *Research Policy* (forthcoming).

KINDLEBERGER, C. (1983), 'Standards as Public, Collective and Private Goods', *Kyklos*, 36: 377–95.

KRUGMAN, P. (1991), 'History versus Expectations', *Quarterly Journal of Economics*, 106: 651–67.

KUPFER, A. (1991), 'The US Wins One in High-Tech TV', *Fortune* (8 Apr.): 50–4.

LIEBOWITZ, S., and MARGOLIS, S. (1994), 'Network Externality: An Uncommon Tragedy', *Journal of Economic Perspectives*, 8: 133–50.

MANASIAN, D. (1993), 'Within the Whirlwind: A Survey of the Computer Industry', *The Economist*, 27 Feb.

MATUTES, C., and REGIBEAU, P. (1987), 'Compatibility and Multiproduct Firms: The Symmetric Case', in L. Gabel (ed.), *Product Standardization as a Tool of Competitive Strategy*, Paris: North-Holland.

—— —— (1988), 'Mix and Match: Product Compatibility without Network Externalities', *Rand Journal of Economics*, 19: 221–34.

McKenna, R. (1989), *Who's Afraid of Big Blue?*, New York: Addison-Wesley.

Nakajima, H., and Kosake, M. (1986), 'The DAT Conference: Its Activities and Results', *IEEE Transactions on Consumer Electronics*, CE-32: 404–15.

Nayak, R., and Ketteringham, J. (1986), *Breakthroughs*, New York: Rawson Associates.

Neil, S. (1988), 'The Politics of International Standardization Revisited: The USA and HDTV', paper delivered at 7th ITS Conference, Boston, June 1988.

Nelson, P. (1974), 'Advertising as Information', *Journal of Political Economy*, 81: 729–54.

Office of Technology Assessment (OTA), (1990), *The Big Picture: HDTV and High Resolution Systems: Background Paper*, US Congress.

Olleros, X. (1992), 'Battles for Share in Hyperselective Markets', mimeo, University of Quebec, Montreal.

Osborne, A., and Dvorak, J. (1984), *Hypergrowth: The Rise and Fall of Osborne Computer Corporation*, Berkeley: Idthekkethan Publishing Co.

Ouchi, W., and Bolton, M. (1988), 'The Logic of Joint Research and Development', *California Management Review*, 30: 9–33.

Pelkmans, J., and Beuter, R. (1987), 'Standardization and Competitiveness: Private and Public Strategies in the EC Colour TV Industry', in Gabel (1987*a*).

Peters, T. (1987), *Thriving on Chaos*, London: Macmillan.

—— and Waterman, R. (1982), *In Search of Excellence*, New York: Harper & Row.

Phillips, A. (1987), 'The Role of Standardization in Shared Bank Card Systems', in Gabel (1987*a*).

Porter, M. (1980), *Competitive Strategy*, New York: Free Press.

Postrel, S. (1990), 'Competing Networks and Proprietary Standards: The Case of Quadraphonic Sound', *Journal of Industrial Economics*, 39: 169–85.

Quantel (1990*a*), 'Pre-Press Definitions', Quantel PLC.

—— (1990*b*), 'The Digital Fact Book', Quantel PLC.

Quinn, J. (1985), 'Managing Innovation: Controlled Chaos', *Harvard Business Review*, May–June: 73–84.

Radiocommunications Agency (1994), *The Future Management of the Radio Spectrum*, Consultative Document, London: Radiocommunications Library.

Rappaport, A., and Halevi, S. (1991), 'The Computerless Computer Company', *Harvard Business Review*, July–Aug.: 69–80.

Recording Industry Association of America (RIAA), (1990), *Inside the Recording Industry: A Statistical Overview*, RIAA.

Rodgers, B. (1986), *The IBM Way*, New York: Harper & Row.

Rosenberg, E. (1976), 'Standards and Industry Self-Regulation', *California Management Review*, 19: 79–90.

Rosenbloom, R., and Cusumano, M. (1987), 'Technological Pioneering and Competitive Advantage: The Birth of the VCR Industry', *California Management Review*, 24: 51–76.

Saloner, G. (1990), 'Economic Issues in Computer Interface Standardization', *Economics of Innovation and New Technology*, 1: 135–56.

—— and Shepard, A. (1992), 'Adoption of Technologies with Network Effects: An Empirical Examination of the Adoption of Automated Teller Machines', NBER Working Paper No. 4048.

SANDERS, T. (1972), *The Aims and Principles of Standardization*, Geneva: International Organization for Standardization.

SCHELLING, T. (1960), *The Strategy of Conflict*, Cambridge, Mass.: Harvard University Press.

SCHERER, F., and ROSS, D. (1990), *Industrial Market Structure and Economic Performance*, 3rd edn., Boston: Houghton-Mifflin.

SCHMIDT, S., and WERLE, R. (1992), 'The Development of Compatibility Standards in Telecommunications', in M. Dierkes and U. Hoffman (eds.), *New Technology at the Outset*, Frankfurt: Campus.

SCHREIBER, W. (1989), 'Withdrawal of Support for the NHK HDTV System', testimony to NTIA, US Department of Commerce, 1 Mar.

SCULLEY, J. (1988), *Odyssey*, New York: Harper & Row.

SHAPIRO, C. (1989), 'The Theory of Business Strategy', *Rand Journal of Economics*, 20: 125-37.

SHUBIK, M. (1982), *Game Theory in the Social Sciences*, Cambridge, Mass.: MIT Press.

SPENCE, A. (1981), 'The Learning Curve and Competition', *Bell Journal of Economics*, 12: 49-70.

—— (1984), 'Cost Reduction, Competition and Industrial Performance', *Economertrica*, 52: 101-21.

STEWART, R. (1988), 'A Strategic View of CT2', *Mobile Communications Guide 1989*, London: IBC Technical Services: 63-9.

SWANN, P. (1987), 'Technology Pre-Announcement as a Competitive Strategy', in Gabel (1987*a*).

TEECE, D. (1986), 'Profiting from Technological Innovation', *Research Policy*, 15: 285-305.

TIROLE, J. (1988), *Industrial Economics*, Boston: MIT Press.

TOKER, S. (1992), *Mobile Communications in the 1990s: Opportunities and Pitfalls*, Report Series, Centre for Business Strategy, London Business School.

Unesco (1988), *Statistical Yearbook*, Unesco.

UTTERBACK, J. (1993), *Mastering the Dynamics of Innovation*, Cambridge, Mass.: Harvard Business School Press (forthcoming).

VERMAN, L. (1973), *Standardization: A New Discipline*, Hamden, Conn.: Arden Books.

VICKERS, J. (1985), 'Strategic Competition Amongst the Few—Some Recent Developments in the Economics of Industry', *Oxford Review of Economic Policy*, 1: 39-62.

WATSON, T., and PETRE, P. (1990), *Father, Son and Co.: My Life at IBM and Beyond*, New York: Bantam Books.

WHARTON, J. (1994), 'The Legacy of Gary Kildall', *Microtimes*, 24 Aug. 1994: 44-50.

WHEELER, E., and GANEK, A. (1988), 'Introduction to Systems Applications Architecture', *IBM Systems Journal*, 27: 250-63.

X/Open (1988), *X/Open Portability Guide*, 3rd edn., New York: Prentice-Hall.

YAMASHITA, T. (1989), *The Panasonic Way: From a Chief Executive's Desk*, Tokyo: Kodansha International.

INDEX